Agenda Setting, Policies, and Political Systems

Agenda Setting, Policies, and Political Systems

A Comparative Approach

EDITED BY

Christoffer Green-Pedersen
and Stefaan Walgrave

The University of Chicago Press | CHICAGO AND LONDON

Christoffer Green-Pedersen is professor of political science at Aarhus University, Denmark, and coeditor of *Dismantling Public Policy*. Stefaan Walgrave is professor of political science at the University of Antwerp, Belgium, and coeditor of *The World Says No to War*.

The University of Chicago Press, Chicago 60637
The University of Chicago Press, Ltd., London
© 2014 by The University of Chicago
All rights reserved. Published 2014.
Printed in the United States of America

23 22 21 20 19 18 17 16 15 14   1 2 3 4 5

ISBN-13: 978-0-226-12827-6   (cloth)
ISBN-13: 978-0-226-12830-6   (paper)
ISBN-13: 978-0-226-12844-3   (e-book)
DOI: 10.7208/chicago/9780226128443.001.0001

Library of Congress Cataloging-in-Publication Data

Agenda setting, policies, and political systems : a comparative approach / edited by Christoffer Green-Pedersen and Stefaan Walgrave.
     pages ; cm
  Includes bibliographical references and index.
     ISBN 978-0-226-12827-6 (cloth : alk. paper) — ISBN 978-0-226-12830-6 (pbk. : alk. paper) — ISBN 978-0-226-12844-3 (e-book)   1. Political science—Europe.   2. Political science—North America.   3. Politics, Practical—Europe.   4. Politics, Practical—North America.   5. Europe—Politics and government.   6. North America—Politics and government.   7. Comparative government.   I. Green-Pedersen, Christoffer, editor of compilation.   II. Walgrave, Stefaan, 1966– editor of compilation.
  JN5.A64 2014
  320.6094—dc23

                                                                    2013035945

♾ This paper meets the requirements of ANSI/NISO Z39.48-1992 (Permanence of Paper).

Contents

Preface

This volume is the result of a lengthy collaborative effort on the part of several research teams in different countries. A group of European and American teams has been collaborating under the common banner of the Comparative Agendas Project (CAP; see www.comparativeagendas.info), which operates as an open network of scholars interested in political agenda-setting processes. The CAP has no formal leaders, no proper institutional structure, and no structural funding. Most teams acquired funding from their national agencies; others (Switzerland, Spain, the UK, Belgium) were funded through the European Science Foundation (ESF). This book would probably not have been produced without this generous support from the ESF.

The CAP has no rules, nor does it have a unified theory. What unites the participants is the simple idea that political attention to issues is a crucial process in politics, that this attention is scarce, and that it is consequential. Drawing on this straightforward core idea, the CAP country teams all gather similar data on political attention to issues in their own countries. The institutions whose issue attention is coded—the coded "agendas" in each country—vary according to the interest of the local research team and the available data (some code media, others demonstrations, still others government decisions, budgets, party manifestos, or parliamentary debates; all teams code bills and passed legislation). The covered periods also vary by country. Some agendas in some of the countries are coded as far back as to the period before World War II; other agendas are only coded for the last ten years or so. The variation is reflected in the country chapters, which cover widely different agendas and periods.

The core of the CAP's collaboration consists of a common coding scheme— basically a structured list of issues with a definition of each issue—and a few rules of how to issue-code political content (each record can get only a single issue code). Another CAP feature is a readiness to share data and a willingness to collaborate.

The CAP's research agenda is thus both very focused in its data gathering and very broad in its application to political-science puzzles. It is highly focused because it analyzes politics in terms of how attention to various policy issues is allocated; at the same time, it is very broad because it uses this lens to analyze many different aspects of politics. The chapters testify to that.

The CAP network is strongly inspired by Frank Baumgartner and Bryan Jones's early work on U.S. agendas, and the national projects owe much to Frank and Bryan in terms of intellectual support in starting the projects. However, the CAP has developed into much more than a comparative test of the ideas presented in their work. For instance, testing the punctuated-equilibrium model is only one among many research questions addressed by CAP scholars. In this volume, it is not addressed at all.

The CAP network has generally moved much more in the direction of the traditional comparative-politics literature, which focuses on political parties, elections, and the workings of political institutions. The primary aim of this book is precisely to show the added value of addressing mainstream comparative politics questions by using a policy agenda–setting lens.

At the CAP network's regular meetings, coding problems are discussed, papers are presented, and plans for future collaboration or meeting venues are made. The idea for this book originated at the third yearly CAP meeting in The Hague in 2009, which was supported by Campus The Hague of Leiden University. The first versions of the chapters were discussed at the 2010 Seattle meeting and some final versions in 2011 in Catania. The book would not have been possible without those great yearly meetings among friendly colleagues and excellent scholars.

Not all CAPs were able to participate in this book; one that was excluded is a CAP on the EU (see www.policyagendas.eu). Furthermore, not all individual CAP members have contributed to the chapters in this book. In many countries other, "invisible" collaborators made contributions in the form of data gathering. We want to thank them for their help. Special thanks also to Frank Baumgartner for his help on this project and to Annette Andersen for excellent secretarial assistance. Thanks also to Rodney Powell and John Tryneski from the University of Chicago Press for their help throughout the process.

Christoffer and Stefaan
April 2013
Antwerp, Belgium; Aarhus, Denmark

1   Political Agenda Setting: An Approach to Studying Political Systems

Christoffer Green-Pedersen and Stefaan Walgrave

T HE IMPORTANCE OF STUDYING POLITICAL AGENDAS—THE LIST
of issues to which political actors devote their attention—was first
argued by Bachrach and Baratz (1962) in their article on power and by
Schattschneider (1960) in his book on American politics. The core idea unit-
ing these two seminal pieces is that defining the locus of conflict, or winning
the conflict of conflicts, is the key "second face" of power, which precedes the
actual decision-making process (the "first face" of power). In other words, the
authors argue that defining which issues should be at the center of political
attention—the process of political agenda setting—is one of the most central processes in any political system. Political elites struggle to gain control
over the political agenda, because this allows them to define the locus of
political conflicts. What politics is about—the issues that enter the political
agenda—not only directly (dis)advantages certain political actors compared
to others (who can or cannot satisfy their constituencies), it also determines
the scope of the conflict (which groups are involved), because it defines in
what venues binding decisions are to be taken (and which actors are allowed
to participate in the decision-making process). In other words, the issues
that are included on the political agenda and those that are excluded, and
the study of the process that leads to their inclusion or exclusion, are related
to the core of political science. If political science is the study of who gets
what when, and why, then the agenda-setting approach can contribute to
the discipline because it studies issues' (what) rise and fall (when) to distinguish powerful from nonpowerful actors (who), and because it addresses the
mechanisms through which issues gain or lose traction (why).

The idea of politics as a struggle for control over the political agenda
raises a series of questions about the conditionality, mechanisms, and consequences of the process: How is the agenda-setting struggle affected by the
character of political systems? What role do various actors such as political
parties and interest groups play in the process? What is the effect of the size
and urgency of real-world problems? And how does elites' ability to define

the locus of conflict affect a society's overall conflict structure? Thus, looking at the process of political agenda setting potentially forms the theoretical starting point for a whole research program on political systems. If defining the locus of conflict is a key process in any political system, and we think it is, studying this process would be a natural way to learn how political systems function and change over time. For example, if a country introduced a federal structure, studying how political agendas change would be an obvious way to study the consequences of devolution. Or, when new parties enter the party system, one could assess their influence by testing whether their presence changed the political agenda at all. The importance of studying the second face of power is widely recognized in political science. The article by Bachrach and Baratz (1962) is the most frequently cited article in the *American Political Science Review* ever (Stone 2006). Nevertheless, a research program on the role of political institutions, actors, and issues in agenda setting did not emerge out of the early agenda-setting literature.

What did emerge was a tradition of agenda research that focused on the role of agendas in policy-making (see, e.g., Cobb and Elder 1983; Kingdon 1995). The core of this policy-agenda tradition consists of case studies showing that an understanding of agenda dynamics is crucial for understanding how and why policy decisions are made. The tradition has provided immense insight into the dynamics of policy decision making and has had a long-lasting impact. Most central is the fact that real-world problems, policy-attention dynamics, and public policy are strongly linked. "Attention" is attention to something, and "something" means problems and solutions, that is, public policy. So, early agenda scholars' focus on policy decisions was not accidental; it was logical when one started to think about attention and its role in politics. A debate that started with Cobb and Elder (1983) is thus about the extent to which characteristics of specific policy issues matter for the policy process (Grossmann 2013). Early policy agenda scholarship also left an important conceptual legacy. Kingdon's (1995) concept of window of opportunities, for instance, is almost universally applied by policy scholars.

However, studies within this tradition have rarely touched upon the broader questions about the role of actors and institutions in political agenda setting. The focus on agendas was tied to specific policies and did not develop into a general framework for asking questions about political systems and political actors and how they relate to the struggle for attention. The object of the focus was policy processes, not politics. Therefore, this volume's first aim is to show that examining the distribution over time of political attention to issues offers a potent framework within which to study politics in general, not only policy.

In fact, inspired by Baumgartner and Jones (1993 and 2009), agenda scholars have gradually started to move away from the policy focus and back toward broader questions about politics that were raised by Schattschneider and by Bachrach and Baratz. Typical policy questions were not abolished, and policy has not disappeared—studies of budgetary developments, for instance, still play an important role (Jones, Baumgartner, et al. 2009; Mortensen 2009). However, the literature has increasingly moved toward questions related to the politics of attention (Jones and Baumgartner 2005), beyond attention to policy. Agenda scholars have started to tackle the questions about political institutions and political actors that follow from the classic work of Schattschneider and Bachrach and Baratz but that until now have hardly been pursued by political science.

This does not imply that policy is forgotten in the shift of focus from policy to politics. "Attention" in this context means attention to specific issues; political actors are thus trying to address real-world problems connected with policy issues. This has implications for how political actors should be studied. Green-Pedersen and Mortensen (20010), Green-Pedersen and Stubager (2010), and Thesen (2013) show that the fact that governments are blamed by the media for whatever policy problems emerge means that governments are often forced to respond to issues raised by other political actors, such as opposition parties.

Accompanying the gradual change from policy to politics, other transformations testify to the broadening of the range of agenda research. To begin with, the scope of the research has increased. Not only were typical policy "output" agendas at the end of the policy cycle (e.g., budgetary and legislative) included, but gradually "input" agendas such as mass media coverage, party manifestos, and parliamentary questions or bills were scrutinized from an agenda perspective. At the same time, political-agenda scholars now increasingly focus on how political agendas interact with and influence each other.

Baumgartner and Jones's original work (1993) mainly assessed patterns of change and stability in attention and policies in relation to specific policy issues or policy questions such as those concerning tobacco, nuclear power, or pesticide use. These studies led to the formulation of the theory of punctuated equilibrium, that is, the idea that in the development of policy there are long periods of stability followed by short periods of large changes before the return to a new, stable equilibrium. This idea, which originated in studies of American politics, has been tested comparatively (see Baumgartner, Breunig, et al. 2009; Jones, Baumgartner, et al. 2009) but is not part of this volume. None of the chapters addresses punctuatedness. Agenda work, also in this volume, has shifted toward the impact of political agendas on one another. How does issue attention "jump" from one agenda to the other, and how do agendas interact? This focus on the mechanisms of agenda change was of course present in the original work of Baumgartner and Jones. But with the explicit and direct focus on how agendas impact each other—for example, how media coverage leads to legislative activity—a gradual shift in focus from agendas to agenda setting has become manifest. The emphasis is on the process, the setting of the given agenda, rather than on the distribution of attention on a given agenda, and its change over time.

This captures the book's second aim, namely to scrutinize the mechanism of agenda setting, not just agenda evolution, and thus attempt to understand the process. Many chapters directly study the process by which issues gain and lose traction by examining how agendas influence each other. Other chapters examine structural breaks or institutional change and their impact on the distribution of attention. In a sense, all chapters follow a causal logic, focus on the process of agenda setting, and try to explain why specific issues rise and fall.

The present volume differs from and contributes to the agenda literature and to political science in a third way. We explained above that early policy-agenda work quite narrowly focused on policy decision making; slowly the emphasis shifted to general politics and to the mechanisms of political agenda setting. In this volume, and we believe it is a first, we employ the political agenda–setting approach to political systems as a whole. As we argue below, we use the agenda lens not to understand why a specific decision has been taken or to examine the power of a specific actor, but rather to measure and understand critical features of each of the political systems under study. Agenda-setting processes are present in the entire political process, and by zooming in on these processes we can assess the streams of influence within a political system. By looking at agenda dynamics we attempt to get a better grasp on how a political system works. In other words, our real units of analysis are eleven political systems—not their issues, agendas, or decisions.

This focus on the system level further broadens the scope of political agenda setting considerably and gears it up to make it a more general perspective on politics. The focus of this volume is much more in line with Baumgartner and Jones's (2013) work after 2000, which examines the entire policy agenda and how it is related to political institutions and the development of political systems.

Finally, the volume goes beyond the quite narrow focus on the United States that has been so typical for early agenda work. All of the above-cited foundational authors examined the United States. The dispersion of the agenda-setting approach outside the United States has contributed to the current boom in agenda studies. This volume testifies to the fact that an agenda approach—examining shifts in political attention over time as they are caused by the agendas of other actors, by institutional changes, and by events—fares well outside the United States. This comparative angle is the fourth characteristic of the essays collected in this volume.

In what follows, we do three things. First, we outline how the classic insights into the importance of agenda setting have developed into a theoretically coherent research program. Obviously there is quite a gap between Bachrach and Baratz's (1962) argument about the second face of power or Schattschneider's (1960) idea about the conflict of conflicts and empirical research on agenda setting, which tackles the functioning of entire political systems. This may explain why research on political systems based on agenda-setting ideas has been slow to emerge. Scholars of agenda setting have tried to bridge this gap theoretically, and we lay out the steps.

Second, the chapter explains that agenda setting is not only a theoretical account but also entails a specific empirical perspective and a distinct methodology for tackling questions about the politics of attention. The core of the approach is a strong focus on issues and on the shifts over time in attention to issues.

Third, we discuss how the approach to studying political systems from an agenda-setting perspective differs from the way political science more broadly has examined the functioning of political systems. The dynamics of political systems and the functioning of political institutions are core issues in political science and have been widely researched based on other theoretical approaches. The contribution of the agenda-setting approach to studying political systems can thus be specified by showing how it differs from these other approaches.

Political Attention Is Scarce and Consequential

The key starting point of agenda setting is twofold: political attention is scarce, and it is consequential. That political attention is consequential means, at the most reductive level, that it is a precondition for political change. The idea that attention is a scarce resource may seem trivial at first sight, but it has many implications. Political actors and their agendas are bound by their carrying capacity. One can thus talk about a "bottleneck of attention" (Jones and Baumgartner 2005, 15–17). The ability of any actor or institution to address issues is constrained. The time, energy, personnel, motivation, money, expertise, logistics, and the like available for attending to issues are limited. But the number of issues or problems begging for political attention is practically infinite. In any society, an endless array of problems, accidents, events, solutions, and so on beg for political attention. This mismatch between an "endless" society and a "limited" political system turns the political prioritization of issues—the choice to attend to an issue at the expense of other possible issues—into a key political process.

The selection of issues that deserve political attention determines all further steps in the political process. When issues are not noticed, political actors do not develop preferences to deal with them, the public does not care about them, interest groups do not bother with them, solutions to the problems are not formulated, political pressure does not mount, and no decision regarding the issue will be taken. In short, without political attention the status quo is extended. (Naturally, the status quo can also prevail even when attention to an issue is raised.) This is why political attention is not only a scarce resource, but also is consequential and a precondition for political action. Both elements are intimately related; attention is scarce because it is a precondition for political action, and vice versa. In short, attention is the gate to politics.

Consequently, the prioritization of attention is a central effect of political institutions and a central goal of political actors. This is basically what Schattschneider (1960) meant when he focused on the scope of conflict and what is implied in Bachrach and Baratz's (1962) second face of power. For instance, if an issue moves from attracting limited attention to being a key political issue, new actors (with other preferences) become involved, electoral concerns (and the preferences expressed through them) become increasingly important for political parties, the media become more interested, and so on. Agenda setting is about how political institutions and the political elites that inhabit those institutions turn societal conditions into political problems.

The main question, then, becomes why political actors devote attention to some issues and ignore others. This is the underlying question all political agenda-setting work addresses one way or another. The answer most agenda-setting scholars have given is tied to the concept of *information* (Jones and Baumgartner 2005, 55–85; Baumgartner, Jones, and Wilkerson 2011; Baumgartner and Jones 2013). Political actors get continuous and unlimited information about all kinds of problems that exist in the real world, and these actors are supposed to attend to these problems and solve them (after all, this is what politics is expected to do). It is impossible, students of agenda setting hold, to understand what is going on in politics without taking into account what happens in society. Politics reacts to the real world and to incoming information about the state of affairs in the real world. Politics is about problems—not in the sense of being a matter of rational responses to objective problems, but in the sense of how conditions become political problems to which politicians try to deliver solutions. Thus the nature and development of the policy problems themselves are important for politics. How can one, for instance, understand the Obama presidency by just focusing on his preferences and the American political system without paying attention to such real-world challenges as the financial crisis, the war in Afghanistan, climate change, or the BP oil spill? Since information on problems in the real world is in principle endless, actors and institutions filter incoming information in order not to get swamped. Political actors are either constantly fighting *against* "issue intrusion" as these new issues threaten to overthrow their present priorities or are fighting *for* issue intrusion as they attempt to garner attention for other issues. As we explained, agenda-setting studies have moved away from policy change as the dependent variable toward studying political attention dynamics, but this does not imply that public policy no longer plays a role in many agenda-setting studies. Attention is attention to policy issues; this is a crucial premise (Baumgartner et al. 2006; Baumgartner and Jones 2013).

This brings us to the second driver of issue prioritization, namely political actors' *preferences*. Arguably, most agenda-setting work has incorporated political actors' preferences much less than issue information. Because information is limitless, actors select the issues they let through their attention gates. Part of this selection process is nondeliberate and unconscious—actors simply have physical and cognitive limits to the attention they can yield—but another part of the selection process is deliberate and based on issue preferences. Actors' preferences are important because they are interested in the allocation of attention to certain issues rather than others: their ideology encourages them to attend to an issue, their supporters care about an issue, they can improve their standing by increased attention to an issue, or they can weaken their competitors when they can generate political attention to a certain issue. Yet, no actor controls the entire agenda-setting process. Further, actors' preferences interact with incoming information: new information may lead to preference updates or to the activation of latent preferences, while preferences filter the information that is let through the gates (Vliegenthart, Walgrave, and Zicha 2013; Baumgartner and Jones 2013). Increasing attention to an issue may even lead to the emergence of new political actors that embody distinct preferences linked to the new issue. The increasing attention to the environment, for example, has resulted in the emergence of green parties in many party systems.

The third factor determining what issues will be attended to is the *institutions* in a political system. Institutions impose rules of collaboration and competition. Political actors are embedded in institutions whose rules constrain the attention actors can extend to issues within those institutions. Institutions create free attention space that begs to be filled with attention, just as they limit the amount of attention that can be spent in a given institution. For example, the weekly question time in many parliamentary institutions creates both an institutional and a regular opportunity for issue attention, but it also restricts this space to a few hours of deliberation time and, consequently, to a limited number of questions to be tabled by each party or MP. Institutions are the venues where preferences and information clash. They constitute different arenas for generating attention to issues. This leads to questions about how different political systems are more or less open in terms of the number of venues they offer for actors to generate attention to issues. At the same time, venues are not neutral. Courts are, for instance, a different political venue from a Parliament or an executive; entry rules, the available space, and the consequences of juridical action differ from those in Parliament or the executive branch.

Summing up, the core of agenda-setting theory is that political attention is scarce and consequential. This makes investigating political attention crucial for understanding politics. In trying to understand why actors devote attention to certain issues, agenda setting puts forward several determinants: information about real-world problems in society, the issue preferences of political actors, and the institutional venues that allow or constrain political attention.

Issues as "Tracer Liquid": Tracking Attention to Issues through Time to Learn about Political Systems

The next question is how these broad theoretical ideas can be translated into specific empirical designs that can provide insights into the dynamics of political systems. Agenda-setting theory comes with a distinct methodological approach. We argue that this typical design makes it possible to learn about political systems, their institutions, and the role of specific actors.

The main feature of the typical political agenda-setting design is its dedicated focus on attention to issues. The agenda-setting approach analyzes political systems through the lens of issues. The idea is that we can learn about political systems by systematically focusing on how they process issues. The basic unit of analysis of almost all agenda-setting studies is the issue(s). This issue focus is the logical consequence of the assumption that politics somehow reacts to incoming information from society about real-world problems. By following how issues flow through the system—how issue attention by one actor or institution is followed by and leads to issue attention by another actor or institution—agenda setting enables us to measure streams of influence and locate power within political systems. Focusing on issues in politics is comparable to, in the medical world, injecting a tracer liquid into a living body to measure the circulation of fluids and determine any deficiencies therein. Zooming in on issues allows us to lay bare the interactions and dynamics between different institutions and actors—how they are linked, affect each other, ignore each other, and catch up later. In other words, focusing on issues allows us to study agenda setting, the crucial process of winnowing the number of potential issues to a workable amount of issues.

Naturally, the scope of the approach remains confined to issue attention; it does not deal with which decisions are taken or which solutions are adopted. Yet, precisely by limiting its scope to issue attention only, agenda setting yields the analytical rigor needed to incorporate many different political actors' behavior and many different types of behavior into a single analytical framework. Agenda setting allows us to investigate relations of influence between very different types of actions, such as demonstrating, budgeting, legislating, asking questions, covering news events, drafting bills, negotiating agreements, and the like. By focusing on issues, the approach not only makes it possible, and theoretically sensible, to incorporate virtually a whole political system in a single analysis; it also offers instruments for the systematic comparison of the workings of different political systems. In any political system, not only is political attention a scarce resource, but (a lot of) political attention is required for political action. In short, students of agenda setting focus on issues such as health, the environment, the economy, and others and learn from them about the political systems in which they are processed.

There is no doubt that measuring issue attention in a quantitative way strongly simplifies the political process. One may ask why many agenda scholars choose to study the quantitative derivative of the political process instead of the process itself. The answer is simple: it makes the incomparable comparable. Different issues, different agendas, and entire political systems can be compared using a similar currency: issue attention. There is a risk that by quantifying attention we miss the point and fail to observe the real processes. But as the chapters in this volume show, the approach seems to make sense and to be capable of capturing meaningful and important features of political systems. A key advantage is, in our opinion, that attention essentially *is* quantitative (with qualitative elements, of course) and can be studied in terms of "more" or "less." The carrying capacity of institutions and the attention spent can almost always be investigated in terms of time spent, length, frequency, or amount of attention. The validity of specific measures can be debated—is the number of words in a law a good measure of its importance and thus of the amount of legislative attention to the underlying issue?—but we hold that it is evident that attention can be assessed quantitatively.

A second key element of the typical agenda-setting design is its longitudinal character. Time is a crucial variable, since students of agenda setting observe how issues flow through institutions through time. Agenda setting is a process, not a one-shot activity, and gauging agenda setting implies taking into account a longer time period. Tracing agenda developments over time— how attention to different issues is prioritized over time—is a central element in understanding political dynamics. Working longitudinally provides a much stronger focus on the dynamic character of political systems than that which is gained from many studies of political systems that focus on a single point in time or short-term dynamics. When viewed in a long-term perspective, political systems are often much more dynamic because they are subject to wildly oscillating flows of information and slowly changing preferences (Baumgartner and Jones 1993).

In addition, the longitudinal design allows students of agendas to make causal inferences. Causality is more than temporal sequence, of course, but it is one of its main components. By adopting a longitudinal perspective, agenda scholars study how one agenda precedes and influences another. And in this case, causality is just another word for power.

Developments over time can be relatively short-term, for example when a political crisis translates into policy change within just a few months. Another example would be how spiking parliamentary control activities challenging the government on a specific issue may lead to swift adjustments or even dramatic short-term reversals of government policy. Or analyses can be really long-term when students assess how structural changes in politics such as the mediatization of politics, the volatility of the electorate, and multilevel governance are changing the patterns and dynamics of issue attention. Very often the starting point for such research is to focus on how agendas develop over time and then see how agendas have been influenced by, for instance, changes in actors (new political parties entering the party system or a government of a different ideological orientation taking office) or changes in institutions (a change in the electoral system or increased decentralization).

To wrap up: agenda setting tackles substantial questions about the role and impact of actors and institutions and offers leverage with which to analyze the workings of political systems by analyzing attention to issues over time. Questions about institutions and actors are asked from a process perspective, that is, from the perspective of how they influence agenda development. For example, we do not study political parties by describing them as formal actors, by analyzing their internal structure, or by counting their number in a political system; rather, we catch them in the act by observing how they affect the prioritization of issues.

Measuring Political Agendas Empirically

The agenda-setting approach not only offers a distinct perspective and a typical design; it also offers a series of concrete guidelines for how agenda-setting dynamics can be studied empirically.

A focus on issues implies that those issues must be identified and labeled. Therefore, agenda-setting research mostly draws upon an elaborate taxonomy of issues—the American original Policy Agendas Codebook is the most common (see http://www.policyagendas.org/). Because the goal is to follow a specific issue, or many issues, over time, the number of issues in the categorization system is high. For example, within the issue of the environment there are often subissues dealing with different types of environmental pollution. The issue codebook more or less resembles a list of the main functions of most states (finances, economy, foreign affairs, defense, etc.), and major issue codes correspond with the major departments of the executive branch. In addition to an issue codebook, measures to map issue attention were also developed by students of agenda setting, which allowed the quantification of attention to issues. In party manifestos, for example, the number of sentences devoted to an issue is defined as a measure of the salience of the issue in the party program. Because it best captures the zero-sum game of attention allocation, the amount of issue attention is usually expressed as a relative measure (share of total attention to all issues in a given time frame). However, agenda space can expand.

Issues do not exist in a vacuum; attention to issues is embodied in various political agendas. Agendas are locations of political attention; each location has its own specific dynamics and constraints. Political systems have many different political agendas. Some agendas are constitutionally or legally established; others are informal and not embedded in formal institutions. For example, one could define a "social movement agenda" as the issues the main social movements in a political system care about most, but this clearly is not a constitutional agenda. Agenda scholars examine a wide variety of agendas using the same issue-classification system, which allows them to map changes in issue attention over time and trace how issues on one agenda affect another agenda.

This book deals with agenda research in eleven countries. In each country nearly identical codebooks were used, all inspired by the original U.S. Policy Agendas Codebook. Small variations on the foundational U.S. codebook were allowed. For example, in the original U.S. codebook the issue "immigration" was included as a subtopic under the broader code of "labor." Since most European countries do not discuss immigration mainly as a labor-market issue, a separate, major immigration code was established, or it was placed within the broader code of personal rights. These small variations in the national codebooks do not affect the results reported in this volume. None of the studies directly compare countries; all studies deal with one country only. However, the cross-national differences are typically minor and can often be handled by moving subtopics to different major codes. Thus, when studies focus on general development across issues, the datasets are comparable. When studies focus on specific issues, they are comparable in most cases, but a look at the national codes is always recommended.

What Is the Difference?

The role of actors and institutions, and how actors and institutions together form a political system, is at the core of political science. The political agenda-setting approach, we have argued, can help us to understand political systems. Of course, many other theories analyze political systems and generate knowledge about their workings. In what respect is the agenda-setting approach different? Why and how would political agenda setting bring something new to the table?

The key difference is that the agenda-setting approach focuses on issues (problems and solutions—e.g., public policy) and on information. We learn about actors and institutions via their dealings with issues. In a sense, agenda setting tackles political systems indirectly by studying those systems in action and focusing on how they process issues. This indirect approach is the legacy of the fact that agenda setting has for a long time been a policy theory. Policy scholars have a keen interest in the content of policy measures, and they focus on the decision-making process as it pertains to specific policy domains or sectors. They are not particularly interested in drawing lessons from the decision-making process about the political system in general, yet this is precisely what political scientists are after.

Putting issues and information center stage differs from the prevailing political-system theories. Most accounts focus not on issues but directly on institutions, analyzing their forms and shape and scrutinizing their rules. Other accounts typically consider preferences as the engine of political action and for the most part ignore information about real-world problems. From preferences as the key concept follows a focus on political actors. Actors who hold preferences and try to implement them are considered to be the main determinants of political action. The agenda-setting perspective does not contend that preferences do not matter. As we explained earlier, preferences and information together determine attention allocation. Preferences and information interact: preferences filter information, and information updates or activates latent preferences. The agenda-setting perspective does claim, however, that the most dynamic element in politics is not preferences, but rather information (Baumgartner, Jones, and Wilkerson 2011). Preferences are more stable and often cannot account for political action; they need to be fueled by information to be turned into factors of political change. Also, the agenda-setting perspective holds that we can observe preferences only by looking at how actors process issues and information.

A few more concrete examples of other political-system approaches can illustrate the point. Tsebelis's (2002) work on veto players is a very well-known example of a preference-based approach to political systems. Its major strength is its ability to predict the effects of different institutional set-ups once we know the preferences of the actors involved. The weakness of the approach lies in its inability to explain dynamics, since both preferences and institutional rules are the more stable aspects of politics. The agenda-setting perspective would argue that only when information is included do we understand the dynamics of political systems. Furthermore, institutions are not just rules for shaping decision-making processes, but also opportunity structures for drawing scarce attention to issues. Venue shopping—where actors are able to move an issue into a different political venue—is thus an important mechanism of political change (Baumgartner and Jones 1993, 31–35).

Another example of an alternative political system theory is that of the Comparative Manifesto Group (CMP), which analyzes how policies adapt following the mandates parties get by means of elections (Klingemann, Hofferbert, and Budge 1994; McDonald and Budge 2005). Parties draft programs, get support from voters (or not), enter government (or not), and implement their programs (or not). CMP scholars focus on dynamics and change, just as agenda setting does. At least in their earlier work, party-manifesto scholars focused on issues and on political content; they implicitly departed from the same idea as that operative in agenda setting: that space on the political agenda is restricted. The main difference between CMP scholars and scholars of agenda-setting theory is that the former consider only one source of political action (electoral mandates) and only one specific actor (political parties). CMP scholars imply that political action comes about only through elections and subsequent changes in the power distribution engendered by the conflicting preferences embodied in parties. This is an arbitrary and unhelpful limitation of the scope of agenda setting and its mechanisms. Obviously, many things happen in society in between elections, and political actors—parties, interest groups, and social movements—are compelled to react, to take a stance, and to act on these new and often unforeseen situations. To

exclude issue intrusion as a distinct mechanism of political action is to neglect a large part of what happens in politics.

About the Book

The chapters all draw on the political agenda-setting approach, and all track
attention to issues over time in eleven countries. Most chapters do not address specific issues but rely instead on the entire range of policy issues.
By tracking attention to issues through time, all chapters aim to uncover
basic patterns and systemic features of the polities under study. Indeed, all
authors' basic assignment was to focus on a key feature of their country's
polity and investigate to what extent an agenda-setting approach could help
explain this primary national characteristic. Each chapter discusses a key
feature of one of the eleven political systems: the federal character of the
state in Belgium, Spain, and Canada; direct democracy in Switzerland; party
fragmentation in the Netherlands; the Westminster system in the UK; the
change in the party system and the breakthrough of new parties in France
and Denmark; the reunification of Germany; the shift from a proportional
to a majoritarian system in Italy; and congressional and presidential alterna-
tions in the United States.

Each chapter tests the extent to which an agenda-setting approach can
shed new light on the distinguishing characteristic of the polity. We explicitly asked authors not to compare their country with others but to focus as
closely as possible on their own country's particular political features. Hence,
the underlying idea of the book is not to further develop agenda setting
theoretically, but simply to see what an agenda-setting approach can yield
when applied to a very diverse set of countries.

The eleven country chapters in the book revolve around two broad
themes. The first six chapters—on the UK, United States, France, Denmark,
the Netherlands, and Switzerland—address the electoral-input side of politics: parties and party competition, elections, government formation, and
government priorities. They mainly examine to what extent party change,
electoral change, and shifts in the partisan composition of government have
led to changes in policy output. In a sense, these chapters examine and challenge the classic account that it is the electoral cycle that leads to changes
in the prioritization of government issues. The remaining five chapters—on
Germany, Belgium, Italy, Spain, and Canada—address changing institutional
structures. They examine political actors' and institutions' issue priorities

but compare them over a longer period and systematically focus on actors' priorities before and after major institutional change. The question is to what extent institutional change, with its changing institutional incentives, forces political actors to adapt their priorities.

Does a political agenda-setting perspective contribute to the analysis of political systems? The proof of the pudding is in the eating. All of the chapters in this book testify to the fact that examining political content tells us something of interest about a political system. Each chapter shows that an agenda-setting perspective of politics contributes to our understanding of the peculiarity of each of the eleven political systems under scrutiny.

PART I

Parties, Elections, and Policies

2   Party Politics and the Policy Agenda: The Case of the United Kingdom

Peter John, Shaun Bevan, and Will Jennings

PUBLIC-POLICY SCHOLARS HAVE NOT PAID VERY MUCH ATTENtion to political parties and spatial models of party competition. In the world of agenda setting, bureaucrats and elected officials compete with interest groups and experts to try to get their preferred topic on the agenda (Baumgartner and Jones 1993/2009). Political attention rises and falls in response to these demands and according to the cognitive capacity of core policy makers. Authoritative decision-making arenas, such as the legislature and the cabinet, provide rules and procedures to ensure that one option is preferred over another.

With such a focus on issues and actors, it is easy to forget that policy makers are very different from each other. Many key participants do not associate only with one sector of activity or policy—they also seek to appeal to wider concerns and constituencies. They may advocate policy positions associated with an ideology, a system of ideas or an outlook aiming to change or preserve the world. Linked to the promotion of an ideology, politicians have an overriding concern with reelection, both to their own districts and also—in a parliamentary system—as possible members of a government. Party organizations generally seek to gain power and to implement their own program of policies when in government. Their leaders occupy the highest office and have places at the cabinet table. They can make an array of appointments across public organizations, and the state's bureaucrats have to do their bidding. They use this power to influence policies in a particular direction and to impose some degree of coherence on policy.

Rather than being analyzed in its own right, party color appears only as a control variable in many studies of the policy agenda. But it is reasonable to expect left-wing parties to concentrate on social policy, and for right-wing parties to focus on international affairs and defense—the so-called guns-and-butter trade-off. The strength of parties in legislatures should, moreover, determine the degree to which it is possible for them to focus on their "owned" issues. The UK should be a strong case of party dominance because of the way in which centralized and disciplined parties command a majority of seats in the legislature, which controls both policy-making and implementation (Norton 2005). An interesting starting point for the study of policy agendas of political parties is to find out whether party dominance in the UK case translates into distinctive policy outputs.

To assess the importance of political parties for the policy agenda, we use data on executive and legislative agendas in the UK between 1946 and 2008, coded according to the policy-content system of the UK Policy Agendas Project (consistent with the coding system for the Comparative Agendas Project).[1] The objective is to analyze the impact of changes of the party in government on issue content. We first consider the policy content of the Speech from the Throne and acts of Parliament, examining the impact of party control on annual executive and legislative priorities of British government. We are interested in the direction and size of the effects of the partisan control of government on attention to issues such as health, education, and defense. We conclude by discussing the extent of the impact of parties on policy agendas in UK politics and the implications of these findings for the comparative study of policy agendas.

Parties and Policy Agendas

The central proposition of the literature is that political parties pursue distinct policy agendas. Parties seek to establish or maintain a reputation for competence and taking ownership on some issues more than others (Budge and Farlie 1983; Carmines and Stimson 1993; Petrocik 1996). Further, parties differentiate their policy positions in order to provide responsible representation of their supporters, sometimes even at the expense of strategic considerations (see Adams 2001). This is partly because they respond to different preferences in the electorate, such as between left and right positions; but also because they are backed by activists and interest groups that articulate an ideology that they seek to put into practice. Parties are likely to prioritize policy issues that link to their underlying preferences. In addition, the public expects parties to represent a diversity of preferences from which they can choose (Ezrow 2007). This expectation plays into the concerns of the activists, but of course too much distinctiveness could precipitate the rejection of the party by the voters at the ballot box. Giving priority to an issue suggests that governments will pursue more policy on that issue, while giving the minimum necessary attention to other issues indicates that the party does not claim ownership of them.

The comparative-politics literature highlights the impact of parties. Output studies show that parties on the left tend to favor higher expenditure on social items (see, e.g., Castles 1982). Researchers from comparative political economy stress that left-wing parties can maintain this expenditure even in the context of a globalized international economy (Garrett 1998; Swank 2002). Parties prioritize different aspects of policy—for instance, those on the left preferring lower unemployment and those on the right, lower inflation (Hibbs 1977). Evidence from the literature on policy and public opinion shows that parties seek to balance defense and welfare expenditure, with parties on the left preferring more social welfare spending and those on the right more defense spending (see Soroka and Wlezien 2010). The party-positions literature shows that parties receive mandates from elections, which they then translate into policy promises and outputs (McDonald and Budge 2005).

Nonetheless, there are factors that reduce the influence of political parties on public policy, such as electoral competition for the median voter, responsiveness to public opinion, the influence of interest groups, and media pressures. Moreover, there is pressure for policy stability when a party enters government (Rose and Davies 1994). Typically its leaders become more separated from the party membership, charged as they are with governing the country; and they do business with nonpartisan individuals and groups, such as bureaucrats and experts. Party effects are not expected to be strong across all areas, especially where policy-making relates to valence issues (Stokes 1963), on which there is broad consensus over objectives. To obtain maximum advantage from selective emphasis or issue ownership (Budge and Farlie 1983; Petrocik 1996), parties need to emphasize those issues that benefit them and respond to the concerns of their activists, yet not depart too far from prioritizing policies that are important for the country and maintaining a reputation for competence and good governance. Moreover, comparative analysis assumes that political parties pursue multiple objectives as vote seekers, office seekers, and policy seekers (Strøm and Muller 1999). The balancing of these objectives takes place within particular national institutional structures that mediates these party effects (Schmidt 1996). It is to the very particular institutional context of the UK that we now turn.

The UK Case

The UK is a party-dominated political system. Rose sums up the conventional wisdom: "party, not Parliament, determines control of British government" (1983, 282). The first-past-the-post (single-member plurality) electoral system usually creates a majority of seats for one party after a general election. With a secure majority—and a centralized party with good discipline over its members in Parliament—the government has a near monopoly over policy-making for an electoral term of up to five years because there are no veto players in the second unelected chamber or at the regional level. The electoral system also benefits one main opposition party and penalizes challengers. With the party in opposition preparing to take on this governing role should the incumbent lose the next election, this strong form of party government is sustained over time.

The traditional framework of British politics has become more complex since the 1990s, which might appear to reduce the autonomy of the executive and the party in government. These changes include increasing numbers of rebellions by MPs against their party whips (Cowley 2005); the growing assertiveness of members of the House of Lords (Russell and Sciara 2007); greater regional autonomy from the devolution of power to governments in Scotland, Wales, and Northern Ireland; the ceding of decision making to the European Union; and the growing power of the higher courts since the passing of the Human Rights Act in 1998, reinforced by the creation of the Supreme Court in 2009. Moreover, the first-past-the-post system no longer so clearly facilitates the electoral dominance of single-party-majority government, since there is a less clear relationship between votes and seats (Curtice 2010). There is also greater electoral support for parties outside the duopoly of Labour and the Conservatives, in particular at the subnational level, where proportional-representation systems are in operation. Nonetheless, the two main parties survive as the key electoral machines for national and local level elections: they win the most seats and usually obtain a working majority in the House of Commons. The governing party is able to enact most of its program through Parliament (Bevan, John, and Jennings 2011) and implement its manifesto pledges (Hofferbert and Budge 1992; Bara 2005), having access to ministerial and prerogative powers like their predecessors. Nor does party control of policy alter much when a coalition is elected into office, as happened in May 2010, when the Conservative Party and Liberal Democrats formed a new government. In a coalition, the leading parties allocate the portfolios between them, agree on a joint policy agenda reconciling their election platforms, and then use their control of the policy process to implement that agenda. A coalition government therefore implements the parties' manifestos, if in moderated form. Nevertheless, it is to be expected that if coalitions become the norm in British politics, parties will trade in their policy preferences on some issues in return for securing ministerial portfolios or policy concessions on other issues. This can weaken the relationship between one party's ideology and the priorities of the policy agenda it pursues when it becomes a member of a government (Müller and Strøm 2000).

Moreover, even if the UK is a perfect example of a party-dominated system, we need not always expect partisan-influenced policy outputs, because there are constraints that prevent parties from pursuing their preferences. Parties can be sensitive to the size of their majority in Parliament, either enabling radical programs or forcing governments to steer toward the center and thereby risk succumbing to paralysis. Some studies suggest that these pressures are so strong that party control does not make a difference to policy outputs in the UK (Rose 1980; Rose and Davies 1994). It may be that the very dominance of parties in the UK system means they are subject to more pressures than there would be in a multiparty system. Factors that push them together are party competition, media pressure, the need to be credible as a governing party, powerful producer groups, and the influence of a centralized bureaucracy. The movement of parties away from their ideological base is a feature of the history of British politics, such as the Labour Party's move to the center in 1990s under a reformist leadership and modernizing agenda. Party leaders created a rhetorical commitment to markets and the need to adapt to a globalized economy to justify a shift of policy toward the center (Hindmoor 2004).

In spite of these pressures, we still expect parties in the UK to seek to establish or maintain ownership of certain parts of the policy agenda, paying more attention to issues that benefit them and less to those that do not. However, there may be issues that parties attend to because they are important and in the national interest. There may be no partisan interest or advantage, perhaps because of the technical and nonpublic nature of decision making in a particular domain. We do not expect party control to impact attention across all parts of the policy agenda.

Data and Methods

To analyze the impact of party control of government on the policy content of executive and legislative agendas in the UK, we use data from the UK Policy Agendas Project (www.policyagendas.org.uk) for the period from 1946 to 2008. We report the nineteen major topic codes that encompass the main domains of public policy with which the UK government is concerned (see Table 2.1).[2] The analyses therefore cover the period of policy-making since World War II, during which time the party system was relatively stable, yielding extended periods of control by the right-wing Conservative Party and the left-wing Labour Party.

This chapter uses two measures of the UK government's policy agenda that reflect different stages of the policy process and over which the governing party has extensive control. The first is the Speech from the Throne—also known as the Gracious Speech and the King's or the Queen's Speech—which is an integral feature of the State Opening of Parliament, when the sovereign addresses the chamber of the House of Lords with members of the House of Commons watching from the galleries. Since 1901 the Speech from the Throne has been a permanent fixture of the political calendar in Westminster, occurring at the start of the parliamentary session.[3] The speech highlights matters of importance to the government and details the legislative program that the government intends to enact in the forthcoming year.

Table 2.1. UK Policy Agendas Project major topic codes

1. Macroeconomics
2. Civil rights, minority issues, immigration, and civil liberties
3. Health
4. Agriculture
5. Labor and employment
6. Education and culture
7. Environment
8. Energy
10. Transportation
12. Law, crime, and family issues
13. Social welfare
14. Community development, planning, and housing issues
15. Banking, finance, and domestic commerce
16. Defense
17. Space, science, technology, and communications
18. Foreign trade
19. International affairs and foreign aid
20. Government operations
21. Public lands, water management, colonial and territorial issues

Note: See www.policyagendas.org.uk for the full codebook with subtopic categories and topic descriptions.

By highlighting certain issues and ignoring others, the speech provides an annual platform on which government can shape the national agenda (Jennings et al. 2011).

The unification of executive and legislative powers in the British political system, combined with its long-standing tradition of party discipline, suggests that there should be a close link between executive and legislative agendas and the other outputs of government. Empirical evidence shows a strong relationship between manifesto pledges, the legislative proposals of governing parties, and actual policy outputs (Hofferbert and Budge 1992; Bara 2005; Bevan, John, and Jennings 2011). The speech has been used as a measure of policy-making (Namenwirth and Weber 1987; Bara 2005; Hobolt and Klemmensen 2005; Jennings and John 2009; John and Jennings 2010; Jennings et al. 2011), as well as in comparison with similar annual executive speeches delivered by heads of state or of government in other countries across Western Europe and in the United States (see Jennings et al. 2011; Mortensen et al. 2011). This statement of the government's agenda is a key part of the agenda-setting process in British politics. Analysis of its policy content provides a means for assessing the institutional function of the speech as a signal of executive priorities and legislative proposals.

The second institutional venue in the UK is acts of Parliament, the name for primary legislation enacted by the UK Parliament. These come into effect after royal assent. The passage of legislation is dependent upon first, second, and third readings of the bill. Most bills that are introduced into Parliament by the government are passed (there is no vote on the first reading, and votes on the second and third reading are—typically—along party lines, although there are exceptions). In practice, the third vote is the only vote that counts, because the first and second readings and committee stages are procedural. The number of bills that are rejected by the House of Commons is low. The 1911 and 1949 Parliament Acts enable the House of Commons to override votes of the House of Lords in the next legislative session (so the Lords act as a weak check on the lower house).

The full transcripts of the Speech from the Throne were blind coded by two researchers first to break them into quasi-sentences (Volkens 2002), demarcated by a policy idea or statement as well as punctuation, and to determine whether each quasi-sentence contained any policy content. The quasi-sentences were then assigned a major topic code and a subtopic code. This procedure led to 90% intercoder agreement for most years. The coders resolved remaining differences through discussion, and the project leaders made the final decision in the few cases where coders could not agree (see Jennings et al. 2011).

The short and long titles of acts of Parliament were blind coded by two researchers, who assigned a major topic code and a subtopic code to each act. This procedure led to 85% intercoder reliability at the major-topic level. The remaining differences were resolved through discussion by the project leaders. For each act, the date of royal assent to the acts of Parliament is the observed time point, and since all acts receive assent prior to the start of a new parliamentary session, which is marked by the Speech from the Throne, we are certain that all acts are properly attributed to the correct parliamentary year and, subsequently, the correct Speech from the Throne.

To test the effect of party control of government on the content of each of these policy agendas, we estimate a time-series regression for each of the nineteen policy topics for the period from 1946 to 2008, with speeches or laws as the dependent variable. In this autoregressive distributed lag (ADL) model, the lagged value of the dependent variable controls for the autoregressive nature of the agenda over time. We test for the effect of party control with a variable that is coded 1 when there is a Conservative government and 0 when there is a Labour government. We also include a variable to control for the short session of Parliament in 1948, which concerned passage of the third act of Parliament to resolve the gridlock between the House of Lords and the House of Commons. In addition, we control for the effect of time to capture long-run changes (i.e., trends) in attention to large issues in our dataset, in particular the decline of agriculture, defense, and international affairs as core topics for the executive.

Analysis

Figures 2.1 and 2.2 report the frequencies of issue attention for speeches and acts by issue. These figures allow us to observe attention to each issue on the agenda and when it changes. The unit of analysis here is the quasi-sentence for speeches and the long title of the legislation for acts. The vertical lines indicate changes in party control of government, of which there were just six during this period because of several extended periods in office by a single party (the Conservative Party, 1951–64 and 1979–97; Labour, 1997–2010). As in previous studies (John and Jennings 2010; Jennings et al. 2011), we observe that the length of the speech remains relatively constant after rising just after World War II. The number of acts has declined since the mid-1970s

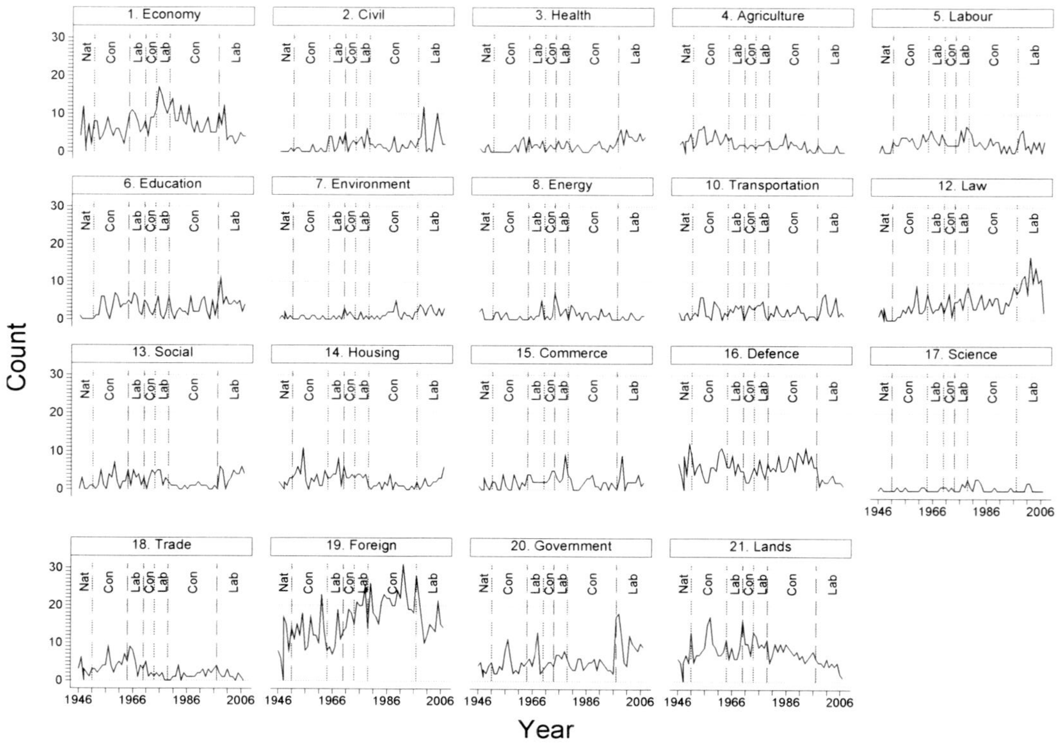

Figure 2.1. Speeches from the Throne, 1946–2008

Note: Vertical dashed lines indicate changes in party control of Parliament.

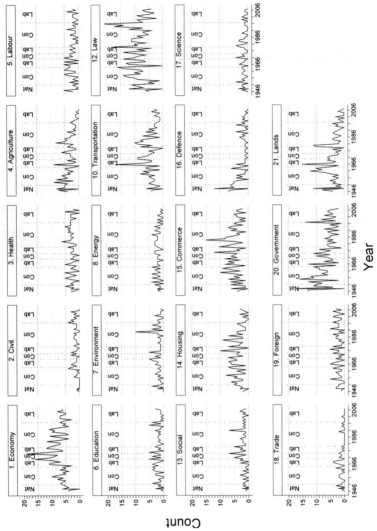

Figure 2.2. Acts of Parliament, 1946–2008

Note: Vertical dashed lines indicate changes in party control of Parliament.

(also see John et al. 2013). Figures 2.1 and 2.2 do not appear to indicate large changes at the point when a new party enters office, with no dramatic shifts in attention to certain issues following party transitions. These observations suggest that following a change of party control, the basic structure of the policy agenda remains stable, responding to long-run forces, such as the gradual weakening of the impact of the economy and foreign affairs on the agenda, the decline of older policy concerns, and the rise of new issues (see John and Jennings 2010). The growth in attention to social policies, such as education and health, appears to be a feature of Labour governments after 1997, as represented in speeches.

The use of time-series regression analysis enables us to analyze the impact of parties on the issue content of the policy agenda, which tests for party influence while controlling for other factors. The results of these analyses are presented in Table 2.2 for speeches and Table 2.3 for laws. For speeches, six out of nineteen topics show the effect of parties to be statistically significant (one topic is significant at the 90% confidence level, the rest at the 95% level). Overall, the size of the effect ranges from 0.8 (for banking and domestic commerce) to 2.6 quasi-sentences (for government operations). The direction of effect indicates that the Conservative Party attends more to international affairs, while Labour tends to emphasize issues involving health, law, crime, family, social welfare, banking and domestic commerce, and government operations. In general, the findings for the speeches are consistent with the issue-ownership model and traditional party images and reputations—the Conservative Party emphasizes foreign affairs, whereas Labour focuses on social issues, confirming findings from earlier research on the effect of public opinion on the Queen's Speech for the period 1960–2001 (Jennings and John 2009, 848) and is consistent with conventional wisdom. As expected, the valence issue of the economy shows no party difference.

The exception to the issue-ownership model is crime, which is commonly viewed as a Conservative-owned issue, but here the effect is negative and significant, indicating that it received more attention from Labour governments. The reverse argument is that a government might want to be seen to be attending to issues where it does not have issue ownership in order to reassure the public; this has been called issue trespass (Norporth and Buchanan 1992; also see Damore 2004). An alternative explanation is that it was New Labour, under the leadership of Tony Blair, which focused on crime, not only as a means of undermining the Conservative government

Table 2.2. The Speech from the Throne, dynamic and party effects, 1946–2008, by major topic

	1. Economy	2. Civil rights	3. Health	4. Agriculture	5. Labor	6. Education	7. Environment	8. Energy	10. Transportation	12. Law
L.Speech	0.521***	0.011	−0.010	0.119	0.380**	0.263*	0.007	0.217†	0.214	0.112
	(0.110)	(0.129)	(0.124)	(0.124)	(0.117)	(0.128)	(0.134)	(0.129)	(0.131)	(0.141)
Time	−0.024	0.045**	0.042***	−0.055***	−0.012	0.024	0.033***	−0.003	0.002	0.109***
	(0.022)	(0.016)	(0.010)	(0.011)	(0.012)	(0.017)	(0.009)	(0.010)	(0.013)	(0.028)
Conservative	−0.591	−1.457	−1.408***	0.372	−0.503	−0.220	−0.206	−0.426	−0.428	−1.494*
	(0.780)	(0.556)	(0.336)	(0.351)	(0.429)	(0.593)	(0.272)	(0.372)	(0.471)	(0.709)
Short	−10.871***	−1.380	−1.274	−3.646**	−3.063†	−1.785	−0.275	−1.865	−1.980	−2.330
	(3.168)	(2.157)	(1.236)	(1.350)	(1.702)	(2.377)	(1.089)	(1.507)	(1.876)	(2.715)
Constant	5.577**	−0.427	−0.401	5.491***	2.792**	0.839	−1.053†	1.354	1.908†	−2.363
	(1.8330)	(1.192)	(0.679)	(0.986)	(0.982)	(1.302)	(0.618)	(0.819)	(1.060)	(1.600)
Adj. R²	0.294	0.216	0.455	0.438	0.151	0.102	0.235	0.007	0.032	0.481

	13. Social welfare	14. Housing	15. Commerce	16. Defense	17. Science	18. Trade	19. International affairs	20. Government	21. Public lands
L.Speech	0.221†	0.137	0.156	0.285*	0.361**	0.422***	0.218†	0.263*	0.352**
	(0.127)	(0.135)	(0.128)	(0.123)	(0.126)	(0.116)	(0.127)	(0.122)	(0.116)
Time	0.001	−0.034*	0.006	−0.027	0.001	−0.039**	0.117***	0.047*	−0.048*
	(0.013)	(0.016)	(0.014)	(0.019)	(0.006)	(0.014)	(0.042)	(0.022)	(0.019)
Conservative	−1.202*	−0.647	−0.830†	1.092	0.158	−0.023	2.660*	−2.257**	1.138
	(0.503)	(0.526)	(0.493)	(0.687)	(0.210)	(0.456)	(1.322)	(0.787)	(0.706)
Short	−3.048	−3.697†	−2.080	−5.332*	−0.546	−5.238**	−9.186†	−4.448	−7.572**
	(1.878)	(2.111)	(1.960)	(2.629)	(0.829)	(1.812)	(4.921)	(2.938)	(2.685)
Constant	2.331*	4.930***	1.855†	5.268**	0.125	4.258***	3.215	2.257	7.719***
	(1.071)	(1.379)	(1.089)	(1.634)	(0.452)	(1.223)	(2.703)	(1.630)	(1.828)
Adj. R²	0.159	0.104	0.049	0.217	0.100	0.351	0.371	0.357	0.375

Note: $N = 62$.

*$p \leq .05$.

**$p \leq .01$.

***$p \leq .001$.

†$p \leq .010$.

Table 2.3. Acts of Parliament, dynamic and party effects, 1946–2008, by major topic

	1. Economy	2. Civil rights	3. Health	4. Agriculture	5. Labor	6. Education	7. Environment	8. Energy	10. Transportation	12. Law
L.Acts	0.347**	0.001	−0.153	−0.186	−0.060	−0.190	−0.123	−0.230†	0.100	0.031
	(0.121)	(0.143)	(0.129)	(0.123)	(0.134)	(0.127)	(0.133)	(0.126)	(0.126)	(0.125)
Time	−0.005	0.013	0.010	−0.092***	−0.017	−0.014	0.005	−0.015†	−0.032	−0.009
	(0.022)	(0.008)	(0.010)	(0.016)	(0.012)	(0.011)	(0.012)	(0.008)	(0.021)	(0.030)
Conservative	−0.169	−0.344	0.418	0.480	−0.153	0.195	0.360	0.718*	1.330†	1.935†
	(0.781)	(0.297)	(0.375)	(0.486)	(0.410)	(0.373)	(0.442)	(0.303)	(0.749)	(1.089)
Short	−6.537*	−0.996	−2.260	−4.881*	−2.310	−2.224	−1.548	−1.723	−4.496	−7.839†
	(3.070)	(1.106)	(1.486)	(1.937)	(1.673)	(1.489)	(1.738)	(1.162)	(2.947)	(4.328)
Constant	5.359**	0.487	2.018*	9.877***	3.288***	2.963***	1.363	2.775	5.376	8.004**
	(1.797)	(0.612)	(0.840)	(1.380)	(0.963)	(0.866)	(0.957)	(0.678)	(1.770)	(2.558)
Adj. R²	0.150	0.037	0.031	0.397	−0.004	0.024	−0.028	0.135	0.102	0.064

	13. Social welfare	14. Housing	15. Commerce	16. Defense	17. Science	18. Trade	19. International affairs	20. Government	21. Public lands
L.Acts	−0.057	0.045	−0.065	0.041	−0.096	0.127	−0.282*	−0.470***	0.081
	(0.133)	(0.128)	(0.126)	(0.127)	(0.127)	(0.126)	(0.127)	(0.106)	(0.128)
Time	0.013	−0.037*	−0.004	−0.067***	−0.022**	−0.025***	0.006	−0.159***	−0.078**
	(0.011)	(0.018)	(0.021)	(0.016)	(0.008)	(0.007)	(0.011)	(0.023)	(0.024)
Conservative	0.139	0.642	1.756*	−0.483	0.157	−0.351	−0.582	−1.714*	0.573
	(0.394)	(0.610)	(0.746)	(0.506)	(0.282)	(0.244)	(0.381)	(0.744)	(0.784)
Short	−1.315	−4.006	−3.940	−4.368*	−1.717	−1.743†	−2.479	−9.293**	−5.987†
	(1.559)	(2.463)	(2.948)	(2.010)	(1.124)	(0.957)	(1.499)	(2.955)	(3.140)
Constant	0.837	5.455***	4.289*	6.803***	2.781***	2.621***	2.513**	21.759***	8.476***
	(0.858)	(1.524)	(1.699)	(1.403)	(0.667)	(0.622)	(0.856)	(2.181)	(1.997)
Adj. R²	−0.020	0.085	0.072	0.262	0.084	0.212	0.071	0.461	0.193

Note: N = 62.

*p ≤ .05.

**p ≤ .01.

***p ≤ .001.

†p ≤ 0.10.

(see Farrall and Jennings 2012), but also to signal that Labour had become moderate after its shift to the left during the early 1980s. Before becoming leader of the Labour party, Blair was opposition spokesman on home affairs and famously used the slogan "Tough on crime, tough on the causes of crime," which subsequently appeared in the 1997 manifesto and became a symbol for a more populist Labour party. If the regression is reestimated to include a variable controlling for the period after 1997, this variable has a significant effect on attention to the issue of crime and renders the party effect statistically insignificant.

We would expect a similar pattern of issue emphasis for acts of Parliament. Even though speeches and acts are distinct venues for decision making, they are closely related parts of the policy process, because governments use the speech to set the legislative agenda for the following year (see Bevan, John, and Jennings 2011). However, acts are different: they are less likely to have been designed for public consumption and agenda setting and are sometimes passed because of a need to respond to external factors or because of internal bureaucratic demands, which might be less popular. The results reported in Table 2.3 indicate the impact of party control of government on acts for each policy topic and show that parties are again important, being statistically significant in five out of the nineteen topics (two of which are significant at the 90% level). The Conservative Party tends to pass more legislative outputs on energy, crime, transport, and banking and domestic commerce, while Labour prefers to legislate more on government operations. The effect sizes for the significant coefficients range from 0.7 (for energy) of an act to nearly 2 for acts (for law and crime). For legislative outputs, then, there is little evidence to support the issue-ownership model, because it is not clear that either of the parties emphasizes these particular topics, nor is there a difference in legislative attention to the core social-policy sectors such as education and health or to defense and foreign affairs. This is surprising given the party differences found in the issue content of the speech, and in light of the evidence of a substantial rate of transmission from the speech to acts. As expected, there is no difference between the parties in attention to the economy. The results also indicate that there is a sign reversal between the two venues for the issues of crime and banking and domestic commerce, with the Conservative Party legislating more on these issues but talking less about them. We would not expect a large party difference in legislation concerning international relations because most government action in this policy domain is conducted through executive decisions rather than legislation.

Conclusions

Parties matter in British politics, but there may be good reason to think that parties do not matter for the policy agenda as much as classic accounts of party government would lead us to believe. Only about a third of the issue domains identified by the Policy Agendas Project coding system are significantly different under Labour than under the Conservatives, both for the Speech from the Throne and for acts of Parliament. For the remainder of the topics, other factors—such as public opinion, events, external changes, and the work of pressure groups—make an impact on public policy. This is consistent with the metaphor of issue intrusion, where new issues are able to become part of the governing agenda irrespective of the partisan cycle (Jones and Baumgartner 2005). Here the dynamics of political attention also make their impact, where issues climb the scale of policy agenda beyond the control of party leaders. More fine-grained analysis using variables that attend to each policy sector, perhaps using case-study methods, could show how issue attention adjusts in response to emergence of these problems. Moreover, earlier work on the issue diversity of the policy agenda shows that party control of government is not a significant factor in determining the overall structure or focus of the policy agenda (John and Jennings 2010).

Party change through elections results in an inflow of new decision makers and new ideas inside government, but there are also pressures to retain a stable level of attention to policy issues once competition for space and time on the parliamentary timetable comes into focus. Parties also compete to ensure that the issues that are on the public's mind are on their agenda too, making the electoral changing of the guard less important than it might be. Parties are still important, however, and the issue-ownership model is plausible for speeches, if less so for laws. There are some exceptions even here, and we have noted the manner in which Labour paid attention to the issue of crime as a means of establishing its credibility, especially during its reinvention as "New Labour" in the 1990s.

The main finding of this chapter is that talking is not the same as doing: party effects differ in executive speeches of policy priorities compared with legislative outputs. Political parties differ in their attention to a number of traditional issue strengths in statements of executive priorities but do not exhibit such a discernible pattern of issue emphasis with respect to lawmaking. This is not entirely surprising: speeches are designed for public consumption and are intended to portray the policy agenda of the governing party in a positive light. Laws are often passed because of regulatory requirements, such as in response to European Union directives. Nevertheless, this finding is unexpected because of the close relationship between speeches and laws (Bevan, John, and Jennings 2011). Whereas the level of attention to policy issues in speeches tends to translate into laws, the partisan aspect of this agenda does not. That is a strong finding. Not only is there a general lack of correspondence between what is important for parties in speeches and what is important in laws, but there are sign reversals for the effects of party for crime and for banking and domestic commerce. For reasons that are not entirely clear, when in office Labour likes to talk more about crime and legislate less on it, while the Conservative Party does the opposite. This finding suggests that parties use these venues for different purposes when in government.

Parties matter, but not for all issues; nor do they have the same impact across institutional arenas. For a party-dominated system, like that in the UK, there are pressures for the two main parties to maintain their attention to many policy issues while establishing or maintaining ownership of some issues to distinguish them from their opponents. The results do not deliver a convincing victory for the politics-matters debate, but at the same time we do not find that party effects disappear. Whether such a pattern extends outside the UK is a matter for further research and debate. If parties matter less because of the compromises of coalition politics, then we might expect fewer party differences in other contexts. Research on executive speeches for Denmark and the Netherlands finds no effect of party control of government on the policy agenda of the speeches and only a marginal impact for the UK (Mortensen et al. 2011). If coalition politics becomes a regular fixture in the UK, maybe the already modest party effects that we observe here will decline.

Notes

1. More information about the UK Policy Agendas Project can be found at www.policyagendas.org.uk.
2. Major topics in the UK differ only slightly from those in the United States. Colonial

and territorial issues have been added to topic 21, and immigration has been moved from major topic 5 to major topic 2.

3. Until 1928 the start of a new parliamentary session generally occurred early in the year, January or February. Since then the parliamentary year has begun in October or November except after an election, where the first act of business for an incoming government is the opening of Parliament with a Speech from the Throne.

Lawmaking and Agenda Setting in the United States, 1948–2010

Bryan D. Jones and Michelle C. Whyman

L AWMAKERS ARE REGULARLY CALLED UPON TO ADDRESS THE pressing problems facing the nation they govern. In the autumn of 2010, politicians in the United States were in a furious debate over whether to extend the expiring reductions in income-tax brackets enacted by George W. Bush and Congress in 2001. Almost all of these discussions centered on the appropriateness of this action given the current economic situation. The effects of the Great Recession, beginning in 2007 and technically ending in the summer of 2009, were still felt far into 2010 in the form of high unemployment, declining home values, inflation, and other measures, leading to a general feeling that the U.S. economy was not recovering quickly enough. In light of these ongoing economic hardships, lawmakers vigorously argued a number of questions. Would the extension of the tax cuts worsen the long-term deficit? Would their elimination increase taxes sufficiently to worsen the slow-growth period that followed the recession? Would the return to earlier rates operate against long-term economic growth? Is it fair or economically efficient to allow continued tax reductions for the most well-off? All of these questions deal with substantive policy issues.

This observation will strike many readers as mundane. Policies are obviously directed at issues. And most critiques of public-policy actions taken by governments center on whether the action was warranted by the problem at hand. As a consequence, it seems elementary that political scientists would address the policy content of policies first and foremost, and that in any decision-making activities prior to lawmaking their focus would be the content of actions. Yet most research on roll-call voting, lawmaking, and virtually any other element of Congress has practically ignored policy content (Lapinski 2008). In the case of lawmaking, most studies have ignored content in favor of focusing on rankings of the "importance" of the act or whether it moved in a liberal or conservative direction. This has led to a great deal of work on the intensity of lawmaking, which goes under the rubric of legislative productivity (Mayhew 1991), and on the effects of public opinion and institutional arrangements on the direction, or liberalism or conservatism, of the laws passed (Erikson, McKuen, and Stimson 2002).

In this chapter we help to correct this oversight by examining the lawmaking process in the United States from an agenda-setting perspective, with particular attention to the reasons for changes in the size and scope of the lawmaking agenda. Agenda setting sensitizes us to the content of issues, not simply the number and importance of laws passed. It prompts us to identify factors that account for changes in the spread of activity across policy issues that the government is addressing (scope) rather than merely changes in the number of laws passed (size). The size of the legislative agenda is only one aspect of lawmaking in the United States. In order to paint a complete picture, we also need to focus on the content and concentration of issues on the legislative agenda and the relative importance of those issues to lawmakers.

Using datasets from the Policy Agendas Project, we first propose a new method for assessing the relative importance of statutes enacted in the United States from 1948 to 2010.[1] Then we use this new resource to examine two aspects of the lawmaking agenda. The first is the *size of the lawmaking agenda*, or the intensity of lawmaking activity over time. The second is the *content of the lawmaking agenda*, or agenda composition, which allows us to address the classic agenda-setting question: how has the distribution of policy topics addressed in the legislative agenda changed over the period of our study?

We find that changes in the size of the statutory agenda can be explained by traditional political variables, especially the size of the partisan legislative majority and public opinion.[2] Changes in agenda composition, while more elusive, are clearly understandable within a framework of the political history and development of the United States. Our tentative conclusion is that standard quantitative counts of activities are amenable to study by techniques that affect lawmaking throughout the period of study—such as the size of the Democratic majority in Congress, public mood, and conditions of unified or divided government. However, we find that examining the policy content of laws requires sensitivity to the temporal context of policy evolution and development. That is, we cannot account for changes in the policy focus and scope of the legislative agenda by studying the aforementioned variables and ignoring U.S. political development.

The Basics

We define the lawmaking agenda as the distribution of issues that are addressed by the laws passed during any given time span. Lawmaking has four distinct components: *intensity, significance, content,* and *direction.* Intensity, or legislative productivity, refers to the number of laws passed during any given period of time. The other three components refer to any single statute. Significance denotes whether the statute has been defined as important (Mayhew 1991). Any single law may also be characterized by its issue focus, or policy content, and how far it moves in a liberal or conservative direction (Jones, Larsen-Price, and Wilkerson 2009).[3]

Our system allows three separate estimates of the lawmaking agenda. The *general lawmaking agenda* is the aggregation of the topical content of laws passed in any given session of Congress (or during any arbitrary time period). Over the period of our study, 19,823 laws were passed, forming the general lawmaking agenda. Within the general agenda, however, some laws occupy a disproportionate amount of time and energy of legislators. We distinguish two subsets of the general lawmaking agenda. The first is the set of laws warranting any coverage by the *Congressional Quarterly Almanac* (hereafter referred to as *CQ*), a specialized media publication that offers extensive and consistent coverage of the U.S. legislative process throughout the period under study. This subset consists of 5,560 laws, which we term the *covered lawmaking agenda.* The second subset is composed of laws that received inordinate coverage, defined as exceeding at least one standard deviation above the mean of lines of *CQ* coverage in a given session, exclusive of those which received zero lines of coverage. This subset is the *prioritized lawmaking agenda* and consists of 551 laws during the period under consideration. Figure 3.1 indicates the relationships among these lawmaking agendas.

We estimate activity in these lawmaking agendas using two datasets from the U.S. Policy Agendas Project: the Public Laws Database, which includes all laws coded according to the nineteen major topics of Policy Agendas Project coding scheme (see appendix), and the Most Important Laws Database, which incorporates a system of associating the statutes with the number of lines of coverage they receive in *CQ*.[4] We then explore shifts in the issue priorities represented both by all laws passed since World War II and by those deemed by our method to be prioritized statutes.

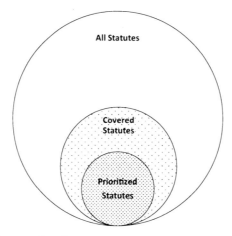

Figure 3.1. Lawmaking agendas: all statutes (N = 19,823), covered statutes (N = 5,560), and prioritized statutes (N = 551)

Note: The figure shows the relationship between three lawmaking agendas. The general lawmaking agenda consists of all laws passed over the period of this study. Covered statutes are a subset of the general lawmaking agenda and include those laws that received any coverage in the *Congressional Quarterly* almanac. Prioritized statutes are a subset of the covered lawmaking agenda and consist of those statutes that receive a disproportionately large share of *CQ* coverage.

Assessing the Legislative Agenda

In 1991 David Mayhew published a study of the relationship between legislative productivity (defined as the number of important statutes passed) and divided government, essentially reporting no relationship. Despite intuitions to the contrary, Mayhew found that important laws win enactment under conditions of divided government just as often as they do under conditions of unified government. This study both stimulated a reexamination of divided government and initiated a new focus on assessing legislative output beyond measures of roll-call voting.

As Mayhew noted, measuring legislative productivity is not straightforward. We could look at the number of statutes enacted as a measure of productivity, but what if Congress in the past enacted lots of trivial laws? Moreover, Congress sometimes passes more omnibus or comprehensive laws in some sessions than in others, and the effect looks systematic. For example, in the 1980s and 1990s Congress used omnibus measures to pass budget reconciliations and complex combined appropriations. Krutz (2000) argues that this is a consequence of a more active party system and the decline of deference to committee recommendations by the chamber, requiring more "logrolling" across arenas to accomplish legislative ends. As a consequence, simply counting statutes may underestimate legislative productivity in the modern era.

It is, unfortunately, also devilishly difficult to assess importance, because importance is rooted in the context of the times (Clinton and Lapinski 2006, 234). What warrants major discussion in a given era may not be viewed in hindsight as particularly important. Conversely, statutes initially passed with little fanfare may become important and occupy positions of great significance in subsequent policy debates. Such is the case with the Clean Air Act of 1963, the first federal legislation on air-pollution control. This act set the stage for future air-quality regulation; however during its passage it was not viewed as particularly important and did not receive any coverage in CQ. Mayhew, in attempting to capture this, developed measures that involved the judgments of both contemporaneous and later observers (1991). His approach was systematic, but the judgments of editors and compilers certainly involved subjectivity. Several scholars have critiqued this aspect of his study and suggested modifications (Howell et al. 2000; Clinton and Lapinski 2006; Lapinski 2008).[5] Moreover, retrospective judgments of statutory importance are irrelevant to the decisions that led to a statute's passage. An effect cannot precede its cause. If we are interested in the examination of public opinion, divided government, or any other variables that are contemporaneous with the statute's passage, we should not include retrospective evaluations. Only the judgments of contemporary observers can affect passage.

Our system relies on the identical content coding by the Policy Agendas Project of CQ stories and of statutes passed. CQ has covered legislative activity in the U.S. Congress since 1945; it is the only consistent and systematic source we have for these matters. We noted whether CQ covered the act in the body of its annual volume. For those included, we weighted the statutes by the amount of CQ coverage on the major topic area of the statute in the articles where the statute was mentioned. This orders by rank all statutes that were passed, but of course it cannot distinguish among those that received no coverage.[6] Unfortunately the CQ volumes vary considerably in size, which could be related to limits on the carrying capacity of the volumes but also to the amount of legislative activity (requiring more coverage).[7]

Our dataset of important statutes has limitations (associated with validity) but it also has major advantages (associated with increases in reliability) over other approaches. It also has the added advantage of carrying with it the systematic content codes of the Policy Agendas Project. This allows us to study how any given session of Congress has prioritized various policies in its lawmaking activities. By examining the statutes that engender the most coverage relative to other statutes in the session, we get a measure of statute prioritization within the context of the session. This is the measure we employ here to distinguish between prioritized legislation and the covered and general lawmaking agendas. It is not a measure of overall statutory significance, because it does not compare, for example, statutes passed in 1969 with those passed in 1995. But it does study directly the realized lawmaking priorities in the year in question.

Legislative Intensity: Counts of Statutes

We begin with a simple count of statutes. During the sixty-two years from 1948 through 2010, Congress passed and the president signed a total of 19,823 general public laws—an average of 319 per year. We judged as "substantive" those statutes that neither addressed individual grievances nor had a simple commemorative objective. In the past, Congress passed many acts for individual relief; many of these concerned immigration issues faced by constituents.[8] Congress also passes lots of commemorative statutes—2,938 of the 19,823 laws passed during this period were commemorative in nature. Many of the substantive statutes are of local interest or limited effect. Sometimes these result from the need to acquire property for federal operations; others address District of Columbia issues or limited regulatory matters. It is straightforward to isolate commemorative acts, but judging acts with limited impacts can be difficult. We need a way of deciding which acts are generally important and which are of lesser interest without relying on a reading of the statute itself. Our weighting system automatically accomplishes this by associating laws with the amount of CQ coverage they receive.[9]

There are some notable differences between the pace of legislation in the general and the covered lawmaking agenda. Beginning in the mid-1950s there is a secular decline in the number of statutes passed in the general agenda.[10] The covered statutes, however, follow a very different pattern. Following a burst of activity after World War II, the number of statutes covered declined during the 1950s and then began a rise in the late 1950s as Democrats came into power. The peak period for coverage was the early 1970s, but aggressive statute making declined only with the election of Ronald Reagan in 1980. After a brief rise during the early years of Bill Clinton's administration, the covered lawmaking agenda collapsed in the late 1990s and remained muted throughout the period of study. On the face of it, the pattern suggests lower levels of lawmaking during Republican administrations.

The Distribution of Lawmaking Attention

By associating the number of lines of *CQ* coverage with laws, we have generated a measure of attention to the lawmaking activity associated with successful statutes. As a consequence, we expect the kind of skewed, leptokurtotic distribution always associated with the disproportionate distribution of attention. Of the 19,823 laws passed during the period, only 5,560, or about 28%, received any coverage at all in *CQ*.

Figure 3.2 plots the distribution of *CQ* coverage associated with all laws over the period of this study. We present both the raw frequency distribution (the number of lines of *CQ* coverage associated with each statute passed between 1948 and 2010) and a log-log plot (log of the frequency count of the number of lines of *CQ* coverage associated with each statute by the log of the upper bin limit of the lines of *CQ* coverage). The characteristic distribution is in evidence. The log-log plot shows that the distribution of lawmaking attention approximates a power function. This distribution is directly related to the agenda distinctions presented in figure 3.1. Most statues are passed with little fanfare; a few take up a disproportionate amount of time (assessed by *CQ* coverage). What is remarkable is how few statutes engender moderate attention: lawmakers either spend a lot of time and energy passing a law or almost no time and energy at all.

The distribution in figure 3.2 is directly related to the agenda distinctions we introduced earlier in this chapter. In effect, the general lawmaking agenda consists disproportionately of laws that generate no interest, even inside the Beltway. The covered agenda consists mostly of laws of specialized interest—they generate only minimal coverage but are worthy of note. The prioritized agenda, consisting of a very limited number of laws, disproportionately captivates attention during any congressional session.

The Causes of Legislative Productivity

In this section we present the results of models for variations in the size of two separate lawmaking agendas: the general lawmaking agenda and the

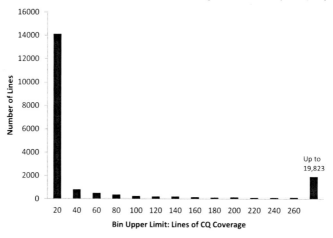

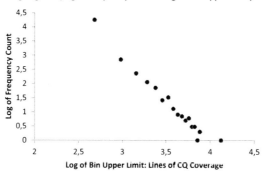

Figure 3.2. Frequency distribution of the amount of CQ coverage for all statutes (N = 19,823) and Log-Log Plot (log of frequency count × log of bin upper limit)

Note: Most statutes are passed without any coverage in CQ, while others attract a disproportionately large share of coverage. The figure shows the relationship between laws passed during the period of this study and the amount of CQ coverage they receive. The distribution is characteristic of a power function and is related to the agenda distinctions presented in figure 3.1.

covered agenda. In each case, the variable of interest is the count of statutes passed, with the size of the Democratic legislative majority (a rough but useful summary measure of legislative party dominance calculated by a simple sum of the Democratic members of the House and Senate),[11] the party of the president, Stimson's (2000) public mood measure, and the number of laws passed the year before (assuming that legislative activity begets legislative activity) as independent variables. We controlled for variations in congressional routines by entering the session in which the activity took place. For the general lawmaking agenda, we added a counter to control for the general trend toward a smaller number of statutes during the period.

Findings presented by other researchers suggest that public mood and governmental activity are in dynamic equilibrium, but with lags. That is, when government grows, the mood becomes more conservative, in a classic negative feedback process (Wlezien 1995; Stimson 2000; Erikson, MacKuen, and Stimson 2002). As a consequence, public mood is entered with one- and two-year lags. These researchers have not examined the totality of laws, as we do here; Wlezien examined budgets, while Erikson, MacKuen, and Stimson examined a directional model of government output which only included Mayhew's important statutes, each assigned a liberal or conservative direction.

For the size of the general lawmaking agenda, only the control variables for the time counter and session are significant. As expected, the raw number of laws passed by the legislature has decreased over the period of this study. Unsurprisingly, a greater number of statutes are passed during the second session of Congress as lawmakers run down the clock and vote on lingering pieces of legislation. None of the substantive explanatory variables reach significance, although mood the year before nears significance and the size of the Democratic majority is in the proper direction. Results are presented in table 3.1.

For the covered lawmaking agenda, results are somewhat clearer. A larger Democratic majority leads to increased statutory output, and the relationship is statistically significant. As the size of the Democratic majority increases, Congress passes more pieces of legislation warranting coverage in CQ. We also find some evidence of the expected complex relationship between public mood and lawmaking. There is an inverse relationship between the public's mood in any given year and the lawmaking activity that takes place in the immediately preceding year, and a direct relationship with the year before that. The number of covered laws decreases in the first year following an increase in liberalism and increases two years after an increase in liberalism.

Here is how we can summarize our findings for the covered agenda:

- Larger Democratic majorities enact more laws warranting coverage in CQ.
- Public opinion affects the size of the covered lawmaking agenda both directly and inversely. More-liberal public opinion causes decreases in

Table 3.1. Regression results for all statutes and statutes with *CQ* coverage (1954–2010); $N = 57$

	Statutes, lagged 1 year	% Democratic majority	Mood, lagged 1 year	Mood, lagged 2 years	Session	Count for passage of time	Constant
All statutes	0.11	51.83	4.82*	−5.47	−179.19***	−3.61***	493.41***
SE	0.15	162.22	3.25	4.04	28.04	0.79	136.60
						$R^2 = 0.771$	Adj. $R^2 = 0.743$
Statutes with CQ coverage	0.28**	310.18***	−5.86**	4.58**	−50.17***	−0.72**	12.91
SE	0.12	91.63	2.23	2.13	9.82	0.34	73.14
						$R^2 = 0.645$	Adj. $R^2 = 0.603$

Note: Changes in the size of the general lawmaking agenda and the covered lawmaking agenda are influenced by traditional political variables. The size of the general lawmaking agenda can be explained by changes in the level of public conservatism in the prior year, session, and the linear passage of time. The size of the covered agenda can be explained by the number of covered statutes passed in the previous year, the public's level of conservatism for two years prior, session, and the passage of time.

* Statistical significance at the 0.10 level.

** Statistical significance at the 0.05 level.

*** Statistical significance at the 0.001 level or above.

statutory output the first year but increased statutory output two years later.

While the relationships are somewhat complex, the forces responsible for increases and decreases in lawmaking are the usual suspects—party and public opinion. Interestingly, there does not appear to be much of a role for the party of the president. The party of the president was included in earlier models; however, since it had no significant effect on either lawmaking agenda, it is not included among the independent variables in the regressions presented in table 3.1. Our findings indicate that it doesn't matter which party currently occupies the executive branch—the amount of statutory activity for both the general and covered lawmaking agendas remains unaffected. This does not necessarily imply that the president has no effect on the size or content of the statutory agenda. However, the effect clearly has little to do with party affiliation; it may have more to do with the unique style and ability of individual presidents.

The Policy Content of Laws

Thus far we have reconfirmed findings about lawmaking that are well established, adding an alternate measure of lawmaking that, happily, leads to results similar to those of other researchers. Moreover, it is clear that the intensity of lawmaking is well explained by traditional variables, although the president seems less involved than one might expect.

However, the simple count of laws tells us nothing about what kinds of matters government is legislating about. Policy makers pursue routine agendas driven by past policy activities and the need to engage in continuous adjustments of these prior commitments (Adler and Wilkerson 2012). They also respond to problems and opportunities—everything from an extraordinary policy challenge to a fortuitous election campaign. Our policy-content coding of statutes allows us to examine these agendas separately.

We know that many laws are simple, routine adjustments to the status quo, but some take up a disproportionate amount of legislators' time and energy. We are particularly interested in these incidents. In any system constrained by the time available to devote to an issue, the amount of time devoted becomes a system of prioritization. Our system of associating laws with coverage in *CQ*, which tracks legislative activities, is essentially a system for prioritizing laws using the activities of legislators, as recorded by *CQ*, to do so.

So we have two different sets of analyses below. One is based on the topics associated with all laws; the second is based on the topics associated with *prioritized laws*. Prioritized laws were selected according to the following criteria: if the number of lines associated with the law exceeded the value of the mean plus one standard deviation of lines in each year, than it was selected as a prioritized law. This process resulted in 551 laws' being selected as prioritized laws, out of the 19,823 passed between 1948 and 2010. The number of lines of adjusted coverage for these selected laws varies from 938 to 19,729.

Figure 3.3 presents the number of total statutes categorized according to macropolicy categories (at the top) and the number of prioritized statutes identically categorized (at the bottom). These macrocategories combine the nineteen major topic areas into a set of six discrete groupings as presented in table 3.2, which shows the discrepancy between the policy content of the general versus prioritized lawmaking agendas: defense and foreign affairs; economics, budgets, and finance; human services; transportation, energy, and the environment; agriculture; and government operations.

There are clear differences between the two types of lawmaking agendas. Most important, the number of statues on government operations

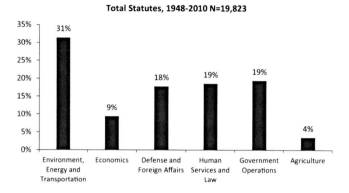

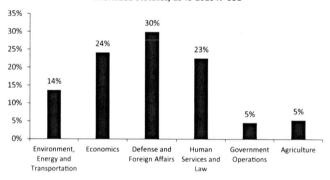

Figure 3.3. Topics of legislation by macrocategory, 1948–2010

Note: Differences in the policy focus of lawmaking are evident across these two agendas. The figure shows the percentage of statutes categorized into each macrotopic area (see table 3.2) between 1948 and 2010 across two lawmaking agendas (all statutes and prioritized statutes).

and on environment, energy, and transportation is much higher for all laws than for prioritized laws. In particular, laws involving general government operations—covering such matters as acquiring land and buildings, agency reorganizations, and specifying the duties of bureaucratic personnel—occupy 19% of the total legislative agenda but only 5% of the prioritized agenda. Environment, energy, and transportation, similarly, occupy 31% of the total agenda but only 14% of the prioritized agenda. Defense occupies a prominent place on both the total and the prioritized agenda but is almost twice as prominent on the prioritized agenda.

We examined the legislative agenda in more detail by using the proportion of laws in each macrocategory as a dependent variable and the set of political

Table 3.2. Macrocategories (see appendix 1 for major policy agendas topics)

---

1. Environment, Energy, and Transportation (Policy Agendas Topics 7, 8, 10, 21)
    Environment
    Energy
    Transportation
    Public Lands and Water Management
2. Economics (Policy Agendas Topics 1, 15, 17, Subtopic 2000)
    Macroeconomics
    Banking, Finance, and Domestic Commerce
    Space, Science, Technology, and Communications
    Subcategory 2000
3. Defense and Foreign Affairs (Policy Agendas Topics 16, 18, 19)
    Defense
    Foreign Trade
    International Affairs and Foreign Aid
4. Human Services and Law (Policy Agendas Topics 2, 3, 5, 6, 12, 13, 14)
    Civil Rights, Minority Issues, and Civil Liberties
    Health
    Education
    Labor, Employment, and Immigration
    Law, Crime, and Family Issues
    Social Welfare
    Community Development and Housing Issues
5. Government Operations (Policy Agendas Topic 20 less 2000)
6. Agriculture (Policy Agendas Topic 4)

---

variables we used to study the size of the lawmaking agenda as independent variables. In no case did these variables reach statistical significance. The content of the lawmaking agenda does not seem to be affected either by the size of partisan majorities or by the public mood, at least according to this first analysis. Because the content of lawmaking is more a function of the information flow—that is, the set of problems facing the political system—this is not surprising.

A Brief Qualitative Assessment of Agenda Change

We have shown above that, in effect, the agenda space expands and shrinks in response to traditional political forces. Congress enacts more laws with CQ coverage when the Democrats enjoy large majorities and when public opinion is supportive. But these traditional political forces fail to account for shifts in the focus of policy-making.

So we at this point need to turn to a more qualitative assessment. Let us first make a cursory comparison of the two peak years in the period of expanded legislative activity, 1965 and 1978. The top five most important acts in 1965 were Medicare, the Voting Rights Act, the Housing and Urban

Development Act, the Immigration and Naturalization Act, and the Elementary and Secondary Education Act. The issues of medical care, civil rights, immigration, housing and cities, and education are classically liberal ones, and legislation relating to them involves governmental expansion in major areas of previously private affairs on behalf of the underprivileged. Three (Medicare, HUD, and ESEA) involved major new agencies and governmental responsibilities, and the VRA extended federal power over states' rights.

In 1978 major topics included taxes, civil service reform, ethics in government, deregulation, energy, and the environment. These represent a far less focused or less condensed agenda, one driven in part by the perceived need to organize and limit the extent of government power. Major new initiatives in energy and the environment were not cut from the same cloth as Lyndon Johnson's Great Society initiatives; rather they represented middle-class horror over coastal oil spills and long gas lines.

Of course, these differences between the high liberalism of Johnson's Great Society and the conflicted and confusing presidency of Jimmy Carter are entirely explicable, but they are not evident from an examination of the pace of legislation alone. And, like understandable complexity in budgets (Jones and Baumgartner 2005), explanation requires a contextual understanding of the political, social, and economic factors of the day.

Next, we turn to a brief examination of changes in the macrocategories over the period of our study. Figure 3.4 shows the division of the issue space among macrocategories for prioritized laws over the time period of this study. The expansion of the size of the agenda space in the 1960s was clearly not a case of a rising tide affecting all boats. Fewer important defense and foreign-affairs bills were passed in this period of legislative intensity than in the statutorily more quiescent 1950s. The increase in legislative activity came primarily in human services, on the one hand, and economics and budgets, on the other. Transportation, energy, and the environment soon joined these topics and were dominant until they were partially displaced by an increasing focus on defense and foreign affairs in the later Carter years.

When a major shrinkage of the lawmaking space occurred in the 1980s under Reagan, not all policies were affected similarly. This era was marked by the utter collapse of lawmaking in human services and in transportation, energy, and the environment. Activity in economics and in defense and foreign affairs, however, increased. This shift in statutory activity followed a major change in the topics of public debate, which was focused primarily on defense due to an escalation of the cold war, tax cuts and reform, and deficit-

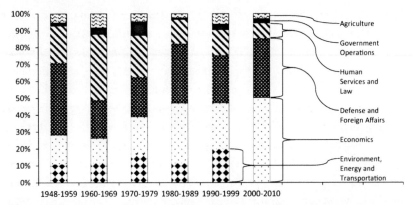

Figure 3.4. Topics of legislation by macrocategory, prioritized laws, 8oth to 111th Congresses (1948–2010), N = 551

Note: The figure shows the percentage of prioritized statutes that fall into each macrotopic area (see table 3.2) between 1948 and 2010 and allows us to track changes in the distribution of attention to policy areas in the prioritized agenda over time and, specifically, over the eras discussed in this chapter.

control measures. It was during Reagan's tenure that Congress passed the Economic Recovery Tax Act of 1981, then the largest tax cut in U.S. history. It is important to recognize, however, that two things happened in this era: the agenda space contracted, and it became more focused.

This view makes clear the changing composition of the issues addressed in the legislative process, especially the human-services focus during the Kennedy-Johnson years; the intrusion of transportation, energy, and environmental matters in the late 1970s; and the dominance of economics and defense in the Reagan and George H. W. Bush years. By the early 1990s, however, human services and transportation and environmental issues had again become the focus of statutory activity—perhaps reflecting a turn toward more supportive public opinion during the late 1980s. But with the shrinkage of the statutory agenda in the late 1990s through the middle years of George W. Bush's administration, defense and economics came to dominate the statutory agenda almost completely.

In brief, the topical agenda of prioritized statutes in the United States has moved first in the direction of human services in the early 1960s, and then into the infrastructure-based policies of transportation, energy, and the environment. The addition of these topics corresponds to the wave of statutory activity associated with Democratic ascendency from the early 1960s to 1980. With the constriction of the size of the agenda in the 1980s, defense and economics increasingly dominated the statutory agenda, a trend that held through the George W. Bush years and to the end of our study period.

These constitute major changes in the concentration and policy focus of the legislative agenda over time, but they are not captured by the traditional political variables we employed in the previous models. At this point they can only be explained as a function of the context of the times, which resists quantitative measurement. We suggest that it is the interaction between information and the problems faced by government, on the one hand, and the political preferences of the dominant legislative party and the president, on the other, that results in changes to the policy content of the statutory agenda. We intend to pursue further research capable of capturing these relationships.

Conclusions

The preceding analyses have revealed factors affecting three estimates of the legislative agenda reflecting prioritization of laws (the general lawmaking agenda, the covered agenda and the prioritized agenda). Some explanatory factors take the form of traditional political variables, which lend themselves to quantitative analysis, while others resist statistical modeling and can only be understood through qualitative assessment.

We find that the size of the general lawmaking agenda has been steadily decreasing and fluctuates according to legislative session, although it remains unaffected by traditional political variables. The size of the covered lawmaking agenda increased in the mid-1960s and attenuated in the late 1970s. After a burst of activity in the mid-1990s, it declined precipitously following the Republican electoral sweep in 1994. We can explain these changes in the number of laws passed warranting *CQ* coverage by traditional macropolitical factors—party control and public opinion—although in the case of public opinion, relations are complicated by dual feedback processes. On the other hand, traditional political variables did not easily explain the topics that were the subject of lawmaking or the concentration or spread of issues on the legislative agenda. We summarize our research in three findings:

Finding 1: The size of the general lawmaking agenda (the number of statutes passed) is affected by a long-run trend toward lower levels of statute production, but not by traditional political variables.

Finding 2: The size of the covered lawmaking agenda (the number of statutes receiving *CQ* coverage) is affected by traditional political variables including party control and public opinion.

Finding 3: The topics that are the foci of statutes are not simply related either to temporal trends or by simple quantitative measures of political forces. They have a logic, rooted in the modern political development of the United States, that is not captured by measures of political forces insensitive to the context of policy development.

Shifts in the lawmaking agenda are certainly affected by politics, but they are also influenced by the objective nature of the challenges facing government. How these interactions play themselves out writes the political history of a nation, but as a consequence they resist simple modeling.

Notes

1. More information about the U.S. Policy Agendas Project can be found at www.policy agendas.org.

2. The statutory agenda (also referred to as the lawmaking agenda here) comprises only written law passed by the legislature and does not include oral or customary law.

3. Although we believe it is a distinct component of lawmaking, the direction of legislation is not addressed in this chapter.

4. We are indebted to Trey Thomas for his help in reconstituting the most important laws dataset presented in this chapter.

5. One way to think about the measurement problem of the importance of statutes is to consider the differences between validity and reliability. Mayhew was fundamentally concerned with validity—getting the measurement right for any one Congress. He was less concerned with the measure's reliability—whether the measure was constant from Congress to Congress. Other scholars, particularly Lipinski, have tried to balance validity and reliability in some mix, but this has led to fairly complex assemblies of assessments and has tended to sacrifice reliability to validity.

6. Howell et al. (2000, 307) report that "CQ coverage is strongly related to apparent legislative significance" and avoids "censoring" problems with newspaper coverage.

7. Whether to adjust for the size of the outlet is not an easy issue. If the vigor of government activity (demand) drives the supply of pages, then one would not want to adjust. Nevertheless, a problematic underestimation of productivity in the 1950s is possible. Additionally, in the late 1990s, there was a shift in *CQ* carrying capacity, as evidenced by the sudden jump in the length of stories and the corresponding decrease in their number.

8. Although in the late 1940s around seven hundred private bills were introduced per year, by the late 1980s the practice had all but disappeared (see Hill and Williams 1993).

9. The use of covered laws avoids the issue raised in n. 4 above.

10. Omnibus statutes, in which several bills on very different topics are combined, cannot account for this trend. The decline in statutory production is too large to be explained by the number of omnibus statutes, which increased after 1980.

11. Entering the two houses separately did not improve the analysis.

4 The Evolution of the French Political Space Revisited: Issue Priorities and Party Competition

*Sylvain Brouard, Emiliano Grossman,
and Isabelle Guinaudeau*

F RENCH POLITICS HAS ALWAYS FASCINATED COMPARATIVISTS ALL around the world. Its rather original political regime, its messy party system, its radical parties, and, at times, its political instability make it an interesting case study. In France or among "pure" specialists of France, these specificities have often led to somewhat anticomparativist stances—an attitude often termed "French exceptionalism." Studies of French politics and French political institutions in the late 2000s have put France into comparative perspective and questioned this particular point of view, showing that France is much less exceptional than is often assumed (Brouard, Appleton, and Mazur 2008; Grossman and Sauger 2009). This is especially true for studies of French party competition, which are dominated by an ongoing debate on the evolution of the French political space. Since the mid-1990s some scholars have argued that this space has evolved from an essentially bipolar political space to a tri-polar space, with the left, the right, and the radical right as the three main poles (Grunberg and Schweissguth 1997). This interpretation has become very popular, as it confirms earlier arguments about dealignment and realignment and the evolution of values. It has also been challenged (Andersen and Evans 2003), however, and some have argued that France has shifted back to an essentially bipolar form of political competition (Grunberg and Haegel 2007).

This chapter suggests that studies of French party competition refocus on a neglected dimension: the issue content of political competition, that is, the issue priorities of political parties and the relationship between the content and the structure of political competition.[1] This focus is promising from the perspective of comparison, given the predominance of salience and issue-competition theories in the study of party competition in other countries. A new perspective is also necessary in order to address the inability of the previous rival theories to account for the decline of partisan (or ideological) identification and increasing electoral volatility (Michelat and Simon 2004), as well as the rise of issue voting (Lachat 2008a). In line with the work of Meguid (2005), we explore the importance of niche parties in the transformation of party competition.

Moreover, we adopt the perspective of the Comparative Agendas Project (CAP). Like other national teams, the Project Agendas France (French Agendas Project) has collected and coded data in a variety of areas. Using an identical classification scheme allows us to observe agenda-setting effects in terms of the relative attention to specific issues. Unlike the Comparative Manifestos Project (CMP), our data do not provide information about direction, but provides a very detailed list of 24 topics and about 250 subtopics. This exclusive focus makes our data superior to CMP data regarding the dimension of salience, even if this is at the cost of letting aside the measurement of positions. Using new data from the French Agendas Project on issue attention in party platforms, we revisit theoretically and methodologically the traditional issue competition approach. We argue that party competition is an essentially endogenous process, in which voters and electoral results play only an ex post facto role. Our results show indeed that the content of political competition is essentially determined by party strategies toward each other. Consequently, debates led in terms of cleavages and alignments cannot be considered to mirror the complex features and dynamics of French political competition.

The following section will elaborate on the actual debate about the nature of French party competition. A second section describes our research design—case selection, methodology, and data. Subsequent sections propose several empirical tests of our argument.

Parties and Issue Competition: Toward a Supply-Side View of French Politics

Scholarship on French party competition has long been dominated by an ongoing debate over the evolution of French political space. This debate is to a great extent centered on the role of voters and originates, obviously, in broader discussions on value changes in Western democracies since the late 1970s. French party competition has, however, never been subject to a systematic analysis of issue competition. Most analyses to date refer to the evolution of electoral cleavages (Bornschier and Lachat 2009; Chiche et al. 2000; Grunberg and Schweissguth 1997). As elsewhere, France witnessed a "silent counter-revolution" against postmaterialism (Ignazi 1992) that was best embodied by the rise of the Front National (National Front [FN]). A second, "cultural" dimension has been said to disturb the classical left/ right divide. This has been challenged by Andersen and Evans, who found that empirical testing of these results had been inadequate. Moreover, they provided data to show that the original left/right divide remains the single most important dimension and that the cultural dimension does not have any significant impact (Andersen and Evans 2003; but see also Tiberj 2012). Most of this debate is concerned with voters and elections: it is essentially a bottom-up or demand-side view of politics. In order to explain the persistent electoral success of the FN, students of elections have focused on the evolution of cleavages, values, and voter alignments.

In line with our supply-side view of politics, we consider that while elections do ultimately select leaders and governing parties, party competition responds only to a limited extent to electoral prospects and incentives. In a context of (electoral) uncertainty, parties mostly pay attention to the strategies of their competitors, perhaps weighted by their anticipated electoral success. Moreover, parties may demarcate themselves from each other not only by adopting distinct positions, but also by addressing different issues. As a consequence, we focus on parties rather than voters, contrary to most of the work cited above.

The French party system experienced profound changes between 1981 and 1993, since which date it has stabilized. Prior to 1981 and beginning with the Fifth Republic, French executive functions had been exerted exclusively by Gaullist and Centrist formations, leaving the two other traditional parties, the Parti Socialiste (Socialist Party [PS]) and the Parti Communiste (French Communist Party [PC]), in opposition.

The early 1980s were a turning point: since then the PCF electoral scores have been in constant decline. They fell from 20.7% at the first round of the 1978 legislative elections to 4.3% at the first round of the 2007 legislative elections. The year 1981 marked the first Socialist victory in presidential and legislative elections and opened a period of systematic alternation between the PS and the alliance between the Gaullist Rassemblement pour la République (Rally for the Republic [RPR]) and the centrist Union pour la Démocratie française (Union for French Democracy [UDF]) that lasted until 2007.

Between 1986 and 1988 France experienced divided government for the first time.[2] A period of left-wing minority governments followed until 1993. Even more important for our concern is the emergence of two niche parties during this period: the far-right FN first entered the National Assembly in 1986 after a strong score in the 1984 European elections (almost 11% of votes). A few years later, the Green Party became electorally significant at the national level, also after having garnered over 10.5% of votes in the 1989 European elections and nearly 14% in the 1992 regional elections.[3] Given the FN's focus on immigration and security and the Greens' emphasis on environmental protection, these two new parties perfectly fit Meguid's definition of niche parties (see below).

In order to study the importance of niche parties, we will focus on issue competition and issue intrusion. Viewed through the lens of issue competition, party competition is about "selective emphasis rather than direct confrontation" (Robertson 1976).[4] Empirical studies of issue competition explore whether parties feature distinctive issue profiles. The scope of differences between parties is also important for understanding patterns of issue competition. A complementary question concerns the issues on which parties differ.

Contrary to issue-ownership theory (Petrocik 1996), research has observed considerable "issue overlap" (Sigelman and Buell 2004; Damore 2005; Green-Pedersen 2007). In the long run, parties have no incentive to avoid issues that another party "owns." Opponents want to contest the incumbent's or niche parties' legitimacy and thus need to devote attention to a given topic, even if it is only to criticize the other party's policy stances. Furthermore, they want to avoid being criticized for ignoring the issue. Finally, when issue intrusion occurs, addressing the issue is a way to keep from losing issue ownership. This logic matches what Sulkin (2005) calls *issue uptake*: the process by which the policy priorities of other electoral contenders are taken up. It is not limited to the electoral challengers, as shown by Sulkin's (2005) study of U.S. congressional incumbents' agendas.

The rise of the FN and the Greens in France makes it possible to analyze the impact of party-system change on issue attention and to test for logics of issue uptake. The effect of the Greens' emphasis on environment and of the FN's focus on immigration and security allows us to explore qualitatively whether mainstream parties' attention to these issues has increased.

Methods and Data

As explained above, we approach issue competition from two different perspectives: issue ownership and issue uptake. We contend that what is at stake in issue competition is the prioritization of issues. Drawing different levels of attention to different issues implies a hierarchy of issues. Sometimes a specific set of issues is at the forefront of a party manifesto. At the same time, another party may rank the same set of issues differently and may include other issues. And both parties may or may not replicate the existing hierarchy amongst issues for the next election. So our investigation will focus on issue prioritization and its changes, looking at how French mainstream parties have ordered the twenty-four general topics of the agendas codebook. To fully acknowledge the importance of prioritization in the study of issue attention and issue competition, we will utilize a seldom-used indicator: the ranking of the amount of attention allocated to each issue as the indicator of issue attention. Going from a cardinal to an ordinal measure presents many theoretical and methodological advantages, from our point of view.

First, using the ranking is a relevant way to study the allocation of attention between issues not only in terms of amount of attention, but more directly in terms of prioritization. In fact, studying the amount of attention per se may be misleading. The amount of attention given to an issue may increase or decrease without changing its rank in the issue hierarchy. Conversely, the ranking of an issue may be affected with or without changes in the amount of attention paid to that issue. Studying issue rankings and changes in them is a way to give credence to the idea that issue competition is first of all a matter of issue prioritization.

Beyond theoretical interest in focusing on issue ranking, a methodological perspective also facilitates the study of "issue intrusion," that is, the emergence of new, previously neglected issues.[5] Furthermore, changes in amounts of attention are only loosely related to levels of change in the hierarchy of issues. The results obtained from our new indicator (ranking) were systematically controlled with respect to both preexisting ones (percentage-percentage method and percentage index).

The CAP provides intriguing opportunities to understand the importance of issue competition in electoral campaigns that compare favorably with expert surveys or comparative manifestos data. The CAP is the first attempt to code party manifestos with an exclusive focus on issue salience. The empirical sources are provided by the corpus of documents collected by the CMP, improved where necessary and possible.[6] With the exception of the 1988 FN manifesto, which could not be found yet, this corpus covers all French parties with more than 3% of votes at the legislative elections: the PC, the PS, the centrist UDF, and the RPR, which has merged with a majority of the UDF to create the center-right Union pour un Mouvement Populaire (UMP). In addition to these four traditional formations, the CAP has coded the manifestos of the two biggest challenger parties: the far-right FN and the Greens.

Party manifestos were split into quasi-sentences—that is, units of sense consisting of a grammatical sentence or a part of a sentence. Each of the over 33,400 delimited quasi-sentences was coded according to its policy content. The topic codebook of the French Agendas Project is a translation and adaptation of the original U.S. topic code, developed by Baumgartner and Jones (2002).[7] The French codebook contains 24 general topics which are subdivided into ten or more subcategories on average. These subdivisions result in a total of 250 mutually exclusive and exhaustive categories, providing a very refined coding scheme.

The CAP approach does not aim at putting an end to the debate between issue competition and spatial models of party competition. For the purpose of this chapter, we measure only issue salience. Further, given that party stances and policy outputs are coded within a perfectly unified scheme, CAP data make it possible to reliably test the relationship between party attention and effective policy agendas. Because of our theoretical perspective, this chapter will focus empirically on the two main political formations, the PS and the alliance between the RPR and the UDF. We chose to analyze their common electoral platforms—that are, de facto, preelectoral coalition agreements—instead of focusing on RPR manifestos,[8] since these documents were systematically signed before the elections and since these two parties mostly presented common candidates. In addition, this choice guarantees a greater continuity in light of the merger of the RPR and of a majority of the UDF in 2002, creating the UMP.

Issue Ownership or Convergence of Issue Profiles?

As mentioned earlier, issue ownership is a traditional way of understanding partisan divides and cleavages. A simple way of testing the issue-ownership hypothesis consists in comparing parties' mean level of attention to each issue. The ownership hypothesis implies that parties stress significantly different sets of issues. Ownership, from this perspective, determines partisan identity among both party members and voters. A party's issue agenda therefore has to be, first, different from other parties' issue agenda. Second, those differences have to be stable over time.

In order to test the ownership hypothesis, we ran a two-group mean comparison t-test on the proportion of attention dedicated to each topic by each party between 1981 and 2007, as well as the ranking of attention. Comparing issue attention across issues, it is striking that the two mainstream parties present very similar profiles in terms of issue attention and issue prioritization. Mean differences are significant for only two issues: unsurprisingly, Socialists pay significantly more attention to labor-related issues ($p = 0.02$ for percentages and ranking) and to civil rights ($p = 0.00$ comparing percentages and $p = 0.03$ comparing issue ranking).[9] While one might have expected significantly higher attention from right-wing parties for questions of justice and crime or immigration, these issues are ranked slightly higher in Socialist manifestos. Similarly, the relatively higher attention paid by the RPR-UDF to education and social policies was unexpected. On the whole, the differences are small and not significant for the quasi-totality of the topics. This finding seriously challenges the issue-ownership hypothesis.

If we assume, instead, that issue ownership is a short-term phenomenon, the expectation is that intrapartisan coherence will be low. Conversely, issue-ownership theory implies stability in the issue attention of each party. We computed an issue-convergence measure, adding up the absolute differences in issue-by-issue attention for each party from one election to another.[10] This indicator was originally developed by Sigelmann and Buell (2004) and has been adapted by Green-Pedersen and Mortensen (2009) to a multiparty context. Looking at issue *ranking*, we see that issue priorities are not frozen. Parties do adjust, confirming evidence obtained by Walgrave and Nuytemans (2009). Between 1981 and 1986, the PS has on average changed its ranking of issues by nearly four ranks. Moreover, the scope of change between two elections has not been stable since 1981. Between 1986 and 1988, the ranking of issues changed on average by 5.5 ranks and only by 2.5 between 2002

Table 4.1. Intrapartisan coherence in issue attention

	Socialist Party		Conservative Party	
	% Index	Ranking	% Index	Ranking
1981–86	76.6	3.9	69.5	3.7
1986–88	63.7	3.8	61.8	5.5
1988–93	61.9	4.4	58.2	5.4
1993–97	74.2	2.8	74.9	3.3
1997–02	75.4	3.2	83.9	2.4
2002–07	85.7	2.3	80.9	2.5

and 2007. Both indicators underscore the existence of significant levels of change in issue attention across time in the party manifestos of the two French mainstream parties. Intrapartisan change in issue attention is far from marginal.

Overall these first analyses appear to disprove and even to contradict assumptions regarding issue ownership. Since issue ownership should lead to differences in each party's issue attention, we computed a measure of interpartisan overlap by adding up the absolute differences in issue-by-issue attention for both parties at the same election.[11] We applied this procedure to both measures of issue attention (relative attention and ranking); the results are shown in Table 4.2. Both measures point to the relative similarity of the two mainstream parties' platforms. On average, party platforms converge on about half the issues. Cross-party priorities remain close for any single election. The level of intrapartisan coherence in issue priority is roughly the same as the level of interpartisan convergence in issue priorities.

In sum, partisan ideology does not seem to restrict the scope of attention or determine the ownership of certain issues. There are good reasons to think along those lines even if the role played by ideology in contemporary party competition is decreasing, as has been asserted. It is true that ideology constrains parties when they are drafting relevant policy proposals, since the party's stances must be consistent with its values. Nonetheless, because an ideology is a worldview, ideology is never at a loss for an answer to any upcoming problem or issue. Thus ideology and values help the party to produce policy proposals for any new problem on the agenda. As a consequence, ideology does not preclude parties from dedicating attention to new problems—indeed, just the opposite. This logic is probably reinforced by the competitive and systemic nature of party systems in electoral democracy.

Table 4.2. Interpartisan convergence in issue attention (between Socialist and Conservative Parties)

Year	Level of attention	Issue ranking
1981	56.4	3.2
1986	48.5	3.5
1988	85.5	3.1
1993	57.6	2.9
1997	41.9	2.9
2002	43.9	2.3
2007	44.4	3.2

Niche Party Power

Unstable issue ownership could be due in part to the fact that we have so far looked at large center parties only. It is true that large parties and "catch-all" parties have to cover a large amount of ground and speak to as many constituencies as possible. As a consequence, it should not be surprising that the major parties show some degree of convergence, as they are in competition for the some of the same constituencies—median or not. Niche parties, to the contrary, draw their legitimacy and electoral appeal from a limited number of issues. Bonnie Meguid has developed a forceful research agenda in this area and provides a useful definition of niche parties:

> Instead of prioritizing economic demands, these parties politicize sets of issues that were previously outside the dimensions of party competition. . . . The issues are not only novel, but they often do not coincide with the existing, "left-right" lines of political divisions. . . . Niche parties differentiate themselves by limiting their issue appeals. They eschew comprehensive policy platforms common to their mainstream party peers, instead adopting positions on and prioritizing only a restricted set of issues. (Meguid 2008, 3–4)

The common wisdom is that the French party system provides two clear-cut examples of such parties: the FN and the Greens. Meguid in fact conducts a case study of the former that she says is in line with her general argument.

An empirical investigation of the specificity of niche parties may first focus on the relative concentration of the policy attention of the different parties. To that end we use the common measure of entropy, Shannon's H,[12] which provides an account of the relative diversity or concentration of party agendas. The indexed version of entropy in Table 4.3 shows the evolution

Table 4.3. Entropy values for party manifestos for each election

	PC	PS	Verts	RPR	RPR-UDF	UDF	UMP	FN	Mean
1981	0.55	0.85		0.72	0.73				0.71
1986	0.79	0.81		0.78	0.84				0.81
1988	0.48	0.69		0.79		0.75			0.68
1993	0.81	0.78	0.74	0.75	0.82	0.71			0.77
1997	0.70	0.83	0.77		0.76			0.84	0.78
2002	0.72	0.81	0.80			0.61	0.81	0.88	0.77
2007	0.87	0.86	0.89			0.83	0.85	0.87	0.86

of entropy for most French parties since the 1981 elections. The measure is simple enough to read: the more it tends toward zero, the more the agendas concentrate on a limited number of issues; in contrast, a score approaching 1 indicates a perfectly equitable distribution of attention across all topics.[13]

Table 4.3 provides several counterintuitive results. While one would expect niche or small parties to be more "monothematic" than centrist catch-all parties, this is clearly not the case. The Greens and the FN scores show average and above-average scores only. The data for the PCF appear to be most representative of such monothematic biases. The platforms for the 1981 and 1988 elections show clear signs of strong concentration on a low number of issues. Quite in line with commonsense expectations for both these years, economic policy and labor take up more than 30% of the overall program, while such issues as rights, health, and energy policy are virtually absent. Yet, the PCF is an "old" party that has played a central role in postwar French politics. It is difficult to consider it a niche party.

Our measure of intrapartisan coherence in Table 4.4 shows above-average stability for both niche parties. The Greens and the FN appear rather more stable than their competitors, but differences are far from impressive and not statistically significant.

A third way of looking at niche party influence is to concentrate on the effect of niche parties' electoral performance on the issues they best embody or seek to embody. Given the relatively few data points—seven general elections—quantitative analysis seems inadequate. Figure 4.1 plots the attention of the two large parties and the electoral performance of the two above-mentioned niche parties for three issue areas.

Meguid insists in her work that it is the *combined* strategy of mainstream parties that will determine the success or failure and—eventually—disappearance of niche parties. In particular, the role of the supposedly

Table 4.4. Intrapartisan coherence

	PC	PS	Verts	UDF*	RPR-UDF**	RPR/UMP	FN
1981–86	41.48	76.59			69.60	68.54	
1986–88	26.15	63.65				54.35	
1988–93	31.25	61.85		64.56	77.93*	56.61	
1993–97	63.60	74.23	72.30		74.91	67.39	
1997–2002	61.95	75.44	78.72	52.33*		80.95	75.20
2002–7	64.33	85.68	69.54	63.54		50.00	83.25

Source: Agendas France. Source: Agendas France.

* The score for 1997–2002 covers 1993 to 2002.

** The score for 1983–93 covers 1986 to 1993.

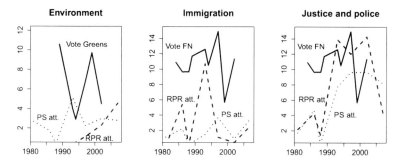

Figure 4.1. Niche party vote and issue attention

farther-away mainstream party is central in this framework. A center-right party may choose to shift attention to—maybe publicly oppose—an issue embodied by a radical-left party in order to hurt its center-left competitor. In comparison, the PS should and did—according to Meguid (2008, 159 ff.)—adopt an "adversarial" strategy consisting of strategically emphasizing the FN's positions, even if it was to denounce them. This was done, according to the author, with the deliberate strategy of hurting the center-right RPR. It translated into specific policy stances about illegal immigration. Moreover, PS leaders are said to have "constantly demonized" the FN in public statements (2008, 160). Most important, the author argues that the introduction of proportional representation was mainly motivated by the will to harm the right-wing RPR by strengthening the FN (2008, 162). This strategy is said to have persisted over the course of the 1990s (2008, 180–82).

While Meguid's research is based on original research and many sound arguments, our study of issue emphasis in party manifestos certainly does not confirm Meguid's general argument. Rather, we find that it is the major party closest to the niche party that reacts to the electoral threat through issue uptake. Issue-uptake theory leads to some qualitative expectations about the effect of the niche parties. First, we would expect the success of the FN in the 1984 European elections as well as its anticipated performance in the 1986 legislative elections to enhance conservative parties' attention to issues of immigration and crime in the 1986 elections. The rise of the far-right FN should thus lead to a sharp increase in attention to immigration issues for conservative parties. Evidence supports our expectations, as figure 4.1 illustrates.[14]

This is largely confirmed by the data. The issue of immigration rose on the conservatives' agenda in the context of the first major electoral result for the FN and reached a peak a little later. "Justice and police," which includes such issues as "social order" and "internal security," is a different topic. Unlike the environment or immigration, it is an "old" topic of which historically conservative parties in many countries have successfully claimed ownership. Yet the FN succeeded in contesting this ownership, leading to a historical attention peak among conservatives during the 2002 elections. The strategy of the incumbent president, Jacques Chirac, proved ultimately successful for him and for the FN and harmful to the PS.

The issue of immigration in 1986 is a perfect example of issue intrusion. The conservative RPR-UDF's program in 1981 paid *no* attention to immigration. Following the electoral success of the FN in the European elections in 1984, its first major electoral breakthrough, and its anticipated success in the 1986 legislative elections, the immigration issue intruded into the RPR-UDF's party manifesto in 1986 and immediately caught almost 5% of attention. Justice and crime also emerged as a new priority for the Conservative Party in 1986, with a corresponding increase in attention of more or less the same magnitude. This empirical result is a clear departure from the previous characterization of the strategy of the conservative mainstream party in response to the FN challenge (Meguid 2005). Moreover, the center-left PS did not take the issue up.

The electoral rise of the Greens should have had similar effects on the issue of the environment in the Socialist manifestos in 1993, because the party had strong showings at the 1989 European (shown) and municipal elections and the 1992 regional elections (not shown). As a consequence, a significant gain was anticipated for the 1993 legislative election. With an increase to nearly 5% of attention, environment gained nine positions in the PS issue ranking between 1988 and 1993.

In sum, this quick glance at niche party features and effects confirms the existence of strong interactions between rising niche parties and mainstream parties depending on the success and issue attention of the former ones. Niche parties are certainly one of the major driving forces of party agenda change, even if the scope of their attention is far broader than usually pictured. Center parties do pay attention to those parties and try to accommodate the views of the ideologically connected niche parties, albeit in a more straightforward way than that described by Meguid.

Conclusions

Shifting the focus from cleavages and alignments to issue competition allows us to gain new insights into French party competition. This is made possible by the new dataset on issue attention in party manifestos collected by the French Agendas Project. Our focus on issue competition and issue uptake between political parties, which departs from classical studies on voters' preferences, provides a fruitful perspective on political competition in France. Focusing on issue ranking and priorities, moreover, provides an interesting additional perspective to the analysis of issue competition.

From a substantive point of view, evidence suggests that French parties do not compete exclusively by adopting positions but also by emphasizing electorally promising issues. The issue competition perspective is thus relevant for understanding French party competition, but our findings contradict classical issue-ownership theory. Issue priorities do not differ significantly from party to party in the long run. The two French mainstream parties have not diverged in terms of lasting differences in focus. In terms of issue attention, commonalities and differences between parties are as important as commonalities and differences between elections within the same party. Parties have regularly adjusted their issue priorities since 1981. In other words, the policy supply has undergone substantial changes in focus over time. The dynamics of issue prioritization may be consistently linked to the ebb and flow of parties' electoral performance by the logic of issue voting, but also by the context of elections and the salience of real-world events. Of course, issue attention during electoral campaigns does not equate to effective political action, but since the late 2000s, studies of public policy have actually come to similar conclusions regarding the limits of the issue-ownership notion: there are hardly any significant differences in policy attention between left-wing and right-wing governments in France (Baumgartner, Brouard, and Grossman 2009; Baumgartner, Foucault, and François 2009). In fact, the result of our party-manifesto analysis may provide a new explanation for this phenomenon.

Now, how does this affect our understanding of the structure of the French political space, as presented in the introduction? The essential message is that the logic of electoral behavior does not necessarily match that of party competition, as measured through issue competition. Concerning the impact of the rise of the FN in the political space, our contribution suggests a different perspective. Without invalidating previous approaches, our conclusions imply that the FN has had a lasting impact on center-right parties' attention to issues usually associated with the far right, such as immigration and crime. A similar conclusion applies to the Greens with regard to the left. Hence, we show that niche parties affect the issue content of bipolar politics. Yet, this only concerns party behavior. It is perfectly possible that there are three or more categories of voters. An exclusive focus on electoral behavior alone, however, may lead to misinterpretation of the evolution of the party system.

Kriesi and colleagues, in their work on the evolution of the European political space (2008), show that the emergence of new cleavages may affect party systems in different ways. In some cases they may permanently reshape the party system; in others existing parties may successfully absorb new cleavages. The French case is often said to belong to the first variety. The focus on issue competition illustrates the strategies and reactions of parties with respect to the emergence of new issues.

Beyond the finding that French issue competition is driven by the logic of issue uptake, a deeper understanding of issue prioritization in political competition presupposes a careful and systematic investigation of the impact of media attention. The role played by the French media in political competition on two levels—voters and parties—seems to be a promising but demanding new research agenda.

Note on Data

We used a new and original dataset collected by the CAP. Thanks to its innovative methodology, the CAP may contribute significantly to the study of issue competition and its evolution by providing the first database to focus exclusively on issue salience in party manifestos. The empirical base is provided by the body of data collected by the CMP, improved where necessary and possible. With the exception of the FN's 1988 manifesto, which could not be found, this corpus covers all French parties with more than 3% of votes in legislative elections: the PCF, the PS, the UDF, and the RPR, which has merged with a major part of the UDF to create the UMP. In addition to these four traditional formations, the CAP has coded the manifestos of the two biggest challenger parties: the far-right FN and the Greens.

Party manifestos were split into quasi-sentences—that is, units of sense consisting of a grammatical sentence or a part of a sentence. Each of the over 33,400 delimited quasi-sentences has been coded according to its policy content. The topic codebook of the French Agendas Project is a translation and adaptation of the original U.S. topic code, developed by Baumgartner and Jones (2002).[15] The French codebook contains twenty-four general topics which are on average subdivided into ten or more subcategories. This leads to a total of 250 mutually exclusive and exhaustive categories, providing a very refined coding scheme.

Notes

1. This chapter would not have been possible without the invaluable research assistance and collaboration of Simon Persico, Caterina Froio, and Zach Green, as well as generous funding allocated by the French National Research Agency (ANR) to the French Agendas Project (Grant "ANR-Gouverner-55"). More information on the project and original datasets can be found at http://www.agendas-france.fr.

2. Divided government in France is called "cohabitation." It designates the situation where the president faces a hostile lower chamber and prime minister, irrespective of the senate majority.

3. Another short-lived ecologist party, Génération Ecologie, was in coalition with the Greens for the 1992 and 1993 elections.

4. This perspective was further developed by Budge and Farlie (1983).

5. The percentage-percentage method—the difference between the percentage of attention at time t_0 and at time t_1 divided by the percentage of attention at time t_0 for each topic T—has up to now been the most commonly used indicator for studying changes in issue attention. It exhibits a bias because of its inability to cope with a total lack of attention (Walgrave and Nuytemans 2009) and because of the overestimation of tiny changes for issues with only marginal attention.

6. For a more detailed discussion of the relative merits of CMP and CAP in the French case, see Brouard, Grossman, and Guinaudeau 2012.

7. For the original twenty-one major topics, see http://www.policyagendas.org. The French codebook is available from the authors upon request.

8. For the 1988 election, for which no common RPR-UDF platform is currently available, we had to rely on the RPR manifesto. The differences between the RPR and the RPR-UDF are small for the other elections.

9. Significance tests were performed on the basis of the percentage of quasi-sentences in each party manifesto.

10. Issue overlap is measured as the sum of issue-by-issue distance between two parties. The exact measure is $H^t = -\sum_{i=1}^{s}(p_i \ln p_i) - [(S-1)/2N]$.

11. This is exactly the measure that was originally developed by Sigelman and Buell (2004).

12. Shannon's H is a widely diffused measure of diversity that has the big advantage of being less sensitive to changes in magnitude than comparable measures such as the Hirschmann-Herfindahl Index. Shannon's H is written as follows:

$$IO = 100 - (\sum_{i=1}^{n}|P_A - P_B|)/2.$$

13. This calculation has here been done using the twenty-four major topics of the Agendas codebook.

14. Figure 4.3 presents indistinctively electoral results for both niche parties at European and national legislative elections.

15. For the original twenty-one major topics, see the appendix.

5 Party-System Development in Denmark: Agenda-Setting Dynamics and Political Change

Christoffer Green-Pedersen

DENMARK IS NOT A FEDERAL STATE AND HAS NO SECOND CHAMBER in Parliament. Courts play a very limited political role, and direct democracy is important only in relation to very specific issues, mainly European integration. Further, the functioning of Danish parliamentarism implies that the distinction between the executive and the legislative branches is of limited importance (Arter 1999b; Green-Pedersen and Skjæveland 2008). Therefore, the parliamentary arena is really the only important political arena in Denmark. What matters in this arena isthe competition between political parties. Danish governments—typically minority governments—depend on their ability to build majorities with other parties in Parliament behind their policy proposals. In short, understanding Danish politics and changes to it means understanding the dynamics of Danish *party* politics.

Looking at the development of Danish party politics over the past forty years, two events stand out in particular: the 1973 election, which doubled the number of political parties in the party system, and the 2001 election, which pushed the majority in Parliament substantially to the right. Studies of the development of Danish party politics have focused on these two events but have struggled to evaluate them and, more broadly, to understand how party politics has changed and the dynamics behind those changes (Arter 1999b; Elmelund-Præstekær, Kjær, and Elklit 2010).

This chapter offers an agenda-setting perspective on Danish party politics. Existing studies typically apply one of two theoretical perspectives: the format of the party system, that is, the number and kind of parties represented (e.g., Arter 1999a; Elklit and Pedersen 2003; Elmelund-Præstekær, Kjær, and Elklit 2010), and conflict dimensions in the party system (Elmelund-Præstekær, Kjær, and Elklit 2010). The latter perspective draws on a broader cleavage approach to party systems (Mair 1997). This chapter focuses on the substance of party politics. It describes changes in Danish party politics as a matter of changes in what is labeled the "party system agenda." In other words, what substantial policy issues have parties focused on? The chapter thus offers a theoretical agenda-setting-based alternative to the two standard approaches to party politics mentioned above, which is of relevance beyond the Danish case.[1]

From an agenda-setting perspective, Danish party politics was quite stable until the early 1980s, focusing on economic and welfare issues. The 1973 election did little to change this, but it significantly complicated majority building on these issues, especially macroeconomic policy. In the early 1980s other issues began to play a more prominent role in the party system. The first major issue was the environment, which was politicized by the left-wing opposition in the mid-1980s. These developments accelerated after the change of government in 1993, when the right-wing opposition began to politicize refugees and immigration in particular. This broadening of the party-system agenda culminated in the 2001 election, in which the issue of refugees and immigrants was highly salient.

Analyzing the development of the party-system agenda provides a new perspective on the development of the Danish party system and thus Danish politics. What has changed in Danish party politics from this perspective is the introduction of new issues into the party-system agenda. The politicization of the issue of refugees and immigrants, for instance, has been central in the success of a major new actor in the Danish party system: the radical right-wing Danish People's Party, which has been highly successful in drawing voters to the right-wing political bloc. This shift in balance toward the right has taken place even though the electorate in the aggregate has not moved to the right (Stubager et al. 2013, 22).

The chapter thus shows the importance of understanding the substance of party politics rather than just focusing on the format, that is, the number of parties. The broadening of the party system agenda has not also implied a more multidimensional party system. Despite the emergence of new conflict lines at the level of the electorate, the conflict structure in the party system has remained stable. The new issues have been integrated into the left-right conflict, and the bloc nature of Danish party politics has actually become more pronounced.

Understanding Change in Danish Party Politics

Party politics has long been a key subject of political science, and the literature on party politics offers several theoretical perspectives on changes in party politics (Mair 1997). One perspective focuses on changes in the number and character of the parties represented in the party system (e.g., Arter 1999b; Grande 2008). This perspective has its theoretical origin in classic work such as Sartori's (1976) on party-system dynamics.

This perspective has also been applied for the purpose of analyzing the development of Danish party politics, especially in the wake of the 1973 election. Until 1973 Danish party politics was dominated by the four traditional parties in the party system: the Social Democrats, the Conservatives, the Liberals (originally a farmer's party, but now a liberal right-wing party), and the Social Liberals, a center party. The only significant addition before 1973 was the left-wing Socialist People's Party in the 1960s. However, the 1973 election doubled the number of parties represented in Parliament from five to ten. The most prominent new party was the radical right-wing Progress Party, which gained close to 16% of the vote. The other new parties were either new center parties or new left-wing parties (Pedersen 1987). The next years were characterized by frequent elections, roughly every other year, and frequently changing minority governments. This development led to an intensive scholarly discussion about the future of the party system (op. cit) and even about a possible crisis of Danish democracy (Svensson 1996). However, as time went by, the Danish party system stabilized, with typically seven or eight parties represented in Parliament, fewer elections, and more stable governments. The scholarly literature settled on an inconclusive evaluation of the 1973 election and its effects on Danish party politics (Elklit and Pedersen 2003).

The other event that has triggered a discussion about change in Danish party politics is the growth of the Danish People's Party in the second half of the 1990s and the 2001 election. The Danish People's Party grew out of internal disagreement in the Progress Party and obtained around 13% of the vote in 2001 with a a platform, which was critical toward immigration. In the 2001 election the party's success was decisive in the Conservatives' and Liberals' gaining government power. Unlike previous right-wing governments, they did not have to rely on support from the Social Liberals but could base a minority government on support from the Danish People's Party. Thus, for the first time since the early 1970s a government was formed without the support of the Social Liberals. This opened a new discussion about change in Danish party politics (Elmelund-Præstekær, Kjær, and Elklit 2010). In sum, Danish party politics has changed considerably over the past decades because of more new parties entering the party system, but the scholarly literature has struggled with how to evaluate these changes.

The other theoretical perspective focuses on the emergence of new conflict lines in the Danish party system. This perspective is based on a cleavage approach to party systems (Mair 1997). Conflict lines in party systems reflect broader cleavages in societies; change comes about when new cleavages in society emerge, which then result in new conflict lines in the party system. The question of new conflict lines in the party system was debated in the 1970s, as a result of the 1973 election (Nannestad 1989). However, it became more relevant in the 2000s, as studies of West European politics began to argue that a new globalization cleavage has emerged based on the conflict between winners and losers in globalization. Radical right-wing parties are the typical agents that mobilize the losers of globalization, generating a cleavage based on issues such as immigration and European integration (Kriesi et al. 2008). In the Danish case, a similar cleavage based on education has been identified within the electorate (Stubager 2010). However, at the party level it has been difficult to identify a second conflict line. Studies of government formation (Skjæveland 2005) and voting behavior in Parliament (Hansen 2008) point to the continuing dominance of the left-right conflict. Actually, the bloc nature of Danish party politics—with competition between a left-wing bloc with the Social Democrats as the main party and a right-wing bloc with the Conservatives and the Liberals—was strengthened after 2001. The right-wing government of 2001–11 did not have to rely on support from the Social Liberal Party, which was part of the left-wing bloc (Elklit and Pedersen 2003; Green-Pedersen and Thomsen 2005). Since the 2011 election, the Social Liberals have thus been part of a left-wing government.[2]

Theoretically, this raises the question of the fruitfulness of understanding change in party politics as a matter of the emergence of a second conflict dimension in the party system reflecting a new cleavage in society. Does the absence of this second conflict dimension in the party system imply that Danish party politics has not changed despite the emergence of new parties, such as the Danish People's Party, which has considerable electoral support? The question is rather whether changes in party politics are not better assessed from a different theoretical perspective.

The Party-System Agenda and the Party System

Party-system change is clearly not the traditional domain of interest of agenda-setting theory. Nevertheless, agenda-setting theory as laid out in chapter 2 offers a number of insights that can be summarized in the concept of a party system agenda (Green-Pedersen and Mortensen 2010). Studying the development of the party-system agenda over time offers a new perspective on party-system change in Denmark and beyond.

The starting point for the idea of a party-system agenda is the question of which policy issues political parties focus on: immigration, the environment, the economy, and so on. Budge and Farlie (1983) argue that political parties compete by attempting to draw attention to issues they find advantageous rather than by assuming different positions on predetermined issues. The same notion about the importance of issue emphasis lies behind Carmines's (1991) model of party alignments and issue competition. As Carmines argues (1991, 75), "All successful politicians instinctively understand which issues benefit them and their party and which do not. The trick is to politicize the former and depoliticize the latter."

When taken to its extreme, the implication of issue-competition logic is that parties talk past each other. All have their preferred issues on which they focus all their attention. However, studies of issue competition consistently find considerable issue overlap (e.g., Sigelman and Buell 2004). Though parties have an incentive to focus on preferred issues, in fact, they address similar issues as well. Green-Pedersen and Mortensen (2010) thus argue that at any given point in time a party-system agenda exists, in the sense that a hierarchy of issues exists, one to which the parties must pay attention while at the same time competing over the future content of this hierarchy. The core of politicization, from the perspective of issue competition, is thus for parties to bring their preferred issues to the top of the party-system agenda because this will force opponents to pay attention to issues that opponents would rather avoid.

The idea of the party-system agenda thus draws on the idea of an agenda as a structure that constrains actors, but that they are able to influence (Dearing and Rogers 1996, 1–3). It also draws on the idea of a party system—the idea that you cannot understand the behavior of a party if you do not understand its competitive relationship with other parties (Kitschelt 2007). The same type of party behaves differently depending on the competitive context in which it finds itself.

Agenda-setting theory, as presented in chapter 2, further offers a number of insights into the dynamics of the party-system agenda. One one hand, the party-system agenda exhibits considerable stability from year to year. The best predictor of the party-system agenda in year t is the party-system agenda in year $t - 1$ (Green-Pedersen and Mortensen 2010). The underlying reason is the importance of parties' perceptions. Once an issue is high on the party-system agenda, parties perceive it as necessary to be given attention, which reinforces the issue's status on the party-system agenda. On the other hand, the party-system agenda also changes, especially over the long term. As argued in chapter 2, policy problems and their dynamics play a key role. For instance, changes in health-care technology present politicians with a difficult trade-off between cost control and citizens' expectation of new treatment opportunities, and political attention to health-care issues has generally been rising (Mortensen et al. 2011). The rising number of immigrants lies behind rising political attention to immigration (cf. Kriesi et al. 2008). However, policy problems and changes in them also are background factors in the development of the party-system agenda. It is party competition that turns policy problems into issues on the party-system agenda. Still, without a rising number of immigrants, for instance, immigration would never have been a potential issue on the party-system agenda.

Why, then, does the development of the party-system agenda offer a fruitful perspective on changes in party politics? The key answer is the increasing importance of issue voting (cf. Thomassen 2005). Issue voting means that a voter bases his or her vote on his or her view of political parties with regard to the issues he or she finds most important—in other words, that are at the top of the agenda. The implication for parties is straightforward: influencing the party-system agenda—that is, issue competition—takes on increasing importance as a way to influence which issues voters focus on when they make electoral choices (Green-Pedersen 2007). Thus, the development of the party-system agenda is a key element of party competition and offers an important window into changes in party politics. Studying how the party system agenda is affected by, for instance, elections and the emergence of new parties offers what existing perspectives on party politics lack, namely a way of evaluating the importance of such developments. What was the effect on the party-system agenda of more parties entering Parliament? What was the impact of a specific election on the party-system agenda? Thus, as argued in chapter 2, issue developments can be used a tracer liquid for evaluating party-system developments.

Measuring the Party-System Agenda

The next question is how to measure the party-system agenda in this chapter about Denmark. The key challenge is to capture its systemic element. As stressed above, the party-system agenda is a systemic concept in the sense that it is more than the sum of the issues parties would like to focus on. Therefore, it is not ideal to consider the party-system agenda to be merely the sum of the issue emphases of individual parties—for instance, as found in party manifestos. The problem is that this sum can be inflated by a few parties focusing strongly on an issue, even if all other parties are ignoring it. We therefore turn to the length of all debates in Parliament as a proxy for the party-system agenda. Debates in the Danish national Parliament occur in relation to four activities: proposals of new bills, policy accounts by ministers, interpellation debates, and parliamentary resolutions. While the two former types of activities are mainly initiated by government parties, the latter tend to be initiated by opposition parties. The length of a specific debate is measured as the number of columns in the parliamentary records devoted to its coverage. What makes the length of parliamentary debates particularly apt as a measure of the party-system agenda is that lengthy debates arise only on issues that many parties from both the government and the opposition deem important. Whereas a single party is able to ask as many questions of the minister as it wants and the prime minister can allocate as much of an executive speech to an issue as he wants, a party cannot on its own set long debates in motion; that would require that many or all parties address the issue at the same time. The measure thereby captures the systemic nature of the party-system agenda.

The parliamentary debates were coded using the Danish version of the policy-agenda coding system (see appendix), which contains 236 subcategories. The 236 subcategories were combined into 24 main categories, such as immigration, economy, health, defense, and the EU, which serve as the main analytical level in the rest of this chapter.

The Development of the Danish Party-System Agenda

The next question is how to analyze the party-system agenda. Agenda-setting studies offer a number of ways to analyze an agenda. One is to focus on the format of the agenda—that is, the number of issues on it and the distribution of attention across these issues, known as "entropy" (cf. Jennings et al. 2011). In terms of the number of issues, figure 5.1 shows how many of the 236 coding categories were actually used to code the party-system agenda in a given parliamentary year.[3] The figure shows a relatively steady rise from the mid-1960s, indicating that more and more issues received attention on the party-system agenda. This would indicate that the party-system agenda became broader, in the sense that parties relate to more issues. However, it does not tell us anything about the distribution of attention across issues. Figure 5.2 shows the development of the so-called h-statistics, which capture how concentrated or dispersed attention is across the 24 issues. Rising numbers indicate that attention is becoming more dispersed across issues, which is in fact the case.[4] In other words, the party-system agenda has become increasingly open in the sense that its concentration of attention on only a few issues is decreasing (cf. Green-Pedersen 2006).

These changes to the format of the party-system agenda—the inclusion of more issues and with attention more evenly dispersed across issues—are found across Western Europe (Green-Pedersen 2007). The reason is the decline of "class politics," that is, politics centered on class (mainly economic) issues. As indicated also by the decline of class voting, class politics has declined. One of the implications of that decline is a change in the format of the party-system agenda. Class politics implied a narrow party-system agenda focused on class issues. A related implication is the increasing importance of issue competition, as argued above. As the party-system agenda has become more important, it has also become more important for parties to influence that agenda.

Looking at this development in the Danish case, figures 5.1 and 5.2 show a relatively gradual development, taking off in the mid-1960s. The 1973 election, with its doubling of parties in the party system, did not seem to have

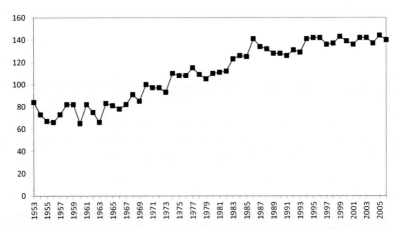

Figure 5.1. Number of subcategory codes used for coding parliamentary debates in Denmark, 1953–2006

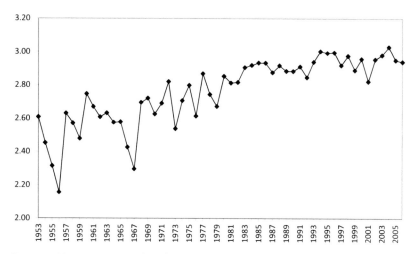

Figure 5.2. *H*-statistic for Danish parliamentary debates, 1953–2006

much direct effect on the format of the party-system agenda; the broadening and more even dispersion of attention was in process before the election and and continued after it. Rather, the 1973 election and the changes in the party-system agenda are rooted in similar changes in the electorate, such as the decline of class voting, increasing electoral volatility, and the rise of issue voting (Pedersen 1988). Nor did the 2001 election directly affect the format of the party-system agenda.

Looking at the format of the party-system agenda has the obvious limitation of being issue-blind. The format can stay unchanged while an issue changes place on the party-system agenda, so we need to look at the development of the issues on the party-system agenda as well. The first way to do this is to look at the development of a number of issue groups. Figure 5.3 shows the development of three issue groups: the economy, the welfare state, and "new politics."[5] The issue development behind the broader party-system agenda is the decline—but not disappearance—of the economy as an issue combined with the growth of "new politics" issues. In terms of timing, this process began in the 1960s. However, during the 1970s the Danish party-system agenda was still relatively dominated by the economy. Welfare state issues have had a more stable, but also somewhat increasing position on the party-system agenda. Finally, neither the 1973 nor the 2001 election seem to have much effect on the issue content of the party-system agenda.

As the next step, it is worth examining which more specific issues have driven the rise of the new politics. Figure 5.4 shows the development of the

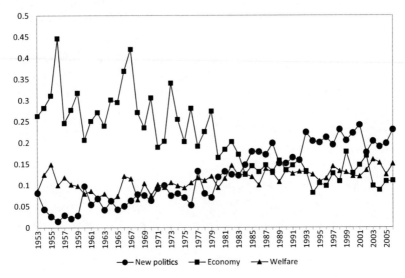

Figure 5.3. The share of the party-system agenda of major issue groups, 1953–2006

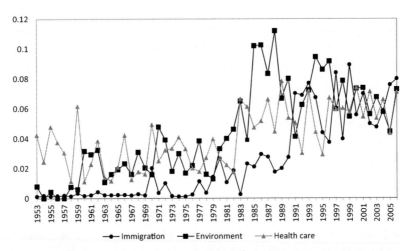

Figure 5.4. The share of the party system agenda of immigration and the environment, 1953–2006

environment, immigration and health care on the party-system agenda. The environment was not an issue before 1960 when it started to gain attention, and then took off as an issue in the early 1980s. Immigration was a nonissue before the 1980s, gained some attention in the 1980s, and then exploded as an issue in the 1990s. Finally, health care is not a new issue, but one that has gained increasing importance in Danish politics. The rise in attention to health care is a major reason for the relatively stable but increasing attention to welfare-state issues.

Summing up, the Danish party-system agenda has become broader and less concentrated on the economy, as illustrated by the growth in attention to the environment and immigration. This development has little to do with the 1973 election, however. Before the election, the party-system agenda was focused on the economy. None of the new parties brought really new issues with them. The Progress Party focused on one part of the economy—taxation—but had no new issues. The Christian Democrats were the only new party with a new issue. The party was founded on opposition to free abortion and liberalization of pornography but has never been able to place these issues on the party-system agenda (Albæk, Green-Pedersen, and Larsen 2012).

This, of course, does not mean that the 1973 election was without consequences. As other studies show (see Green-Pedersen 2001; Green-Pedersen and Thomsen 2005), the main effect was that it significantly complicated majority building on economic issues. The new parties entering Parliament, such as the Progress Party and the radical left-wing parties, were quite unreliable coalition partners, which made it hard for the two blocs in Danish party politics to build and sustain majorities, especially with respect to economic policy (Green-Pedersen 2001). The 2001 election by itself also does not seem to have been a significant event for the issue content of the party-system agenda. In 2001 the broadening of the party-system agenda was a fact: new issues, such as the environment and immigration, were well established on the party-system agenda. Thus, the outcome of the 2001 election can be seen as the culmination of the broadening of the political agenda in Denmark.

This description of the long-term development of the party-system agenda raised the question of the dynamics of the individual issues. While the broader party-system agenda can be explained by long-term structural changes such as the rise in issue voting, this does not explain why some issues rather than others gain attention on the party-system agenda. Even though party attention has become more evenly dispersed, party attention is still something issues compete for, and understanding the dynamics of the party-system agenda means understanding why some issues succeed and not others. Looking at the individual issues might also offer a new perspective on the consequences of both the 1973 and the 2001 election.

As argued above, Danish party politics continues to be dominated by left-right competition, so a starting point for understanding the appearance of issues such as the environment and immigration on the party-system agenda requires an understanding of how these issues have been integrated into left-right competition and thus, as argued elsewhere (Green-Pedersen 2012), an understanding of the electoral and coalitional incentives the issues offer the major parties in the Danish party system: the Social Democrats, the Liberals, and the Conservatives.

The first significant attention to the environment in Denmark was in the early 1970s, including the establishment of the Ministry of the Environment in 1971. However, as can be seen from figure 5.4, the issue lost attention again, and the 1973 election brought no new political party with a strong focus on the issue into Parliament. The issue did not really enter Danish party politics until the mid-1980s (Green-Pedersen and Wolfe 2009) when a center-right government consisting of the Liberals, the Conservatives, and two small center parties (with support from the Social Liberals) focused on restoring the Danish economy after the economic crisis of the 1970s (Damgaard and Svensson 1989). For the Social Democrats and the left-wing opposition, the environment constituted an ideal issue for moving attention away from the economy and challenging the government. The Social Democratic Party had a well-established green profile in terms of issue ownership (Goul Andersen 1990). With respect to party position on the environment, the only difference from the left-right structure was the more left-wing position of the Social Liberals, which implied that the party was not necessarily willing to support the government on environmental matters as it did on economic matters (Damgaard and Svensson 1989). The fact that the Social Liberals were further to the left on the environment than on the economy actually made the issue more attractive for the Social Democrats, because it implied that the government found itself without a clear parliamentary majority. The issue thus offered both electoral and coalition incentives for the Social Democrats, who, together with the rest of the left-wing opposition, then used cases of pollution, especially those related to intensive farming, to drive politicization of the issue (Andersen and Hansen 1991; Green-Pedersen and Wolfe 2009). The result was that the environment rose substantially on the party-system agenda as part of the left-right conflict in Denmark.

In many ways, the focus on immigration is the mirror image of that on the environment. Immigration appeared on the party political agenda during the period of Social Democratic and Social Liberal governments from 1993 to 2001. The issue has been owned by the major bourgeois parties, the Liberals and the Conservatives. In terms of party positions, the structure is also similar to that regarding the environment—that is, with the more left-wing position of the Social Liberals as the only exception to the traditional left-right structure. When in government from 1982 to 1993, the Liberals and Conservatives relied on the Social Liberals and avoided noneconomic issues in order not to lose their parliamentary majority.

In opposition after 1993 (and not dependent on the Social Liberals, who had joined the Social Democratic government), the Liberals and Conservatives systematically tried to politicize the issue (Green-Pedersen and Krogstrup 2008). The extreme right-wing Progress Party had already tried in the 1980s, but its efforts were in vain—the mainstream bourgeois parties ignored the issue. However, once the mainstream bourgeois parties started to push the issue, it provided fertile ground for the Danish People's Party (ibid.).

The rise of the environment and immigration on the party-system agenda has thus happened within the existing left-right format. Moreover, the rise has been driven by the major parties. The Social Democrats pushed the environment in the 1980s because they had issue ownership, and the issue drove the left-right balance in Parliament toward the left. Along the same lines, the Liberals and Conservatives had issue ownership over immigration and pushed this issue when in opposition, driving the political balance toward the right.

The rise in attention to health has been ongoing since the 1980s. With health care being a central part of the Danish welfare state, the issue has traditionally been owned by the left-wing parties. This bloc started to focus more on the issue during the 1980s. The right-wing government was under pressure due to the need for fiscal austerity and rising expectations of health-care services owing to technological developments in the field (Green-Pedersen and Wilkerson 2006). Health care became the policy area where people wanted the most increases in spending (Mortensen 2006, 61). When the government changed in 1993, the right-wing parties took over the opposition focus on health care, and the same was the case with the left-wing opposition from 2001 to 2011. In other words, health care seems to be an issue to which the opposition, regardless of party color, finds it attractive to draw attention because having government responsibility implies an unpleasant trade-off between cost containment and rising expectations of health-care services (Mortensen et al. 2011).

Summing up, it is also worth stressing that elections have played a limited role in the intrusion of these three issues into the party-system agenda in Denmark. Thus neither the 1973 nor the 2001 election is an important event in this development. The agenda-setting dynamics happen in between elections. The key to understanding this dynamic is studying the coalitional and electoral incentives that different issues offer to the major actors in the Danish party system.

Conclusions

Looking at the development of Danish party politics by studying the development of the party-system agenda offers a new assessment of the past forty years. The Danish party-system agenda has become broader—it includes more issues and spreads attention more evenly across the issues. The clearest example of this is the growth in party attention to the environment, immigration, and health care. This change in the substance of party politics has had important implications for the format of the Danish party system as well. The increasing attention to immigration in particular has been crucial for the establishment of the Danish People's Party in the party system. This development has again been important for the right-wing change in Danish politics after 2001, which deprived the Social Liberals of their decisive role in the party system.

In terms of the underlying dynamics of change, our analysis shows that elections play a rather limited role. The 1973 election had limited long-term impact, whereas the 2001 election was the culmination of a long-term change in the substance of the party-system agenda. It also shows that focusing strongly on elections is not a useful starting point for understanding party-system change. This is in line with other studies within the policy-agendas tradition that find elections to be a limited source of agenda change (cf. Mortensen et al. 2011; Baumgartner and Jones 2009, 287–88). Agenda-setting dynamics are important in explaining elections such as the Danish one of 2001, but the opposite rarely seems to be the case. The main agenda-setting dynamics happen between elections, and the main importance of elections is when they reshuffle coalition incentives in the party system—which, again, is important for how the major parties evaluate the potential politicization of issues.

Further, the emergence of new and important issues on the Danish party-system agenda has occurred while the Danish party system has stayed within a one-dimensional left-right framework. This shows the danger of defining the questions of change in party politics as a matter of the emergence of new conflict lines in the party system, which would be the typical perspective on party-system change from a cleavage approach (Mair 1997). It is remarkable how much the substance of Danish party politics—the party-system agenda—has changed within a stable conflict format. Paradoxically, this points to the importance of a key insight of the cleavage approach, namely the stability of conflict lines in party systems despite broader societal change (Mair 2006, 373–74). At the same time, however, new issues can be incorporated into existing conflict lines, and this process is crucial for understanding which issues gain substantial attention on the party-system agenda.

In terms of the format of the party system—that is, the number of parties—the analysis shows the limitations of focusing on this question when evaluating party politics. New parties are of course important, mainly for how they affect coalition building; they have direct impact on the party-system agenda. Actually, it seems that the development of the party-system agenda is the key to understanding the long-term fate of new parties. The parties that entered Parliament in 1973 are now all gone; the reason, from an agenda-setting perspective, is that none of them were rooted in new issues on the party-system agenda. One of the parties, the Christian Democrats, tried to bring morality issues such as abortion into the party system but failed; today they are out of Parliament and close to extinction (Albæk, Green-Pedersen, and Larsen 2012). The Danish People's Party, which entered Parliament in 1995, is in a very different situation because its key issue, refugees and immigrants, is well established on the party-system agenda. According to the literature on the establishment of new parties (Hug 2001), the conclusion about the importance of new issues is not new. However, the policy agenda-setting perspective provides an answer to the question that immediately emerges when the importance of new issues is highlighted: when do new issues emerge—that is, when do they become politicized?

More generally, this chapter—with its focus on the development of the party-system agenda—shows the potential contribution of studying the development of this agenda for understanding the dynamics of party politics. It provides considerable added value compared to perspectives focusing on format (number and type of party) and conflict lines. Its contribution lies in the fact that studying the party-system agenda provides a standard for assessing such changes, for example, an increase in the number of parties or the emergence of new parties, using issue developments as tracer liquids, as argued in chapter 2. In relation to the Danish case, it thus shows that the most important change over the past decades has been the broader party-system agenda, which provides fertile ground for the long-term success of a party such as the Danish People's Party, which has become a well established in the party system. The financial crisis has most likely led to increasing focus on the economy on the party-system agenda.[6] The economy was also the major issue in the 2011 Danish election, in which a left-wing government gained office (Stubager et al. 2013). However, other issues still play an important role for vote choice, and the Danish People's Party suffered only a limit loss. Thus the expansion of the party-system agenda and, especially, the politicization of the immigration issue has left a long-term mark on Danish politics because it has led to establishment of the Danish People's Party as a significant actor in the Danish party system. This party has gained a substantial part of its electorate by drawing voters from the Social Democrats, and thus from the left-wing bloc based on the issue of immigration. Still, the party has positioned itself as a stable member of the right-wing bloc. Its emergence has therefore shifted the political balance in the Danish party system significantly to the right—not because Danish voters have moved to the right in general (Stubager et al. 2013), but because the expansion of the party-system agenda to include immigration has drawn voters to the Danish People's Party, which is part of the right-wing bloc.

Notes

1. More information about the Danish Policy Agendas Project can be found at www.agendasetting.dk.

2. In the 2011 election the right-wing bloc lost its electoral majority; thus, the balance between the blocs has shifted toward the left. However, thanks to the emergence of the Danish People's Party, the right-wing bloc is now able to strive for government power without the support of the Social Liberals. All opinion polls since the 2011 elections have shown that the right-wing bloc would regain power.

3. A parliamentary year in Denmark runs from 1 October to 30 September 30. The year (say, 2006) in the table refers to the beginning of a parliamentary year. Data for 2006 thus cover the period from 1 October 2006, to 30 September 2007. Data are shown beginning in 1953, the year Denmark got a new constitution. Among the important constitutional changes was the abolishment of the first chamber.

4. The h-statistic is defined as $-\Sigma\ P(x)^*log(P(x))$, where P is the share of attention for each category, and based on the natural log. With 24 categories, the h-statistic varies between 0 and 3.18, where 0 means all attention is concentrated on one category and 3.18 indicates a completely even distribution of attention.

5. The economy includes all economic issues, such as inflation, unemployment, public budgets, and current accounts, as well as taxation. Welfare-state issues include general social-policy issues, health care, pensions, unemployment benefits, housing, and child care. New politics issues refer to immigration, the environment, law and order, and personal-rights questions such as freedom of speech. See also Green-Pedersen 2005.

6. Unfortunately, data for the party system agenda are not available after 2007.

6 The Policy Agenda in Multiparty Government: Coalition Agreements and Legislative Activity in the Netherlands

Arco Timmermans and Gerard Breeman

I N COALITION GOVERNMENTS, SETTING THE LEGISLATIVE AGENDA is a balancing act. While parties entering a new government together usually advertise their shared good intentions, the real and somewhat hidden world of making priorities for the years to come is a matter of extensive bargaining. This bargaining between parties happens at an early stage during coalition formation following parliamentary elections, because the collective responsibility of cabinet ministers for legislative decisions must be well secured. This is often done by negotiating a coalition agreement that includes policy intentions for the coming term in office.

One country where coalition agreements feature as an institutional mechanism of agenda setting and coalition governance is the Netherlands. Negotiating a coalition agreement in the Netherlands is not just a ritual dance between prospective partners in office; it is substantive and usually takes several months. Parties building a coalition government in the Netherlands consider the negotiation of a policy agreement to be an investment for the term in office. Their sense of commitment sometimes even leads the parliamentary groups to lock themselves into policy deals to such an extent that legislative scrutiny of proposals following from these deals is reduced to a marginal task (Timmermans 2011).

The properties of coalition agreements and the conditions for their existence received attention in the early 2000s (Müller and Strøm 2008), but except for some studies focusing on a limited number of governments, their agenda-setting effects on legislative activity are still largely unknown (Timmermans 2003, 2006). In this chapter we analyze agenda dynamics during the lifetime of coalition governments in the Netherlands.[1] We show how the initial policy agenda included in the coalition agreement relates to the legislative agenda set each year during the term of a government. If the coalition agreement is a policy equilibrium set in government formation, what happens in subsequent years? Do governments stick to the allocation of attention to policy problems as fixed in the coalition agreement, or do they move away from it? Our expectation is that after a short warming-up period, governments in the Netherlands set the legislative agenda in correspondence with the coalition agreement but then move away from it owing to pressures from the political and social environment as well as changing priorities of the coalition parties themselves. One possible reason for this drift is the limited capacity of the legislative agenda set each year. We use a dataset of some nine thousand content-coded statements in coalition agreements and government bills in the Netherlands for the period 1981–2009.

An Agenda Perspective on Coalition Governance

For several decades theories of government coalitions dealt almost exclusively with their formation and termination, and scarcely at all with their actual life and activities in office. Initially assumptions of rational behavior were operationalized in terms of coalition size, predicting that parties form minimal winning coalitions to maximize political utility (Riker 1962; Dodd 1976). Later studies considered policy aspects but still focused mostly on the formation and duration of governments (Axelrod 1970; Laver and Schofield 1990; Warwick 1994). Policy-oriented approaches typically focused on ideological distances between parties (Klingemann, Hofferbert, and Budge 1994; Budge et al. 2001; Laver, Benoit, and Garry 2003; Laver and Benoit 2006) and on their policy horizons when coalescing (Warwick 2006). While they add to the theoretical to empirical knowledge of coalition formation, these approaches say little about the policy activities of governments during their term in office.

Most of the literature also showed skepticism about coalition agreements, which were seen as artifacts of symbolic politics—window dressing, with little relevance to policy-making (Luebbert 1986; Laver and Schofield 1990; Laver and Shepsle 1996). However, since 2000 we have seen an increase in the scholarly interest in these policy documents and their possible effects (Müller and Strøm 2000; Timmermans 2003; Martin and Vanberg 2004 and 2011; Moury and Timmermans 2008; Strøm, Müller, and Bergman 2008). The analysis of the substantive effects of these coalition policy agendas thus has taken off, but there is still much work to be done.

Coalition agreements are pieced together by parties to reduce uncertainty, address matters of dispute, and increase the likelihood of parliamentary majority support when policy proposals are on the legislative agenda. Although negotiated in secret, most coalition agreements are made public. This public display of attention enhances the significance of credible commitment on deals over issues made between political parties. Written policy agreements are, as Strøm and Müller (1999: 255) put it, the "keys to togetherness" between coalition parties: they are meant to bind representatives of the coalition parties in the cabinet and often also in parliament to a common course of action in policy-making. The bonds that agreements create between coalition partners are not legal but political. Enforcement and monitoring agencies are informal and must be designed from within the coalition.

The institutional machinery developed in countries with coalition governments may facilitate loyalty and enforcement and even reallocations of attention, but they do not by themselves determine agenda development after a government has been inaugurated. Societies experiencing social change, mediatization, and exposure to national and international events put pressure on coalition governments when they try to convert plans in the coalition agreement into formal legislative proposals. New issues intrude into the policy agenda and compete with matters that have already been scheduled. And ministers face party colleagues in the legislature who must act on behalf of their constituencies. For this reason, the legislative agenda involves complex information processing within executive coalitions and their supporting parliamentary parties.

When it comes to analyzing the legislative agenda in governments that begin their term in office with a coalition agreement, the policy-agenda approach and the data collection it involves has considerable added value (Breeman et al. 2009). It enables a much more comprehensive view of the dynamics of legislative agenda setting in multiparty governments during their lifetime than provided thus far. The substantive coalition policy agenda is set during government formation after (or sometimes even before) parliamentary elections, and then the process of legislative agenda management really begins. Many factors influence this process. The cumulative experiences of coalition partners—positive or more frustrated—induce these partners to continue or withdraw from collaboration. Next to scheduled elections, interparty dispute is the second most frequent reason for government termination in European countries with a multiparty system (Damgaard 2008). Multiparty systems have designed institutional arenas for coalition governance (Andeweg and Timmermans 2008; Müller and Meyer 2010) wherein parties make legislative timetables and other more or less formal arrangements to facilitate

smooth processing and accommodate the preferences of the coalition partners (Döring and Hallerberg 2004; Martin 2004; Rasch and Tsebelis 2011).

The Legislative Agenda in the Netherlands

Political parties in the Netherlands incur considerable costs when negotiating a new government. The electoral system of proportional representation
includes no real threshold, and this facilitates the presence of many parties in
the chamber of representatives. Since 1945 no single party has ever obtained
a parliamentary majority, so coalition building in government formation is
imperative. After the elections of June 2010 there were ten parties, of which
five have a governmental track record and the other five have always been in
the opposition. With differences in the vote shares of parties decreasing and
electoral shifts between them increasing, building a viable government coalition has become a hard task for the *informateur* called by the head of state
to lead this process. Since 1945 there have been twenty-eight governments
(including some with short-term caretaker status), most of which have lasted
for the majority of their term in office but have ended prematurely.

The costs that political parties incur in coalition formation relate to their
intention to hammer out a coalition agreement in which party leaders go
beyond paying lip service either to their followers or to the general public.
In the Netherlands coalition agreements have become comprehensive multi-
issue documents beginning in the early 1980s. Figure 6.1 shows the size of
coalition agreements.

While not all content is truly substantive and doable, the coalition agreement can be seen to represent the legislative agenda at the point of departure
of a new government. Ever since written coalition agreements were first
published in the 1960s, their length has varied. The document produced in
1998 contained almost forty thousand words. Although since then parties
have expressed concern about long and detailed agreements that "precook"
policies before legislative chambers can debate them, few governments have
produced short texts.

In-depth empirical analysis of coalition agreements and their effects in
the Netherlands is still limited, but case studies of governments suggest that
these effects are substantive and politically important. Policy deals in agreements are found to provide a basis for resolving conflict in cases where such
conflict was already present during government formation, and they contribute to disciplining members of coalition parties (Timmermans 2003). Similar

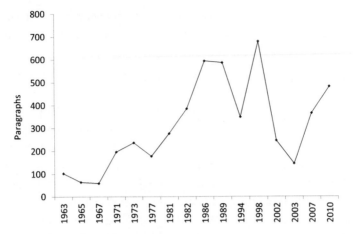

Figure 6.1. Length of coalition agreements, 1963–2010

initial work on governments in other countries such as Belgium and Italy indicates that conflict containment and substantive agenda setting during the term of governments are visible functions of coalition agreements (Timmermans and Moury 2006; Moury and Timmermans 2008; Moury 2012).

Studies of legislative agenda setting in European parliamentary democracies all point to the existence of a de facto institutional privilege for the executive (Heller 2001; Döring and Hallerberg 2004; Martin 2004; Bräuninger and Debus 2009; Rasch and Tsebelis 2011). In the Netherlands executive's political primacy in initiating bills is emphasized by the institutionalization of coalition agreements. The formation of majority governments has helped to create a relatively stable support basis for enforcing these agreements.[2] Of course, legislation always needs parliamentary approval, and each bill can be subjected to amendment. Executive information and initiative advantages do not change the fact that constitutional rules lead the legislative process through both legislative chambers. On average, bills in the Netherlands spend some two years in the legislative pipeline, but the time period varies considerably, as bills sometimes are extremely controversial or are considered inadequate. Nonetheless, the reality is one of disciplined legislative behavior.

A Hypothesis on Legislative Agenda Dynamics

As pointed out above, in coalition systems the legislative agenda is exposed to different pressures that help to sustain or disrupt the equilibrium set in the written coalition agreement. One source of pressure, mostly internal to the coalition, consists of institutional arrangements designed—and often reproduced from one coalition government to the next—to maintain and implement the initial policy agenda (Martin and Vanberg 2004; Andeweg and Timmermans 2008; Müller and Meyer 2010). These mechanisms of coalition governance are meant to uphold what Shepsle (1979) calls a "structure-induced equilibrium." The policy agenda, set at the government's point of departure, contains promises not only to the public, but first of all to the coalition partners, which need to keep the government on track. In the Netherlands, this element of credible commitment is particularly important because the involvement of the coalition parties' legislative branches in formulating the agreement may reduce their political leeway to propose changes later on (Timmermans 2011). Such commitments raise the costs of renegotiating the policy agenda.

The other, more external type of pressure works against the stability of the coalition policy agenda. New information and issues intruding onto the legislative agenda require flexibility and responsiveness, and such matters may begin to drive away prioritized topics at any point in time during the life of the coalition. Yet, if issues on the legislative agenda must make place for other urgent matters, which ones should be sacrificed? Parties may disagree on this question, but they must act in concert to avoid the risk of coalition collapse. Though most governments in the Netherlands reach the end of their constitutional term in office, most of those that end prematurely do so because of interparty policy dispute (Timmermans and Andeweg 2000). In short, issue intrusion on the legislative agenda is an important fact of life for coalition governments, and addressing such issues may push them to the limits of coalition governance mechanisms that are meant to sustain equilibrium and stability.

The likely consequence of these types of pressure is that during the coalition government's term in office it becomes increasingly difficult to maintain an equilibrium in attention to the legislative policy topics set in the coalition agreement. Time works against policy equilibrium, even if mechanisms of coalition governance exist for keeping the coalition in balance. Our hypothesis is that *the correspondence of the coalition agreement to the annual legislative agenda declines over the life of a government*. The dependent variable is thus the allocation of attention to topics on the legislative agenda in successive government years relative to the coalition agreement. We expect a linear decline in agenda correspondence from the first full year in office to subsequent years.

Though there are many possible reasons that agenda stability and change are a part of coalition governance (Strøm, Müller, and Bergman 2008), we focus in this first longitudinal empirical analysis of coalition life cycles on an explanation linking institutional conditions to the phenomenon of selective attention and intrusion of information on policy problems. More specifically, we consider the effect of information intrusion and agenda capacity on legislative-agenda development. As pointed out earlier, the coalition agreement emerges in a setting allowing flexibility. Peterson and De Ridder (1986: 565) call government formation an "institutionalized extra-institutional arena." In this arena, political parties increase agenda capacity whenever they find it necessary. These conditions of dealing with different issues at the same time and producing package deals are conducive to establishing an equilibrium. The fact that the prospective coalition parties rarely reject the results at their congresses or conferences prior to the inauguration of the new government speaks not only to their eagerness to govern but also to the substantive payoffs the coalition agreement is seen to provide.

But as conditions change during the government's term in office, the capacity of the agenda is more limited. Governments cannot table an infinite number of bills in a legislative year, and even if they might wish to do so for political reasons, they face constraints of administrative preparation and formal legislative calendars. There is no formal maximum in legislative production in the Netherlands, but in practice the number of bills placed on the legislative agenda has a limit of some two hundred per year. Strategies of agenda management and informal arenas of coalition governance may help to maintain political balances, but these mechanisms do not change the fact that governments are often forced to focus all their attention on one or just a few issues at a time and thus must set priorities within annual capacity limits. They must do this while the political detectors of governments must manage a constant flow of information and new problems intrude on the agenda, putting even more pressure on the process of prioritization.

Thus, our hypothesis of declining agenda correspondence is grounded in the institutionally limited capacity of the legislative agenda and the constant pressure implied by the intrusion of new issues. Bottlenecks in information processing occur when all these issues begin to compete for attention with electoral promises and programmed policy decisions. For this reason, we expect governments in their first full year to try to use the agenda in full and schedule their various legislative intentions as stipulated in the coalition agreement, following the consensus on the allocation of policy attention.

Of course, governments that are just beginning their term have a political honeymoon and must warm up the legislative machinery. Most governments between 1981 and 2009 took office well into the second half of a calendar year, and we consider the remaining of that year the honeymoon period.[3] By "high correspondence" we mean a legislative agenda that is close to the distribution of attention in the coalition agreement. As the memory of government formation and the ensuing honeymoon fades, all kinds of information alarm bells begin to ring, and in subsequent years we would expect to see increasing drift from the distribution of attention in the coalition agreement. Moreover, if political problems occur, they also may reduce the actual capacity of the legislative agenda, because controversial issues consume disproportionate political energy that might otherwise be expended on different policy topics. In sum, we analyze legislative agenda development in the Netherlands, confront a parsimonious model of declining agenda correspondence based on the application of policy agendas theory to our data, and then consider how institutional bottlenecks play a part in legislative agenda setting.

Data Strategy and Research Design

To empirically examine our expectations, we use two datasets constructed within the Comparative Agendas Project, following a uniform approach to content-code data sources across countries (see appendix). For this we developed a Dutch version of the topic classification scheme that contains a limited number of subtopics specific to the Dutch context (Breeman and Timmermans 2009). We content-coded all paragraphs of all coalition agreements published in the Netherlands between 1963 and 2010, and all bills submitted in the Tweede Kamer (chamber of representatives) from 1981 to 2009. Both data sources were coded by trained coders working in pairs but coding independently and comparing and discussing cases of coding disagreement. This resulted in an intercoder reliability of over 90% in both data-collection projects.

In this chapter we use data on coalition agreements from 1981 to 2007 in order to synchronize these data to our data on bills from 1981 to 2009. In coding paragraphs in coalition agreements, we also used a variable indicating whether statements actually had policy content; we excluded statements referring to the government-formation process or to some very general point about government with no substantive relevance to the agenda. The dataset of coalition agreements from 1981 to 2007 contains some four thousand content-coded paragraphs. The dataset on bills contains nearly five thousand bills, the titles of which we used for topic and subtopic coding. Both datasets are analyzed at the level of main topics.

With these two datasets for analyzing the policy agenda of Dutch coalition governments, we carried out descriptive statistics and then applied a more intensive research design for analyzing legislative agenda correspondence in the nine governments in office between 1 January 1981 and 31 December 2009. Thus, in relating coalition agreements to annual legislative agendas, we made observations for each year these governments were in office. In the section below we begin by mapping the general empirical picture of both types of agendas, with findings at the aggregate level, and briefly discuss their meaning. Then we proceed with the analysis of legislative-agenda dynamics during each government's term in office and confirm our hypothesis with the findings.

Analysis: Legislative Agenda Development

FEATURES OF THE COALITION AGREEMENT AGENDA

As the baseline policy agenda set when a government takes office, we saw that coalition agreements vary in size. Empirical work on these policy documents in the Netherlands and other European countries shows that the initial size of the agenda has no clear relationship to the length and complexity of the government-formation process, but that policy relationships between the coalition parties do matter to the content of the agreement (Müller and Strøm 2008, 191–93). Coalition parties have discretion when it comes to expanding or contracting the size of the initial coalition agenda (Müller and Meyer 2010). This finding speaks to the policy agendas approach: parties change the size of the agenda as necessary when allocating attention to problems. It therefore seems reasonable to expect that the content matters to the partners when in office. As mentioned above, the coalition agreement can be considered the policy equilibrium on which further legislative agenda setting is built. This equilibrium was set differently between governments, as coalitions changed their emphasis on major policy themes.

The scope of government expanded with the establishment of the welfare state in the 1960s and 1970s. From the 1980s onward, issues relating to social security, the labor market, health, and justice and crime acquired more prominence in the development of the welfare state and its boundaries; matters of the macroeconomy and government operation in general also

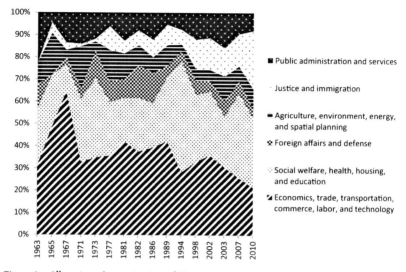

Figure 6.2. Allocation of attention in coalition agreements, 1963–2010

appear central to any government. Some topics, such as public housing and science and technology (mainly television broadcasting policy), were politically prominent in the 1960s but declined in the 1980s. Overall, the allocation of attention to major policy topics became more equal over time. This finding, of course, is due in part to our relative measurement, since we consider the proportional distribution of attention. Some topics received more absolute agenda space in coalition agreements in order to express concern with certain problems or hammer out detailed deals if the topics were disputed. Figure 6.2 shows the allocation of attention to major topics in coalition agreements over time. We clustered the major topics into six broader categories to make the patterns in the graph easier to interpret.

   While governments face general expectations and a degree of path dependency with regard to the policy agenda in the coalition agreement that may lead them to reproduce the emphases of their predecessors, they do redistribute attention. Newly formed coalition governments sometimes do so more drastically, but there is no clear pattern here. We found no indication that the party composition of coalitions made a difference. Governments including Christian Democrats and Liberal Conservatives (1982, 1986, 2002, 2003, and 2010) and governments with the Social Democrats on board (1981, 1989, 1994, 1998, and 2007) (table 6.1) produced agreements of comparable length, and center-right and center-left coalitions both varied relative to their predecessors in the extent to which they reallocated attention to major

Table 6.1. Dutch governments, 1981–2010

1981–82	Van Agt II	CDA-VVD-D66
1982–86	Lubbers I	CDA-VVD
1986–89	Lubbers II	CDA-VVD
1989–94	Lubbers III	CDA-PvdA
1994–98	Kok I	PvdA-VVD-D66
1998–2002	Kok II	PvdA-VVD-D66
2002–3	Balkenende I	CDA-VVD-LPF
2003–6	Balkenende II	CDA-VVD-D66
2006–7	Balkenende III	CDA-VVD, caretaker government
2007–10	Balkenende IV	CDA-PvdA-CU

Key: CDA: Christian Democrats

PvdA: Social Democrats

VVD: Liberal Conservatives

D66: Liberal Democrats

LPF: Party List Pim Fortuyn

CU: Christian Union

policy topics. Nor did the number of coalition parties seem to make a difference. Coalition agreements thus are not simply cumulative wish lists of all partners taking office.

We acknowledge that changes in attention do not automatically imply changes in tone, and that relative stability in attention to topics does not equal continuity in the specific content of policies pursued. Nonetheless, the distribution of attention to topics in the coalition agreement is an important point of departure for governments in legislative agenda setting.

FEATURES OF THE BILLS AGENDA

The dataset constructed for analyzing the legislative agenda contains some five thousand bills submitted in the Tweede Kamer between 1 January 1981 and 31 December 2009. Not included in this dataset are bills that formally present annual departmental budgets. The bills included are truly the legislative agenda, in that they were submitted, not yet adopted; thus the reflected the input of the legislative agenda in the chambers of Parliament. The adoption rate of submitted bills is very high in the Netherlands, so in effect the legislative agenda (bills) is almost similar to the legislative output (laws). Of course, formal legislation represents only a part of government activity, even of regulatory activity, and not all bills are equally important in this respect. Some bills are truly policy innovations, while others are technical corrections or updates of existing legislation. Still, we believe that analyzing the legislative agenda can tell us much about the way in which governments allocate attention to problems. The vast majority of bills submitted in the Tweede Kamer also are adopted, usually after amendments are made during the legislative scrutiny process.

There is an institutional and administrative limit to the legislative agenda capacity of some two hundred bills per year. This figure excludes budget bills, which are routinely given the form of legislation and are fixed in number— one for each government department. The period between 1981 and 2009 shows some ups and downs, most clearly when governments are resigning and new ones are starting up. The features of the legislative agenda during years in office differ from coalition agreements not only in terms of agenda size. Figure 6.3 shows the average attention differences in policy topics be- tween the two types of agendas for the period 1981–2009.

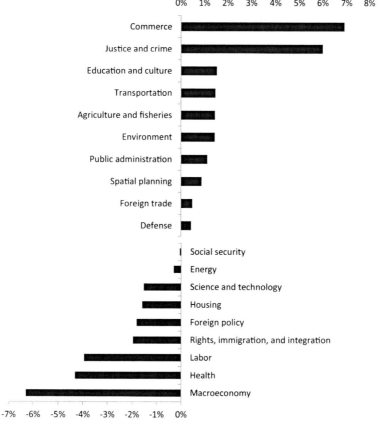

Figure 6.3. Attention difference between bills and coalition agreements (1981–2009)

This difference suggests that emphases change when governments are in office. However, some of the variation between the two types of coalition policy agendas relates to the institutional properties of policy domains, some of which are more typically domains of regulatory policy than others and thus are likely to be represented more prominently on the bills agenda. While the prominence of commerce and of justice and crime on the bills agenda (they are the topics that appear most frequently) speaks to the political attention paid to such matters, they are also typical regulatory domains. Conversely, coalition agreements contain topics central to government formation because they are manifest or potential sources of division between the partners, though this salience is not always expressed in legislation. As noted earlier, legislation is one of the tools of government. Thus, the macroeconomy is of major importance to the coalition agenda but involves other tools besides legislation, while domestic commerce and business rarely are central to coalition building but are a relatively important domain of legislation.[4] Further, the formal legislative agenda is influenced and even mandated to some extent by European policy, in particular directives that are to be transposed into national laws. The extent of this influence of European policy over the national legislative agenda has increased over time, but it is nowhere near the situation of dominance that politicians sometimes claim for it (Breeman and Timmermans 2012).

We mention these general differences between coalition agreements and bills here because they mean that the baseline correspondence between the two types of policy agenda in an ideal world of enforcement of the coalition agreement is not perfect but is at some point below a correlation of 1.0.

LEGISLATIVE AGENDA CORRESPONDENCE

The observations above indicate the validity of a comparison between the coalition agreement and legislative agenda development in the years in office following a government's inauguration. As already pointed out, there are pressures that help to maintain equilibrium and others that may lead to interruption. Our hypothesis is that agenda correspondence declines over time during the term of a government. We expect an institutional agenda capacity effect: coalition agreements contain a comprehensive policy agenda, but the annual legislative agenda–setting capacity is limited for institutional and political reasons. This may push coalition partners to engage in sequencing when submitting bills. But *what* sequencing?

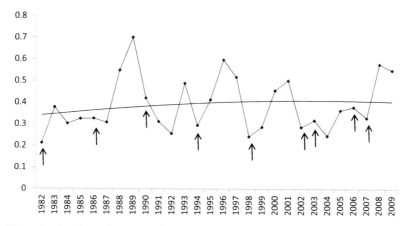

Figure 6.4. Correlation between coalition agreements and bills introduced from year to year (arrows: new coalition)

Figure 6.4 shows the correlation between the distribution of attention in the coalition agreement and the distribution of attention to topics on the annual legislative agenda between 1981 and 2009. The pattern shows steep rises and declines in agenda correspondence, between just above 0.70 and a mere 0.20 in some of the years. In a weak trend over the entire time period, the average level of agenda correspondence developed slowly from 0.35 to 0.40.

The expected pattern of rise and decline would display time intervals in which governments begin high and end rather low. As noted, we consider the first full calendar year in office to be the first year in which legislative production is expected to follow the coalition agreement closely. Low levels of correspondence are expected to occur in transition years, where one government is outgoing and the next is formed and needs some time for the political honeymoon and for setting the administrative machinery in motion. The years of hypothesized low correspondence are 1982, 1986, 1989, 1994, 1998, 2002, 2003, and 2007. This mostly conforms to the results we obtained, but 1989 stands out as an exception: in that year the legislative agenda of the second Lubbers government corresponded quite strongly to the coalition agreement of 1986, despite its outgoing status for a large part of 1989 and a new government, the third Lubbers government, taking office also in that year.

More important than this high level of agenda correspondence in a transition year is that our findings contradict the hypothesis. The first full calendar year in office is not typically the year of greatest adherence to the allocation of attention set in the coalition agreement. Coalition partners do not appear to stick to their mutually agreed-to allocation of attention to policy topics more strongly in their first full year than in later years. In fact, most governments work toward more agenda correspondence in their second and third years in office and only then show the expected decline in their remaining years (provided they last long enough). On average, agenda correspondence in the first year is 0.35 and rises to 0.45 in the second and third year, then declines. Coalitions that lasted only a very brief time also show little if any adherence to the agenda set in the coalition agreement. This was the case in 1982 with the second Van Agt government (September 1981–May 1982), which foundered over the interpretation of the coalition agreement; and the very early collapse of the first Balkenende government in October 2002 after just three months in office also rendered its policy agenda during its outgoing period in 2003 meaningless. Governments that stayed in office longer began to set the legislative agenda selectively earlier than expected, move closer to the policy-attention distribution made in government formation, and then move away again.[5] As figure 6.4 shows, some governments reached a mid-term peak level of agenda correspondence of 0.50 or 0.60, but some, such as the first Lubbers government (1982–86) and the second Balkenende government (2003–6) never moved closer than 0.35 (almost all annual observations for these governments are below the average trend line). This may indicate that mechanisms of coalition governance help in preventing too much drift from equilibrium; however, the modest agenda-correspondence levels also suggest that such internal-correction mechanisms are not devices of automated government following the coalition agreement. Our findings tell us that in legislative agenda setting during the term in office, coalition partners experience pressure to alter the distribution of attention set initially in the coalition agreement.

CAPACITY LIMITS AND LEGISLATIVE AGENDA CHANGE

In this adaptive behavior to new information and changing circumstances, some legislative topics are prioritized more strongly than in the coalition policy agreement, while others receive less or are placed on the legislative waiting list. As already stated, there are some intrinsic differences between the two types of agendas that even in an ideal world of enforcement lead us to expect a correspondence of less than 1.0. But our findings show that even topics that are generally over- or underrepresented on the bills agenda do vary in emphasis throughout the years that a government is in office. For example, the economy is almost always more prominent in the coalition agreement than on the bills agenda, but the first Lubbers government, composed of Christian Democrats and Liberal Conservatives, made this topic a matter of first priority in legislating after taking office in 1982. The next government, led by the same prime minister, made this topic its first legislative priority only in its final year, in 1989 (this government broke down prematurely). The second Balkenende government (2003–7) set out with an ambitious agenda of reform in public administration and government operations but began its legislative activity with a focus on education and justice and crime issues and followed public alarm over climate change by enlarging legislative attention to environmental issues.

Some major policy topics announced prominently in the coalition agreement never reached a similar priority level in legislative activity. Health reform was prioritized in the coalition agreement of the first Kok government in 1994, but this topic was suppressed by other matters until the following second Kok government raised it again for the legislative agenda, and it obtained the proportion of attention corresponding to the coalition agreement in that government's final year, 2002. Social policy and labor-market policy also show a pattern of attention shifts from year to year relative to the coalition agreement of governments.

Thus, governments do shift to different matters of political importance to them in successive years of their stay in office. In his comparative study of the government agenda, Martin (2004) found that at early stage in office, governments mostly focus on salient but also uncontroversial matters. Our findings for coalition governments in the Netherlands suggest that governments varied considerably in the set of topics prioritized in this way, which often implied deviations in attention relative to the initial agenda set in the coalition agreement. In their allocation of attention from year to year, coalitions often cut in attention as much as they increased. Although the changes for any given topic on the bills agenda were modest and rarely extreme, such modest changes in legislative attention add up to deviations from the coalition agreement.

The present analysis shows the first overall picture and does not unravel the specific strategies of coalition parties. Martin's finding that coalitions begin their legislative activity with relatively low-risk issues is one path that parties faced with priority choices may take. However, our analysis also suggests that coalitions not only select annual legislative priorities from a given agenda set as the initial policy equilibrium, but also address legislative matters left unfinished by a preceding government and respond to new issues intruding on the political agenda. In order to respond to urgent matters, coalitions must sacrifice some of those included in their policy programs. Some of this response may be symbolic, but legislative agenda setting requires also a more "effective" type of responsiveness (Hobolt and Klemmensen 2008: 309).

Our basic point in this chapter is that coalition and party strategies in legislative agenda setting happen in a context of scarcity of attention and limits to the capacity of the annual legislative list of bills to be introduced in Parliament. Causal thinking about the annual size of the legislative agenda and agenda correspondence requires extreme caution. Not only might low agenda correspondence result from a lower rate of bill production, but also coalition governments may submit fewer bills precisely because they stumble over the topics in the coalition agreement when making priorities. The point to appreciate is that the existence of a limited capacity of the annual legislative agenda and the intrusion of issues with regard to which coalition parties cannot simply refer to written deals in the coalition agreement pushes the government to deal with issues one by one. Such cases of adapting priorities involve political transaction costs that limit the capacity for legislative digesting by the government and its supporting coalition parties.

Conclusion: Agenda Dynamics in Coalition Life Cycles

Coalition governments in the Netherlands draft comprehensive agreements to set policy equilibrium between their members and present the legislative agenda for its term in office. During the period under consideration, as these agreements got longer they also raised expectations of parties and the general public. Ostensibly this mechanism of coalition governance would reduce uncertainty and conflict and lead to a smooth process of implementing policy intentions secured by a stable parliamentary majority. When the government is actually in office, however, this scenario of policy programming does not appear to hold. Coalition governments face the intrusion of new issues onto the agenda and expectations of responsiveness that press them to reconsider priorities. And when in office, governments face the institutional constraint of the legislative agenda's limited carrying capacity. Although coalition agreements are made in an informal and flexible setting, the formal legislative agenda involves not only tight rules but also bureaucratic structures that limit time, space, and scope. Internal governance mechanisms are used to guard the policy equilibrium, but coalition partners must adapt to circumstances they cannot always control. And they often disagree over how to respond to them.

We hypothesized that governments set the annual legislative agenda close to the coalition agreement in their first full year in office and then drift away from it. The data presented in this analysis show agenda drift, but not in a linear way. Coalition governments in the Netherlands appear to set a different course of attention to legislative topics in their first full year, and in following years they move closer to the coalition agreement. When in office long enough, they then drift away to the level at point of departure. By and large, agenda correspondence levels vary between some 60% and 20%, with an average at midterm of 0.45. Skeptics about the role of coalition agreements may argue this is nowhere near the level of credible commitment that party leaders proclaim when negotiating and presenting such joint policy programs. But this level of correspondence for the entire policy agenda is politically significant. Given the institutional differences between agreements and the annual bills agenda and the length of time that Dutch governments stay in office, we can conclude that coalition agreements do provide a basis for Dutch governmental legislative action.

The Dutch system of multiparty government has received much criticism, and some have presented somber diagnoses (Andeweg and Thomassen 2011). The strong emphasis on proportional representation and "inputism" is seen to be out of balance with the capacity of domestic political institutions to set priorities and be responsive when conditions change or when the public expresses dissatisfaction. But considering the period since 1981, the dynamics of legislative agenda setting do not point only to inertia in the political system and "coalitionability" under stress. Analysis of the legislative agenda during the life cycle of a coalition may not tell us all we need to know about responsiveness, but it does inform us that governments do not just stick to the initial allocation of attention if they receive signals from the public and pressure mounts to alter governmental attention in legislative agenda setting. At the same time, the institutional properties of the legislative agenda constrain its flexibility, given capacity limits and rules of procedure that may become weapons in the hands of parties within the two legislative chambers. Informal rules of coalition discipline may help in keeping the partners in office on track, but executives face limits to their degree of agenda control. This limit of internal control has become more important and visible as electoral incentives for responsiveness to public opinion have increased and incumbent parties have become more sensitive to opposition parties playing the populist card.

A recurring pattern in Dutch governments since 1981 points to a cyclic process in which agenda correspondence increases and decreases during the life of a coalition. This finding calls for further work on policy agendas in coalition governance. One line of research is to include other dependent variables central to coalition studies—government stability and duration, the electoral fate of parties in office, and legislative-executive relationships—and link these to agenda dynamics. Work including independent variables such as the level of interparty dispute over policy topics (using policy-distance models of preferences or other approaches) also may be fruitfully combined with empirical data on attention patterns and their consequences. Further work on agenda dynamics in governments may use more rigorous models for testing hypotheses. Such work can and should be comparative. In short, in the years to come, the policy-agendas approach and research on coalition governments face many possibilities for cross-fertilization.

Notes

1. More information about the Dutch Policy Agendas Project can be found at www.mi-cdh.nl.

2. After almost a century of majority governments, a minority coalition was formed in October 2010. This two-party minority government negotiated a support agreement with the right-wing populist Freedom Party. In April 2012 this government resigned when the Freedom Party withdrew its support. After early elections a majority government was formed.

3. The only government that began its formal term early in a calendar year was the fourth Balkenende government, in February 2007.

4. The figure does not include the 2010 coalition agreement, in which justice and crime became more prominent than before and the macroeconomy was given the smallest proportion of attention ever. We exclude the 2010 agreement here because we analyze the bills agenda up to 31 December 2009, for which the agreement of 2007 was relevant.

5. The fourth Balkenende government had this kind of early rise in agenda correspondence in its first full calendar year, 2008. But here we note that this government had been in office already since February 2007, so the warming-up period did not differ much from that of other governments.

7   Agenda Setting and Direct Democracy: The Rise of the Swiss People's Party

Frédéric Varone, Isabelle Engeli, Pascal Sciarini, and Roy Gava

O N 29 NOVEMBER 2009 SWISS CITIZENS WERE CALLED TO THE voting booth to ban the construction of minarets, the distinctive architectural feature of Islamic mosques.[1] This proposal resulted from a popular initiative launched by two conservative right-wing parties, the Swiss People's Party (SPP) and the Federal Democratic Union. Despite the fact that the government and parliament, along with most political parties, interest groups, and religious organizations, recommended a "no" vote, a clear majority of voters (58%) and cantons (nineteen and a half out of twenty-three) accepted the proposal. Even though there are only four minarets in the entire country, a majority of the Swiss people supported the initiative's view that these minarets constituted a symbol of the growing religiopolitical power of Islamic groups and a first step toward the Islamization of Swiss society.

Exactly one year later, on 28 November 2010, Swiss citizens again accepted a popular initiative from the SPP. This time the target was not a specific culture or religion, but criminal foreigners in general: the initiative called for the automatic deportation of foreigners who had committed various types of criminal offenses—ranging from murder and breaking and entering to welfare fraud. Swiss voters were faced with a choice between the hard-line option of the SPP and a compromise submitted by moderate-right parties that would have allowed for a case-by-case examination of criminals' deportation. The majority of the voters (53%) and cantons (seventeen and a half) nevertheless opted for the more extreme proposal, which would lead to the automatic removal of convicted foreigners and contradict both the European convention of human rights and the bilateral agreements on the free movement of persons with the European Union.

These two popular votes offer fine examples of the impact that direct democracy can have on agenda setting and policy punctuation. They demonstrate the political opportunities that direct-democratic instruments grant to populist right-wing parties, which can use these institutional venues to attract political attention, voice their policy preferences, promote their vote-seeking strategies, and possibly induce policy changes. These cases illustrate the decisive influence of both institutional venues and actors' preferences on issue prioritization. At first glance they appear to confirm the core assumptions regarding the two key drivers of agenda setting put forward by Green-Pedersen and Walgrave in the introduction to this volume.[2]

However, the question remains as to whether these two votes are representative of the agenda-setting power of the SPP or are exceptional cases. To answer this question, and to analyze agenda-setting dynamics through issues and time (as is required by the classical agenda-setting approach), this chapter looks at the changing patterns of the vote-, office-, and policy-seeking strategies of the SPP over the last three decades. Based on a careful examination of the parliamentary motions and the popular initiatives launched since 1979, we investigate the party's issue prioritization and "venue-shopping" strategy, as well as its success in controlling the political agenda.

In the next section we provide background information about the Swiss party system in general, and about the electoral rise of the SPP in particular. We show the programmatic transformation of the party from an agrarian to a populist right-wing party over the last two decades. Since the 1991 national election the party has been the uncontested champion of cultural protectionism, advocating, for example, isolation from Europe, and the tightening of immigration and asylum policy. To map these changes in issue attention over time, we apply the issue classification system developed in the Comparative Agenda Project (see appendix) to the manifestos of the SPP from the 1979 to the 2007 national elections. We then briefly present the main institutional venues for agenda setting that a political party has at its disposal in Switzerland, namely parliamentary motions and popular initiatives. Based on that we formulate two expectations regarding the SPP's agenda-setting strategy. First, we expect the party to focus on its "new" issues regarding Swiss identity, immigration, and law and order. Second, we anticipate that it relies extensively on direct democracy (i.e., popular initiatives) to promote these issues and set the political agenda. Our empirical results, which appear in the section titled "Empirical Comparison of Agenda-Setting Activities before and after 1991," confirm these expectations.

Our analysis shows that a combination of cultural protectionism and economic neoliberalism, along with the transformation from a governmental to an antiestablishment party (albeit one still seated in the governing coalition), has enabled the SPP to win parliamentary elections and to significantly influence the political agenda since 1991. It also demonstrates that the agenda-setting power of the SPP is higher in the realm of direct democracy than in the parliamentary arena; it is more successful with its popular initiatives than with its parliamentary motions. In other words, we show that with its far-reaching direct democracy, the Swiss political system offers favorable institutional conditions for a populist right-wing party such as the SPP. In conclusion, we discuss the broader implications of this result for the agenda-setting approach.

Conversion of the Swiss People's Party into a Populist Right Party

The Swiss party system has long been viewed as a paradigmatic case of stability, with low electoral volatility and only small changes in party strength across elections. As a result, the composition of the government (Federal Council) has remained unchanged from 1959 to 2003 (two seats for the Social Democrats, two for the Liberals, two for the Christian Democrats, and one for the Swiss People's Party).

Against this backdrop, the dramatic rise of the SPP since 1991 has certainly been the most spectacular event in contemporary Swiss politics. While the vote share of the SPP remained fairly stable (around 12%) from the end of World War II to the late 1980s, it more than doubled (from 12% to 29%) between 1991 and 2007. This came at the expense of both Liberals and Christian Democrats, as well as nongovernmental (mostly far-right) parties.[3] The repeated electoral gains that the SPP has accumulated during the last fifteen years are exceptional not only according to Swiss standards; they are also highly unusual from a comparative perspective, at least in fragmented multi-party systems such as the Swiss one. They also stress the relevance of a study focusing on the SPP and evaluating whether and to what extent its electoral rise has been associated with a rise in its agenda-setting power.

The electoral success of the SPP has had far-reaching consequences for the Swiss party system as a whole, turning power configuration on its head (Lachat 2008; Giugni and Sciarini 2009; Nicolet and Sciarini 2010): Once considered the junior partner of the governing coalition, the SPP has become the first party in the National Council (the lower Chamber of Parliament), where it now holds 62 seats out of 200, as many as the other two right-wing governing parties put together (31 seats for the Liberals and 31 seats for the Christian Democrats). Additionally, the rise of the SPP has not only concerned vote seeking, but has also extended to office seeking. After a lively debate, the party gained a second seat in the Federal Council in 2003 at the expense of the Christian Democrats. This additional governmental seat was offered to the charismatic party leader, Christoph Blocher.[4]

Up until the late 1970s, the freezing hypothesis (Lipset and Rokkan 1967) provided a convincing explanation for the stability of the Swiss party system (Lijphart 1979). However, both religious and class cleavages have declined since then, and a new conflict between the "losers" (the working class and the old middle class) and "winners" (the new middle class and upper class) of globalization has emerged. This new cleavage translates into a conflict over the country's desired level of openness to international cooperation, European integration, migrant workers, and asylum seekers—that is, a conflict over the openness/closedness or demarcation/integration dimension (Brunner and Sciarini 2002; Hug and Trechsel 2002; Kriesi et al. 2008; Lachat 2008).

This change on the demand side went hand in hand with a dramatic change on the supply side, with the SPP turning into a radical-right party since the late 1980s (Mazzoleni 2003; Oesch 2008; Skenderovic 2009). Moving away from its traditional center-right, agrarian, and governmental profile, the SPP has radicalized and has increasingly opposed Switzerland's openness to the rest of the world. As a response to the growing political, ethnic, and cultural competition associated with globalization, it has supported the isolation of the country with respect to European integration, the defense of Switzerland's key institutions (neutrality, direct democracy, and federalism), and the tightening of the country's immigration and asylum policy. By so doing, it could establish itself as the main protector of Switzerland's traditional concept of national identity and therefore increase its distance from—and hence reduce competition with—the other two right-wing governmental parties (the Liberals and the Christian Democrats).[5] By contrast, the SPP does not differ much from its right-wing competitors on the economic dimension. It is a pro-market party, albeit with some selective tendencies; and while it opposes all welfare-state developments, it nevertheless supports state interventionism for some specific segments belonging to its core electorate (farmers and the elderly).

In sum, since the late 1980s the SPP has substantially updated its ideology and transformed its issue profile, articulating the interests of globalization's losers. By combining a national-conservative stance on the cultural dimension and a liberal program on the economic dimension, it has successfully applied Kitschelt's (1995) famous winning formula. Its electoral rise owes much to its transformation from a moderate-right to a radical-right party, and more specifically to its clear cultural-protectionist profile (Brunner and Sciarini 2002; Kriesi and Sciarini 2003; Kriesi et al. 2008; Lachat 2008).

This transformation of the SPP evidently stems from its party manifestos. Figure 7.1 presents the evolution of issue attention during the period 1979 to 2007. In this figure, as in the remainder of this chapter, we divide the period into two subperiods, and we use the 1991 national election as a cutoff point to separate the "old" and the "new" SPP.

Although the party addresses a wide range of issues, we see from figure 7.1 that some topics have been more salient since 1991. More specifically, we can see a sharp rise in attention (from 10% to 18%) in the category of immigration and integration, civil rights, and law and crime, which clearly addresses the openness/closedness dimension. The SPP also put more emphasis on issues directly linked to globalization such as defense and foreign policy, whose weight has increased from 9% to 13% since 1991. Finally, macroeconomic, labor, and employment issues have attracted increased interest over time (from 12% to 14%), which is also in line with the (neo)liberal profile of the "new" SPP. Altogether, then, these three groups of issue topics account for half of the electoral manifestos of the SPP after 1991, though they made up less than one-third of such manifestos before 1991. By contrast, figure 7.1 shows that the party has disregarded issues not belonging to its new programmatic

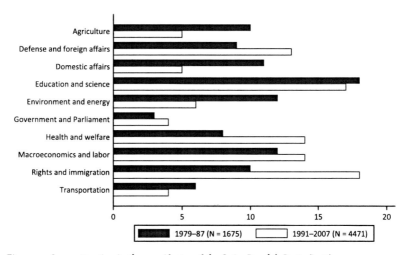

Figure 7.1. Issue attention in the manifestos of the Swiss People's Party (in %)

core. The relative attention dedicated to the category of domestic commerce, regional development, and housing has decreased markedly, from 11% to 5%. A similar reduction in issue attention is also seen for environmental protection and energy policies, as well as for agriculture policy.

These results regarding party manifestos are in agreement with a study of media coverage in the six months leading up to the national elections (Kriesi et al. 2008). This study confirms the strong focus of the SPP on immigration and foreign (European) policy since 1991. Furthermore, it demonstrates the stark increase of the overall weight of SPP issue campaigning in media coverage, as compared to the other parties: the SPP accounted for only 15% of all issue-related claims in newspaper articles during the 1991 election campaign, but up to 30% in 1995 and 40% in 1999. This was the first indication that, at least since the mid-1990s, the SPP had successfully set the public and media agenda during election campaigns.

Institutional Venues in the Swiss Political System

From a comparative perspective, Switzerland stands apart with respect to its political system, which is neither parliamentary nor presidential. As in a parliamentary system, the seven members of the Federal Council are elected, on an individual basis, by the Parliament for a mandate of four years. Unlike in a parliamentary system, however, they cannot be dismissed before the end of the legislature; the Parliament and/or the people may well reject their policy proposals, but this does not have any effect on the composition of the Federal Council. Conversely, the government cannot dissolve the Parliament or call for new parliamentary elections before the legislature is over. Further, while the Swiss government comprises several parties, it is not a true coalition, since parties do not negotiate a coalition agreement before entering the government. Switzerland is not a presidential system either, since the government is not elected by the people. More important, the executive power is shared by a collective and collegial body, in which each of the seven members has exactly the same rights and duties. Collegiality essentially means that even if some members do not share the opinion of the majority of the Federal Council and are outvoted, they must nonetheless endorse the government's decision and defend it before Parliament and the public.

Switzerland is often characterized as a paradigmatic case of consensus democracy (Lijphart 1999). The preference for the peaceful resolution of conflict through negotiation and for compromise or even consensus is a hallmark of the Swiss political system. According to a widespread view, Switzerland's consensus democracy has been strongly influenced by the existence of direct-democratic institutions, in particular the referendum (see, e.g., Neidhart 1970; Kriesi 1998), which limits the control that the government and Parliament can exert on the decision-making process.[6] Acting as a sword of Damocles over the entire decision-making process, the referendum always forces the elite to take into account the risk of defeat in a popular vote. To reduce this risk, the executive has developed sophisticated formal mechanisms in the early phase of the decision-making process, intensively consulting interest groups and other stakeholders when drafting a policy proposal. To further reduce the risk of referendums and popular defeats, all major political parties have been integrated into the governing "coalition."

From the point of view of the agenda-setting approach, the Swiss political system offers several institutional arenas in which to put a new proposal on the political agenda. We investigate the two main venues: parliamentary motions and popular initiatives. While the former is a standard instrument in all democracies, the latter is a powerful nationally specific instrument for setting the agenda: by collecting 100,000 signatures in eighteen months, a group of citizens, a political party, or an interest group can call for a total or partial revision of the federal constitution. Irrespective of the preference of the Swiss government and Parliament (for or against the initiative), the proposal is submitted to a popular vote. The adoption of the constitutional amendment requires a double majority of both the people and the cantons.

This direct-democratic instrument puts heavy pressure on both the government and the Parliament, which lose their monopoly over agenda setting and must share it with the people. Launching a popular initiative is costly, since initiators not only need to collect 100,000 signatures but must also take an active part in the campaign prior to the popular vote. In addition, the capacity of political actors to directly impact policy through popular initiatives is rather limited since, on average, nine out of ten initiatives are rejected. However, even if it is rejected, a popular initiative may have positive side effects (Kriesi and Trechsel 2008). First, by attracting attention from media and voters, and by giving political parties the ability to profile themselves on key issues, it offers important agenda-setting and vote-seeking opportunities. Second, a rejected popular initiative may still lead to policy changes indirectly, because the demand raised by the initiative may be addressed at least in part in another legislative act, that is, in a law or an executive decree (Werder 1978).

The SPP, like any other party, may launch or sponsor a popular initiative. Historically, this instrument was first used by the Social Democrats and the Christian Democrats against the Liberals to introduce a proportional representation system for the election of the National Council. Later, the political left often resorted to popular initiatives to initiate social reforms and to support the expansion of the welfare state. Since the 1980s, the popular initiative has been frequently used by new social movements, including the Greens, to promote progressive policies, but also by far-right parties to limit immigration and tighten asylum policy (Linder 2007).

Alternatively, or additionally, the SPP may launch a motion in Parliament. If supported by a majority of Members of Parliament (MPs), this motion can force the Federal Council to submit a legislative act to the Parliament or to take appropriate measures about the issue at stake. An accepted motion thus fulfills an agenda-setting function and may disturb the government's legislative priorities.

Finally, we make note of an additional specificity of the Swiss political system. Because of the very loose definition of governmental coalition at work (i.e., because of the absence of any coalition agreement or requirement regarding governing parties' loyalty toward governmental policy proposals), the distinction between government and opposition does not make much sense in the Swiss context (Kerr 1978, 52–55; Helms 2004, 45–49; Church and Vatter 2009). Even if they belong to the same government, and even if collegiality is the rule for the seven members of the Federal Council, governmental parties may occasionally or even frequently behave as opposition parties in Parliament. In other words, they can launch or support motions that run against the government. The same holds true with respect to direct democracy: a governing party can oppose governmental decisions by launching or supporting popular initiatives and optional referendums and by campaigning against the governmental proposal during referendum campaigns. As a matter of fact, since the mid-1990s decision-making processes ending with a popular vote have rarely included all four governing parties: either the SPP or the Social Democrats (or both) have defected, expressing voting recommendations that ran counter to the government (Sciarini 2007, 486). In other words, in Switzerland's consensus democracy, parties are in fact allowed to play the double game of government and opposition. Although the SPP was a true government party up until the late 1980s, it has increasingly defined itself as both a government and an antiestablishment party since the early 1990s.

The SPP's Agenda-Setting Strategy: Issue Attention and Venue Shopping

Based on both the programmatic transformation of the SPP in the 1990s and the institutional opportunities offered by the Swiss political system, we formulate two expectations regarding the agenda-setting strategy of the party since 1991. When developing such an agenda-setting strategy, the leaders of the SPP have to answer two basic questions: (1) what policy issues do we put on the political agenda? and (2) which institutional venues do we use to increase our agenda-setting power?

Our first expectation builds on the selective issue competition (Carmines 1991; Riker 1996) and issue ownership (Petrocik 1996) approaches and concerns the policy issues that the SPP is likely to promote through its agenda-setting strategy. As a populist "opposition party," the "new" SPP is likely to address issues that are important to its own constituency and that account for its electoral success. More specifically, we expect the SPP to emphasize issues pertaining to cultural protectionism and targeting immigrants, asylum seekers, foreign workers, Muslims, criminals, and others perceived to be a threat to Swiss identity. The rationale for this first expectation is threefold. First, this choice enables the party to differentiate itself from its two right-wing competitors (the Liberals and the Christian Democrats). Second, to increase its electoral support, the SPP is expected to promote the same issues in the parliamentary and direct-democratic arenas that it does during electoral campaigns. And our analysis of party manifestos clearly demonstrated a sharp increase in attention to issues of immigration, minority rights, and law and crime. Third, but still mostly for electoral reasons, the SPP needs to distance itself from the overall consensus that praises the Swiss political system and to signal to its electorate that a credible governmental alternative does exist. In sum, we argue that the agenda-setting activities of the SPP strongly follow a vote-seeking logic, even if they contradict its governmental status (i.e., run counter to governmental policies).[7]

Our second expectation relates to the SPP's venue-shopping strategy. To put an issue on the political agenda, the party may introduce parliamentary motions and/or launch a popular initiative. Although popular initiatives are costly, we nevertheless expect the SPP to rely increasingly on this institutional venue after 1991 for three main reasons. First, if the SPP is able to collect the 100,000 signatures for its own popular initiative, then it can be sure that it will influence the political, media, and public agendas: the government, the Parliament and the citizens will all have to address this issue and decide whether to accept or reject the popular initiative. The control of the agenda-setting process is much weaker in the case of a parliamentary motion. To influence the political agenda, the motion has to be accepted by a majority of MPs in both chambers, which is empirically quite infrequent: the adoption rate of motions is low, especially for motions submitted by nongovernmental parties (e.g., the Greens) and/or for motions asking for a major policy change. Second, agenda setting through popular initiative allows the SPP to frame the policy problem and to draft a proposal that fits its own interests and beliefs. This is not necessarily the case for a parliamentary motion, because the government is the bill drafter, and because Parliament may further amend and oppose it in various ways. Besides rejecting a motion, Parliament may delay the formulation of a bill, modify its content, or challenge the resulting law through a referendum. In other words, and according to the punctuated-equilibrium approach (Baumgartner, Breunig et al. 2009), institutional friction is higher for parliamentary motions than for popular initiatives. Third, the popular vote resulting from a popular initiative offers the SPP an additional—and highly mediatized—opportunity to communicate its own preferences to the public. Furthermore, it is also a clear signal that the people, and not the political elite, should be the ultimate and more legitimate decision maker. The medium thus becomes the message. This is of course highly appealing for an antiestablishment, populist, and vote-seeking party such as the SPP.

Empirical Comparison of Agenda-Setting Activities before and after 1991

To check whether the agenda-setting power of the SPP has increased since its ideological transformation and electoral rise in the early 1990s, we first look at issue attention and party success in Parliament, and then in direct democracy.

PARLIAMENTARY MOTIONS

The parliamentary agenda-setting activities of the SPP have substantially increased since the 1990s. During the first period under scrutiny (1978–91) it submitted far fewer parliamentary motions (98 motions) than the three other governing parties (845 motions). From 1991 to 2008 its share of motions doubled from 10% to 21%, reaching an absolute number of 422 motions, as opposed to 944 motions for the Liberals and Christian Democrats and 614 for the Social Democrats. Despite this impressive increase, we note that the share of the SPP's motions does not exceed its share of seats in the National Council (15% in 1995, 22% in 1999 and 27% in 2003). In other words, since 1991 the agenda-setting activity of this party has been fairly proportional to its parliamentary strength.

If we look at the issues articulated in the motions submitted by the SPP during the two time periods (table 7.1), three striking results emerge. First, the party has indeed integrated some core issues of the right-wing populist parties. Since 1991, and in line with the change observed in the party manifestos (fig. 7.1), it has reoriented its legislative proposals toward policies on immigration and integration, civil rights, and law and order (i.e., cultural protectionism). The share of this category doubled from 7% to 14% in the second period under study. Similarly, one also witnesses a slight increase in the category of defense and foreign policy, from 10% to 12%. The rise in attention is even greater with respect to the second dimension of the party's winning formula, namely economic neoliberalism: the motions on the macroeconomy and labor and employment policy have quadrupled (from 3% to 14%) between the two subperiods. The slight increase in the category of government and Parliament (from 8% to 10%) is also compatible with the new antiestablishment profile of the party, which proposed several budget cuts and institutional reforms, such as in the field of direct democracy. Second, as in the case of the electoral manifestos, since 1991 the party has paid far less attention to topics such as environmental protection, energy, and agriculture: in these policy domains, the share of motions has halved. We note, however, that agriculture still represents 10% of all motions raised by the party, which is a high share in comparison both with other issues and with other parties.[8] Therefore, the SPP's legislative agenda-setting strategy tends to mix a growing attention to right-wing populist issues with a stable emphasis on more classic issues. This strategy speaks to the two main categories of globalization losers: the working class and the old middle class of farmers and small business owners.

The comparison with the agenda-setting activities of the two other right-wing governmental parties, the Liberals and the Christian Democrats, highlights the specificity of the SPP. On the one hand, these two parties do not differ from the SPP with respect to the economic dimension: their attention to macroeconomic and labor issues has also strongly increased between the two subperiods. On the other hand, their agenda-setting activity on immigration and integration, civil rights, and law and order, unlike that of the SPP, has remained fairly stable over the entire period. The same holds true for government and parliamentary affairs. These results confirm that it is especially with respect to the cultural dimension of politics that the SPP has differentiated itself from its right-wing competitors. On their side, the two moderate-right parties seem to refrain from competing with the SPP over its new core issues. Interestingly, this does not hold true for the party located at the other end of the political spectrum, the Social Democratic Party, which has not remained unaffected by the change of the SPP's profile: we see from table 7.1 that the Social Democrats also display a strong increase in attention to immigration and law and order (from 12% to 19%), that is, to issues that do not belong to their programmatic core. The same is evident, albeit to a lesser extent, with respect to defense and foreign policy. This result can be interpreted as a counterreaction to the drift of the SPP toward national-conservative right-wing stances: wishing to profile themselves as the "antidote" to the SPP, the Social Democrats were forced to target their agenda-setting activities in Parliament on issues pertaining to the openness/closedness dimension.

Figure 7.2 illustrates the success of the SPP in setting the parliamentary agenda on its core topics: the macroeconomy; labor and employment;

Table 7.1. Issue attention in parliamentary motions (in %)

	1979–91			1991–2008		
	Liberals and Christian Democrats	Social Democrats	Swiss People's Party	Liberals and Christian Democrats	Social Democrats	Swiss People's Party
Government and Parliament	13	6	8	10	6	10
Defense and foreign affairs	6	10	8	7	12	10
Environment and energy	16	18	17	8	7	7
Macroeconomics and labor	8	15	3	16	16	14
Health and welfare	6	9	11	9	12	8
Agriculture	8	5	21	6	2	10
Rights and immigration	12	12	7	12	19	14
Education and science	9	6	2	10	10	7
Transportation	12	9	12	9	6	14
Domestic affairs	10	11	9	14	11	7
N	410	435	98	944	614	422

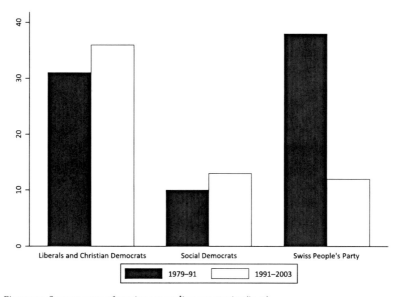

Figure 7.2. Success rates of motions regarding new topics (in %)

Note: New topics include four policy categories: macroeconomics, labor and employment; immigration and integration, civil rights, and law and order; defense and foreign affairs; and parliament and government.

immigration and integration; civil rights; law and order; defense and foreign affairs; and Parliament and government.[9] Before 1991, when the SPP was still a loyal coalition partner, the success rate of its motions was substantially higher than that of the Social Democrats (38% vs. 10%), and even higher than that of the Liberals and the Christian Democrats (31%). The picture has changed dramatically since 1991: the success rate of the SPP abruptly fell (to 12%); it is now far below that of its two right-wing competitors (36%) and very similar to that of the Social Democrats (13%). In other words, the strong increase in SPP parliamentary agenda-setting activities after 1991 went hand in hand with a sharp decrease in its success rate.[10] This result, which is presumably due to the extreme character of its motions, is a clear indicator of the SPP difficulty to win support for its policy proposals in Parliament, and to translate its electoral gains into agenda-setting power in the legislative arena.

POPULAR INITIATIVES

As we argued above, popular initiative constitutes a key institutional opportunity for agenda setting and policy-making in Switzerland. The picture emerging from the analysis of popular initiatives promoted by the SPP tells us a lot about the transformation of its political profile. First, between 1979 and 1991, the SPP did not launch or even support any popular initiatives. Its strategy has changed considerably since then: between 1991 and 2010 it launched or supported thirteen initiatives. In so doing the SPP has come closer to the oppositional strategy of the Social Democrats, who supported twenty-four initiatives during the first subperiod and up to forty-three during the second subperiod. However, the Social Democratic Party is in a very different governmental situation. As the only left-wing party of the governing coalition, it is frequently in the minority camp, which in its view justifies its oppositional profile. By contrast, the two moderate right-wing parties (the Liberals and the Christian Democrats) did not modify their strategy toward popular initiatives in the second subperiod. Rather, they supported very few initiatives and remained loyal to the government the entire time.

Second, the SPP has used popular initiatives to define itself on typical core issues of the new populist right. Eleven popular initiatives promoted by the party focused on its "new" policy issues (table 7.2): immigration and asylum policy (e.g., the initiative "against illegal immigration" in 1996, the policy "against misuse of the asylum policy" in 2002, and the policy on the "automatic deportation of criminal foreigners" in 2010); law and order (e.g., the initiative for "unlimited incarceration of sexual and violent offenders" in 2000); and the limitation of state intervention in direct democracy (e.g., the initiative "for people's sovereignty without governmental propaganda"

Table 7.2. Number of popular initiatives launched and/or supported by Swiss political parties

	1979–91				1991–2010			
	SPP	SD	S	NO	SPP	SD	S	NO
Government and Parliament	0	0	0	0	0	2	1	0
Defense and foreign affairs	0	2	0	1	0	6	2	2
Environment and energy	0	5	0	1	0	7	1	1
Macroeconomics and labor	0	3	0	0	1	4	0	0
Health and welfare	0	1	0	0	1	13	1	3
Agriculture	0	1	0	0	0	1	0	1
Rights and immigration	0	1	1	2	10	3	0	1
Education and science	0	2	0	0	0	2	0	0
Transportation	0	6	0	1	0	4	0	0
Domestic affairs	0	3	0	1	1	1	0	0
N	0	24	1	6	13	43	5	8

Key: SPP: Swiss People's party support only

SD: Social Democrats support only

S: Support from more than one governmental party

NO: no support from governmental party.

in 2008). Thus, not only has the SPP devoted more resources to popular initiatives since 1991, but it has also used direct democracy as a platform from which to promote its new key issues in the cultural openness/closedness dimension, which has also been at the core of its party manifestos since 1991. In short, the SPP has used popular initiatives to establish itself as the main political supporter of globalization's losers and of the traditional concept of Swiss national identity.

The SPP's intense focus on new cultural issues in the arena of direct democracy contrasts starkly with its agenda-setting activities in the parliamentary arena: while it has multiplied the number of motions on the macroeconomy or labor in Parliament, it has supported only one popular initiative in this field (the popular initiative on Swiss National Bank profits for the pension scheme in 2002). In sum, the SPP seems to follow a differentiated strategy in the parliamentary and direct-democratic arenas, extending its agenda-setting activities to both the economic and cultural dimensions of electoral competition in the former and focusing on the cultural dimension in the latter.

The Social Democrats, like the SPP, have used popular initiatives to set the agenda and to voice their policy preferences on their core topics, such as health and social welfare (thirteen initiatives supported), environment and energy (seven initiatives), foreign affairs and defense (six initiatives), the macroeconomy and labor (four initiatives), and transportation (four initiatives). There is, however, an important difference between the two parties: the SPP enjoyed popular support of its proposals, whereas the Social Democrats did not. Five of the thirteen initiatives launched or supported by the SPP since the early 1990s were accepted in a popular vote and therefore resulted in policy change. By contrast, the Social Democrats were successful in only two cases out of forty-three. Therefore, while the usual success rate of popular initiatives is less than 10%, the SPP has been incredibly successful over the last few years with 38% of their supported initiatives accepted. The Social Democrats, for their part, have been particularly unsuccessful with only 5% of their supported initiatives accepted.

Conclusions

This chapter has analyzed the dynamics of change in the vote-seeking and agenda-setting strategies of the Swiss People's Party since its dramatic ideological shift in the beginning of the 1990s. A careful examination of party manifestos, parliamentary motions, and popular initiatives of the SPP shows two main sets of results. The first set regards the agenda-setting activities of the SPP. On the one hand, and as a result of the transformation of the SPP into a populist right and "opposition" party in the 1990s, its agenda-setting activities have increasingly focused on issues related to cultural protectionism. However, this overall result needs some qualification, for we noted a differentiated strategy between the parliamentary and the direct-democratic arenas. In the latter, the SPP has strongly focused on its new cultural issues (immigration and asylum policy, and law and order). In the parliamentary arena, by contrast, it has extended its agenda-setting activities to economic neoliberalism and has submitted a growing number of motions in this field since the early 1990s. On the other hand, but again as expected, since 1991 the SPP has strongly relied on popular initiatives to increase its agenda-setting power, whereas before that it had not supported a single initiative.

The second set of results regards the success of these agenda-setting activities. Here the picture is more mixed. On the one hand, the SPP has performed poorly with respect to parliamentary motions since 1991: as if there were a price to pay for radicalization, its success rate on motions has dramatically dropped, including on the issues it owns. Consequently, the party has not exerted a decisive direct impact on the parliamentary agenda in this second subperiod. On the other hand, the party has been more successful in launching popular initiatives. In addition, and even more important, it has also been successful in winning popular support for its initiatives: the two votes of November 2010 (automatically deporting convicted foreigners) and November 2009 (banning minarets) are cases in point. More generally, its success rate with respect to popular votes on initiatives lies far above that of other parties and is in fact exceptional by Swiss standards. This demonstrates that the SPP has acquired a significant capacity to promote its core issues through direct democracy.

Finally, it should again be noted that the success of the agenda-setting activities of the SPP must not be evaluated through the lens of policy seeking only, since it is also oriented toward vote seeking. In fact, our study even suggests that the strategy of a party resorting to venue shopping may not be primarily oriented toward policy change, but rather toward vote seeking, which thus becomes a goal in and of itself. Going one step further, one may even claim that direct-democratic venues have strongly contributed both to the electoral rise of the SPP and to its agenda-setting power and influence over legislation. By the same token, the absence of direct democracy in general, and of popular initiatives in particular, may help explain why other radical-right parties did not reach as high an electoral share as the SPP in other European democracies or, if they did, why they then suffered from severe electoral drops and failed to stay in power, as was the case with Jorg Haider's Freedom Party of Austria (Freiheitliche Partei Österreichs).

Of course, this interpretation is only suggestive, and the question of whether our Swiss results can be generalized remains open. Our analysis clearly indicates that institutional rules do matter with respect to party agenda-setting strategies. It thus confirms the need to better cross-fertilize the agenda-setting approach by putting it in a comparative perspective (Baumgartner, Breunig et al. 2009). More specifically, an extension of our study to other populist right-wing parties in Europe (Vlaams Belang in Belgium, the Danish People's Party, and the Dutch Party of Freedom) would provide further important insights. In future work we would also like to look more closely at the interactions between the SPP and other governmental parties. Our analysis of parliamentary motions suggests that the programmatic reorientation of the SPP led the Social Democrats to address issues that they might otherwise have avoided (Green-Pedersen and Mortensen 2010). The same holds true, of course, if policy proposals are put forward through a popular initiative: in this specific case, all parties would have to address the issue and express their own preferences. Finally, our research would also benefit from a media analysis (Tresch, Sciarini, and Varone 2013). If the core strategy of the SPP is to attract the attention of voters by focusing on "new" issues in various institutional venues, then it is highly relevant to ask how these various agenda-setting activities are depicted in the media.

Notes

1. This chapter is a product of the Agenda Setting in Switzerland (ref. 105511-119245/1) and Mediatization of Political Decision-Making (National Center of Competence in Research "Democracy") projects, funded by the Swiss National Science Foundation.

2. This chapter does not address the impact of new information (about problems that exist in the real world) as a third determinant of agenda setting. For example, it does not investigate how external events affect the way a political party prioritizes its own issues when elaborating its electoral manifestos, launching a popular initiative, or submitting a parliamentary motion.

3. In the last national parliamentary elections of October 2011, the SPP suffered a defeat for the first time since 1995 (-2.4%).

4. The government changed again in 2007, when Parliament did not reelect Christoph Blocher but opted instead for another member of the SPP who was not supported by the party.

5. The SPP's successful opposition to Switzerland's membership in the European Economic Area (EEA) is a case in point in that respect. This opposition, which greatly contributed to the rejection by the Swiss people of the EEA treaty on 6 December 1992, has become a symbol and provided the basis for the electoral rise of the party and its leader, Christoph Blocher.

6. Constitutional amendments require a "mandatory referendum," whereas fifty thousand citizens may launch an "optional referendum" to oppose a given federal law or international treaty. The popular acceptance of a constitutional amendment (the mandatory referendum) requires a double majority of the people and the cantons, whereas the popular acceptance of a law (optional referendum) requires only a majority of the people.

7. This is in line with Bräuninger and Debus's (2009, 813) finding that even in parliamentary democracies, governing parties' issue-ownership may lead governing parties to propose bills that go against the government.

8. Similarly, the SPP has maintained a fairly high level of parliamentary agenda-setting activity on transportation issues.

9. For reasons of comparability, the second subperiod ends in 2003, when an institutional reform was introduced: from that year on a motion could no longer be transformed into a "postulate" (a less constraining but also less powerful parliamentary instrument, which results in a governmental report on a given topic only, and not on a proposal for a policy change).

10. Note that this poor performance holds not only for the "new" issues promoted by the SPP, but for all its motions. In addition, its success rate has not improved during the period of 2003–8: it is still more than two times lower than that of the Liberals and Christian Democrats, and no higher than that of the Social Democrats.

PART II

Issue Priorities and Institutional Change

8 Content and Dynamics of Legislative Agendas in Germany

Christian Breunig

THE CONVENTIONAL WISDOM ON GERMAN POLITICS IS THAT IN response to the political volatility of the Weimar Republic, the architects of the post–World War II political system valued stability above all other concerns.[1] As a consequence of this preference, the Basic Law introduces numerous veto points in the political process and counterbalances a strong executive branch headed by the chancellor with a powerful upper chamber (Bundesrat). Federalism and a corporatist socioeconomic structure provide additional sources of stability. Given this configuration, political conflicts are typically managed by cooperation and agreement among political elites. Consequently, scholarship on cross-national comparisons of democracy has categorized Germany as a consensus democracy (Lijphart 1999) or a semi-sovereign state (Katzenstein 1987).

These categorizations of German politics are not shared by all scholars. Authors working within a rational-choice institutionalist framework, especially those who examine the role of the upper chamber in lawmaking (Bräuninger and König 1999; Manow and Burkhart 2007), characterize the political process as competitive. They argue that majoritarian and power-sharing components are simultaneously at play: Germany is generally governed by a fairly narrow majority coalition of two or three parties who rarely control the upper chamber at the same time. As Lehmbruch (2000) has pointed out, this setup is delicate. It pits competition among parties against the need for federal cooperation.

Given the ambivalent role of political institutions, scholarly accounts commonly waver between admiration and exasperation when assessing public policy-making. On the on hand, the German political system delivers a stable environment for incremental and deliberative policy-making that allows for long-term policy commitments among political actors. On the other hand, consensus-type politics relies too heavily on small-scale policy change (von Beyme 1985, 21), lacks new policy initiatives (Katzenstein 1987, 4), and is slow to respond to crises. In contrast to majoritarian systems such as that in the

United Kingdom, only hard-won consensus among the major institutional and parainstitutional actors delivers the rare legislative ruptures of political reform and innovation. The resulting public policy–making style is labeled "policy of the middle way" (Schmidt 1987), sitting between a Social Democratic welfare state and North American capitalism.

In this chapter I explore these two features of German politics: the multifarious influence of institutions and centrist public policies. I ask whether the suggested outcomes—stable and consensual public policies—occur across all policy domains and travel across different institutional settings. I address this question by relying on more than three thousand laws enacted between 1978 and 2005, classifying them according to the issue areas specified in the Comparative Agendas Project (CAP) coding scheme. I show that public policy–making in Germany is dynamic—that is, policy issues change substantively over time. I then explore how large-scale transformations (particularly reunification and Europeanization) and different institutional settings (such as government partisanship and upper-chamber control) influence the content of legislative agendas.

The analysis of legislative content and its dynamics delivers two payoffs. First, it provides an alternative conception of legislative politics. Building on theories of public policy, the chapter concentrates on the content and not the mechanisms of legislation. While it is important to understand how legislation comes about, which problems are addressed by government and which ones are neglected is a central interest of a polity. Policy makers, bureaucrats, and the affected public at large are concerned not only with how policies emerge and are enacted, but also with what types of issues are addressed and what types of tools government employs to meet the public's demands and remedy their worries (i.e., "who gets what?"). In order to provide even a preliminary answer to these matters, it is insufficient to examine particular policy areas. Instead, this chapter considers all laws and all policy areas in order to elucidate what German governments do. In short, it shows what overall policy change looks like (Schattschneider 1960, v).

A second, related payoff centers on the study of policy dynamics. By studying policy dynamics, I am able to formulate some new expectations regarding the nature of policy outcomes in Germany. Scholarly works on American policy-making and increasingly on comparative public policy (as this volume attests) examine some general properties of policy dynamics across all political issues and across the policy cycle. The guiding research question for students of policy dynamics is why government prioritizes some policy problems over others. Jones, Baumgartner, and their coauthors (Jones and Baumgartner 2005; Jones, Baumgartner, et al. 2009; Baumgartner, Breunig, et al. 2009) contend that, owing to their penchant for the status quo, legislative organizations process information disproportionally. Consequently, government is forced to catch up sequentially to the changing reality. Different institutional settings exacerbate this processing ability (Breunig 2011). In studying the dynamics of German legislative agendas, I probe into whether large-scale changes of the polity and different institutional configurations ease or hinder policy-making in particular domains.

I proceed as follows in order to scrutinize the content and dynamics of legislative agendas in Germany. First, I introduce data on German legislation and discuss the topic coding of all laws. Using these data, I then illustrate which issues the German Parliament legislates over time. Briefly, although legislative activity fluctuates over the years, economic issues dominate the legislative agenda. In addition, issue areas differ substantially in their size and volatility; some creep onto the agenda slowly and stay put, such as law and order, while others, such as environmental concerns, suddenly peak and then fall back. Third, I explore whether two large-scale transformations of German politics—reunification and Europeanization—led to shifts in legislative agendas. The short answer is: postreunification legislation covers more law-and-order as well as environmental issues at the expense of economic and welfare topics; a European impulse is most prevalent in the environmental and economic areas, much less so for issues related to welfare and, unsurprisingly, governmental operations. I also examine and discuss how different institutional features—namely the party of government, upper-chamber control, and ministerial portfolios—shape the agenda dynamics.

The Content and Dynamics of German Legislative Agendas

DATA

In the following, I explore the content and dynamics of German legislative agenda setting based on all enacted legislative initiatives from the eighth to the fifteenth *Legislaturperioden* (legislative sessions [LP]) of the German Parliament. The time span of the data covers the years 1977 to 2005. All data are based on the Dokumentations- und Informationssystem für Parlamentarische Vorgänge (Parliamentary Material Information System [DIP]), which is available online and includes detailed information on legislative processes in the Stand der Gesetzgebung des Bundes (German Bundestag

[GESTA]). The dataset employed here was compiled by Burkhart (2008) and is distributed by the Data Archive for the Social Sciences. The GESTA data are widely used for the analysis of German parliamentary activities (see, e.g., Bräuninger and König 1999; Manow and Burkhart 2007; Lehnert, Linhart, and Shikano 2008). The dataset contains 3,138 laws.

Following the Comparative Agendas Project coding scheme, the legislative data are coded into nineteen major topic areas (see appendix). For the purpose of this chapter, these nineteen major topics are aggregated into six macrosubjects: economy (macroeconomy; labor and employment; and banking, finance, and domestic commerce), welfare (social welfare; health; housing and urban development; and education), environment (the environment, energy, transportation, and agriculture), law and order (law, crime, and family; civil rights; minority issues; immigration; and civil liberties), foreign policy (international affairs and foreign aid; defense; and foreign trade), and other (space, science, technology, and communications; government operations; and public lands and water management). Unique to the German codebook is a separate category for topics related to reunification. Laws are coded under reunification if the item directly mentions unification or clearly links to the consequences of unification. Subsequent amendments of these laws are coded into the appropriate issue category. We opted for this restrictive approach as a balance between capturing this unique historical incident and recognizing the political challenges of the new Germany.

The division into seven issue categories roughly corresponds to qualitative accounts of German politics that examine several policy areas at the same time. Two of the most prominent accounts are Katzenstein (1987) and von Beyme (1998). Katzenstein examines six policy areas: economic management, industrial relations, social welfare, migrant labor, and administrative and university reform in order to cover intergovernmental, economic, and state- and society-related problems. Von Beyme's analysis of 150 key policy decisions covers foreign, legal, economic, social, environmental, housing, and education policy. In contrast to the comprehensive dataset here, there is very little explanation in either work of why these policy areas were selected or how representative they are.

THE GERMAN LEGISLATIVE AGENDA

As a first step for empirical generalizations about German legislative agendas, it is important to illustrate the content of policy issues over time. Figure 8.1 provides a visual summary of the content and dynamics of the

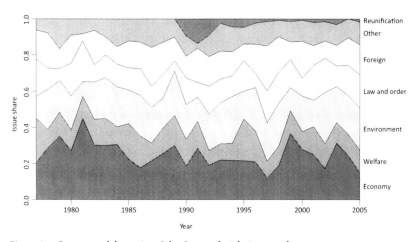

Figure 8.1. Content and dynamics of the German legislative agenda

The stacked area plot displays the composition of legislative issues by year. The issue shares are in percentages across the seven macrotopics (N = 3138).

German legislation. It plots the percentage share of each macrotopic area over time. In the following I use shares instead of total counts because the agenda space is limited—only a limited number of topics can be addressed during a given period.

Some initial observations are in order. First, the largest macrosubject on the German agenda is the economy, a substantial proportion of which consists of macroeconomic concerns. Roughly 23% of all laws passed between 1977 and 2005 deal with economic issues. Second, and somewhat surprisingly, environmental issues receive approximately 20% of government attention, comprising 9% transportation, 5% agriculture, and 5% environment. Government operation covers 9% of all laws. On the other end of the spectrum, we identified only sixty-nine of the more than three thousand laws to be directly related to reunification.

Second, some interesting dynamics can be seen over time. Among all issues, economic issues dominate throughout the entire time period. This category occupies 44% of the agenda space in 1981 (and is similarly high throughout the ninth LP) and 37% in 1999. At both points in time Germany was in rather poor economic shape. Welfare issues were at the forefront of the legislative agendas (24%) in 1977 and in 1996. The roughly simultaneous peak of welfare and economic issues might suggest that government is responding to economic hard times with a flanking maneuver: macroeconomic steering and social-welfare restructuring. This is an interesting insight; gov-

ernmental response to unemployment is legislative activity and is not necessarily based on automatic triggers, such as fulfilling certain eligibility criteria.
Figure 8.1 suggests that during crisis government works on the parameters
of entitlements.

Third, three issue areas that have received increasing attention since the
1990s are the environment, foreign affairs, and law and order. By 2002, 28%
of the issue space was covered by environmental issues. Across time, environmental issues are the most volatile. The 1990s and early 2000s also saw
a surge in foreign policy issue, peaking in 1997. Many legislative activities
during this time were a response to the Balkan crisis and then to international terrorism, commencing with the 11 September attacks in New York.
Foreign policy was a central topic of the thirteenth LP. Issues pertaining to
law and order steadily grew beginning in the mid-1990s and reached close to
20% of all laws by 2001. While legislation on individual rights and liberties,
especially in the area of immigration, were substantively important, the bulk
of law-and-order legislation concentrated on the organizations of courts and
changes in the criminal and civil codes.

Finally, it is astonishing how little German reunification changed the composition of major legislative issues. Reunification-related legislation peaked
in 1991, when it occupied 13% of the issue space. The increase in reunification
issues came largely at the expense of environmental and law-and-order concerns. After 2000 only 1–2% of all laws dealt with reunification-related issues.
One is tempted to conclude that by 2005 the unification of the once-divided
Germany had been accomplished, at least in the legislative arena.

This introductory inspection of the German legislative agenda points toward two intuitions. First, a limited number of issues, most prominently the
economy, continuously occupy a substantial amount of space on the issue
agenda. These issues, which include budgeting and macroeconomic management, are central to lawmaking and to our understanding of what government does for its citizens. Second, the content of the German legislative
agenda is animated. The agenda space is peppered with sudden spikes in a
particular issue at the expense of a fourfold drop in some other areas. At
the same time, some issues, such as law and order, creep onto the legislative agenda and rarely vanish. In short, stark differences in both the size
and the volatility of the legislative topics addressed by the German Parliament exist. Minimally, this initial description hints that some issues receive
a steady stream of legislative attention, while others burst onto the agenda
and quickly disappear. So far we know relatively little about why these differ-

ent dynamics prevail across issues in general and in the German Bundestag specifically.

This chapter develops a tentative inquiry into the sources of variation in legislative agendas and examines two forces: large-scale transformations and legislative institutions. Agenda-setting theory (Baumgartner, Breunig, et al. 2009) holds that both political attention to a particular issue and institutions influence agenda dynamics. Since selecting issues is a precondition for legislative action, I expect that large-scale changes, such as reunification and Europeanization, serve as powerful focusing events that grab legislators' attention and shift the legislative agenda temporarily. At the same time, certain institutional configurations enable or thwart legislators' ability to legislate on those issues. For the purpose of this chapter, I examine whether three legislative venues—partisanship in the Bundestag, opposition control of the Bundesrat, and ministerial portfolios—change the content of the legislative agenda. I examine each source in turn.

The Role of Large-Scale Transformations

German politics has witnessed two large-scale transformations since the 1970s: Europeanization and reunification. Although scholarly literature on the influence of both forces on specific public policies is enormous, in this section I will examine whether and how Europeanization and reunification change the German legislative agenda—in other words, whether different issues are legislated (1) in the absence or presence of a European impulse for legislation and (2) in the period before or after reunification. In order to address both questions, I rely on simple contingency tables and display their results in figure 8.2.

REUNIFICATION

In 1990, reunification profoundly altered the shape and character of the German polity. The union of the former communist German Democratic Republic and the German Federal Republic was largely accomplished by transferring West German legal, political, and economic institutions to the Eastern states. This accession established the most populous country in Western Europe and, in a very short period of time, created a culturally and economically more fragmented polity. Among the most important political modifications of the new Germany are (1) an important shift in Germany's federal system, with the addition of five new *Länder*, and (2) the inclusion and rise of a new

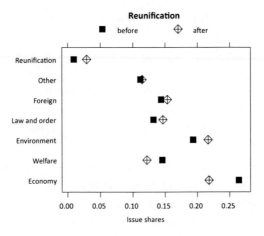

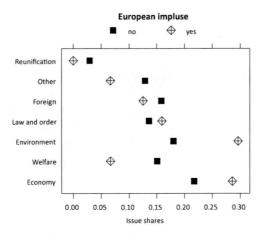

Figure 8.2. The German legislative agenda and two historical transformations

Note: The top plot displays the shares of legislative issues before and after reunification. The bottom plot shows the shares of legislative issues with or without a European impulse. Issue shares are in percentages across the seven macrotopics (N = 3138).

left-wing party, the Left Party of Democratic Socialism (PDS/Linke), emerging out of the former East German Communist Party. These two political changes are linked: the upper chamber incorporated the resulting new states and redistributed its seats among the *Länder*—a reshuffling that tipped the political balance toward poorer and more leftist states.

Along with political changes came a gamut of pressing policy problems. Given the desolate state of the East German economy, the government of Helmut Kohl promised to respond with immediate macroeconomic and labor policies aimed at boosting the economic well-being of East German citizens (*blühende Landschaften*). Derelict industrial and military constructions called for an environmental policy that repaired the ecological legacy of the collapsed socialist state. In addition, unification forced German policy makers to rethink its foreign policy by addressing how a unified Germany should and would assert itself within Europe and on a global scale. Given the large-scale regime change and pressing policy needs, how did the legislative agenda respond?

A simple comparison of the legislative agenda for the time period before and after the official date of reunification provides some answers. As the top-right plot of figure 8.2 shows, when comparing legislative outputs for the period between 1977 and 1990 with those for the period between 1990 and 2005, no stark differences exist. Economic (-5 percentage points) and welfare (-2 percentage points) issues receive a bit less attention, while law and order, reunification, and environment gain between 1 and 2 percentage points. The plot indicates that legislative output and public policy did not vary dramatically after reunification.

At least for the legislative agenda space, reunification, in pure numbers, never occupied a central role for an extended period of time. Only 69 of 3,138 enacted laws directly dealt with reunification. Going back to figure 8.1, the reunification issue surged on the legislative agenda in 1990. From then until 1992, reunification occupied between 9% and 13% of the total legislative agenda. Within this topic area, macroeconomic and property-rights issues were a major concern immediately after reunification, while legislation on civil rights and liberties (including affairs related to Stasi, the East German state security service) became more prominent thereafter. Admittedly, it might be charged that the relatively meager share of reunification issues is due to the coding protocol. But even if we had continued to code all amendments and revisions as reunification-specific issues, our recoding revealed that the topic of reunification hardly ever surpassed a 5% share of the total agenda space.

The historical consequences of reunification are profound. In the early 1990s some legislative decisions, such as the unification treaty, not only were fundamental legislative accomplishments in the post–World War II era but also generated life-changing experiences for large parts of the citizenry. However, these substantively important policy shifts did not, by and large, alter the legislative agenda. The postreunification legislative era started with a modest increase in legislation related to reunification and marginally moved the composition of legislated issues away from welfare and the economy toward environmental concerns and law and order. In addition, it is hard to sustain the argument that this small shift in the composition of issues should be attributed solely to the reunification process.

Instead of major discontinuity, the German Parliament responded with legislative continuity. Thus, the significance of reunification was not just an institutional transfer (*Institutionentransfer* [Lehmbruch 1990]) but also a thematic transfer (*Thementransfer*). There was no transformation of the issue space; instead, the German Parliament legislated on similar issues before and after reunification. This observation suggests that the inclusion of new states and a leftist party did not dramatically alter the composition of legislative issues. Instead, new problems and issues, such law and order, intruded onto the legislative agenda after the brief surge of reunification issues in the early 1990s.

EUROPEANIZATION

While reunification rapidly transformed German politics, the foundations of European integration had been laid in the 1950s. Since then national governments have adapted to this creeping, gradual process by coordinating public policy at the domestic as well as the European level. With regard to public policy, Europeanization is generally understood as a cross-national convergence of policy styles and outcomes. The vast literature on this topic (e.g., Hix and Goetz 2000; Risse, Cowles, and Caporaso 2001) highlights three broad mechanisms for convergence: national-level adaption of European Union decisions and regulation, common interests and values of political elites across countries and within the EU institutions, and strategic exploitation of different policy levels by domestic actors in order to achieve their preferred policy outcomes. All of these mechanisms suggest that attention to various policy issues becomes increasingly homogenous and coherent across European polities and that Europeanization crowds out domestically instigated policy change.

From European institutions' earliest inceptions, policy-making, particularly market regulation, was a primary motivating factor in the integration process. Without doubt, by the beginning of the twenty-first century the influence of Europeanization had been documented across several policy fields, most notably for agricultural, environmental, human rights, and immigration issues. The obvious question is if a European impulse has a uniform effect across all topic areas or some policy issues are more receptive than others. In order to address this question, I rely on the parliamentary records that specifically mention European involvement. A European impulse comes in a myriad of ways, such as responses to EU directives and recommendations, decisions by EU institutions (Parliament, council, court of justice), agreements, conventions, and treaties.

For the period between 1977 and 2005, I find that 24% of all laws respond to a European impulse. Although large fluctuations in the percentage of laws with a European impulse occurred during the late 1970s and early 1980s, at least 30% of all laws passed by the German government after 2000 were based on European impulses. The bottom plot in figure 8.2 displays how this effect is distributed across the different macrotopics. It is instantly apparent that a large variation of Europeanization exists across the seven policy topics. Welfare and government operations receive over 5 percentage points less agenda space from European impulses. On the other hand, Europeanization can be easily detected for economic topics (which include regulatory issues) and environmental topics (which include agricultural issues). The differences are a 7 and a 12 percentage-point increase in the issue share respectively. A simple χ^2 test indicates that there is a statistically significant difference in the composition of issue shares across topics for laws with and without European impulse ($\chi^2 = 129$ with 6 degrees of freedom, $p < 0.001$). When viewed over time, it also becomes apparent that the share of economic topics with a European impulse rose after 2000.

All in all, the comparison of legislative agendas with and without European impulses largely confirms the previous efforts of scholars on European politics. First, Europeanization of the German legislative policy agenda becomes more common. Second, distinct patterns of Europeanization prevail across policy issues. As Börzel (2006) argues, the breadth and depth of Europeanization varies across policy areas. For agricultural and environmental issues, Europeanization is most highly developed. Other policy areas, such as social welfare, labor, and education, operate for the most part domestically. In short, Europeanization focuses legislators' attention on a small set of policy areas for which their decision-making authority is constrained.

Legislative Politics and Legislative Agenda

The institutional foundation of legislative politics in Germany conjoins majoritarian and nonmajoritarian features of democracy. The government is headed by an institutionally powerful chancellor (*Kanzlerdemokratie*) and is represented by a minimum-winning coalition in Parliament. Consequently, the majority of legislation originates from the executive branch. At the same time, the strong executive faces multiple veto points in the legislative process. The strategically most important hurdle is the upper chamber (Bundesrat) because policy-making across most policy areas is a process of joint decision making (Scharpf 1988). Opposing majorities in the Bundesrat and Bundestag paired with partisan competition among a small set of parties contribute to conflict-laden parliamentary decision making and policy-making. I therefore expect that two features—partisan control of government and opposition control of the upper chamber—affect the legislative agenda.

First, literature on the role of parties in government offers two opposing logics on how government parties shape public policy–making and legislative agendas. The first strand essentially argues that partisan preference makes a difference in policy outcomes. It maintains that public-policy outcomes can be derived from ideological positions of the executive. Once in power, parties aim to implement their policy agenda. Both rational-choice accounts of partisan politics and more substantial descriptive accounts on the role of the chancellor in German lawmaking therefore hold that the policy content of the legislative agendas varies depending on which parties rule in parliament. The second strand maintains that ideologically derived policy preferences have at best a limited influence on public policy, for two reasons. First, given the multiple veto points and the strength of parapublic institutions, the German political system encourages power sharing and consensus seeking within the governing coalition and the larger institutional environment. This logic contends that, in general, Germany is governed from the center, and policy content changes little. Second, some public-policy literature (Jones and Baumgartner 2005) argues that governing parties are not utility maximizers; instead, they serve as problem solvers. Consequently governments, regardless of their partisan stripe, are forced to attend to and address pressing policy needs. This urge stymies preference-based policy-making and leads to similar (if environmental stimuli are random across governments) and dynamic legislative agendas.

The second source of changes in legislative agendas is partisan control of the upper house. Interchamber relations are typically characterized by a strong form of symmetrical bicameralism and by partisan competition between government and opposition across the two legislative institutions. Scholarly works on German bicameralism bemoan the persistence of political immobility and legislative gridlock (Scharpf 1988; Lehmbruch 2000) because the Bundesrat (1) represents a crucial veto point in the passage for a considerable share of all bills and (2) is seldom in the control of the government coalition. Two arguments for legislative delays and failure are put forward. First, given that the different partisan majorities prevail in each chamber, a typical veto game ensues that produces either legislative failure or lowest-common-denominator policies. Second, government might be able to anticipate the veto by the opposition-controlled upper chamber and therefore will not even consider introducing a bill requiring Bundesrat consent (Manow and Burkhart 2007). Both logics support the idea that the two houses operate differently depending on whether government controls the Bundesrat. Consequently, one would expect that distinct policy agendas are legislated under different types of upper-chamber control.

In addition to partisan control and bicameralism, the literature on comparative politics argues that a core function of parliamentary government is choosing a cabinet and ministers (Budge and Keman 1990; Laver and Shepsle 1996). An essential aspect of coalition bargaining and government formation is the creation and control of individual ministries. By heading a particular ministry, political parties are able to control policy outcomes on that policy dimension. The literature offers two mechanisms on how ministerial agenda control influences policy. Both understand ministers as agents of their parties. First, ministerial discretion induces stability in the multidimensional policy space and enables dimension-by-dimension policy-making (Laver and Shepsle 1996). Second, individual ministers push for policies in their policy realm in order to reward constituency groups (von Hagen and Harden 1996). Both mechanisms suggest that ministerial agenda control should be concentrated on each ministry's legislative jurisdiction.

This brief discussion introduced three institutional features—governing parties, bicameralism, and ministerial control—that should alter the legislative agendas. Large bodies of literature propose significant policy differences depending on the constellation of each of these three features. I examine each area in turn.

Government Parties

Differences in the legislative agenda across government parties can be assessed by the three different coalitions during the time period examined. From 1974 to 1982 the social-liberal government was led by the Social Democratic Party (SPD) under Chancellor Helmut Schmidt, with the FDP as the junior partner. After a constructive vote of no confidence in 1982, Kohl took over the chancellorship, and his Christian Democratic Union (CDU) governed in coalition with the Christian Social Union (CSU) and FDP until 1998. After the Red-Green victory in the 1998 election, the SPD's Gerhard Schröder headed the government, with the support of the Green Party, for two legislative periods until 2005.

The top plot of figure 8.3 displays the issue shares for each governing coalition. An initial visual inspection hints that the composition of the legislative

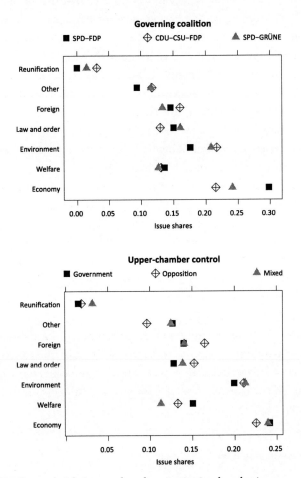

Figure 8.3. The German legislative agenda and two institutional mechanisms

The top plot displays the shares of legislative issues for each of the three government coalitions. The bottom plot shows the shares of legislative issues depending on the three types of upper-chamber control. Issue shares are in percentages across the seven macrotopics (N = 3138).

agenda is fairly stable across the three governing coalitions. In fact, the difference in the size of the issue shares is hardly more than 2 percentage points for three policy macrotopics: foreign, economic, and other. The most stable of all macrotopics is welfare: partisan difference in government attention is less than 1 percentage point!

When comparing each government transition, some policy shifts become discernible. The switch from a social-liberal to a CDU-led coalition led to an 8 percentage point drop in economic issues, which was replaced by a 4 percentage point surge in environmental topics (split about equally between agriculture and the environment) and a 3 percentage point rise in unification-related legislation. Drilling down to the major topic level reveals that the main difference between the two governments is macroeconomic issues. Of all Germany's governments during this time, the SPD-FPD coalition was the most active in this area. It was also the government with the most exclusive focus on one area: 18% of all laws were related to macroeconomic management. This finding correlates well with the scholarly perception of the SPD-FDP government. In the mid-1970s the government was able to keep unemployment fairly low and incomes up owing to active macroeconomic and labor-market policies, including deficit spending. However, different opinions on how to respond to worsening economic conditions and rising debt ultimately broke the SPD-FDP coalition apart in 1982.

The switch from a conservative to a Red-Green coalition in 1998 produced a less pronounced shift in the legislative agenda. Foreign-policy topics dropped by nearly 3 percentage points, while legislation on the economy and law and order increased by roughly 3 percentage points. When compared to ideological placement, this small change in the legislative agenda seems surprising. Despite the SPD's move to the ideological center during the 1990s, the two major parties were ideologically distinct. This is even truer for their respective junior coalition partners. Overall, this brief inquiry indicates that the legislative agendas of the three different governing coalitions are fairly similar overall. This finding hints that governing coalitions cannot simply translate their partisan position into legislative outputs. Given that the legislative agenda is disjointed and episodic (see fig. 8.1), the lack of partisan differences might be due to which issues governments attend to and how they are addressed once they land on the legislative agenda. This logic suggests that although governments legislate on various policy issues in a serial manner, legislative agendas across governing coalitions are similarly composed in aggregate. The resemblance might simply be due to similar external shocks.

Interchamber Relations

The bottom plot of figure 8.3 displays the composition of issue shares among the three constellations of Bundesrat control. Three types of upper-chamber constellations are considered: Bundesrat is in the hand of the governing coalition; opposition parties control the Bundesrat; and mixed majorities of government and opposition parties prevail. For the time period examined, only 24% of laws are passed under unified control. The plot offers three insights.

First, the composition of legislative topics differs among the three types of upper-chamber control. A χ^2 test ($\chi^2 = 24$ with 12 degrees of freedom and $p < 0.05$) indicates that a statistically significant difference among chamber control and legislative agenda composition exists. The plot allows us to see that welfare topics (especially social welfare and labor policy) are more likely to be legislated when government parties control the Bundesrat. The difference between government and opposition control is a reduction of nearly 2 and 4 percentage points when the upper chamber holds a mixed majority. One might speculate as to why welfare is lower under mixed than under opposition control of the Bundesrat. A potential answer might be that under mixed majorities, interchamber bargaining might be too costly and vague in terms of time and payoffs.

Second, issue shares for most topics, notably the economy, other, and foreign affairs, as well as education and energy when examined at the major topic level, hardly differ (i.e., a change of less than 1 percentage point) between government and mixed control. For a host of policy topics, whether or not the Bundestag is in government or mixed control makes no difference in terms of legislative agendas.

Third, the issue shares of some policy areas, most notably the environment (especially transportation) and law and order, increase when the Bundesrat is controlled by mixed or opposition majorities. When government is not in control in the Bundesrat, some policy topics appear to generate less resistance and to attract cross-chamber attention more easily.

Taking all this together, I find more nuanced evidence for the influence of the Bundesrat on the legislative agenda. The key insight is that different majority constellations result in distinct legislative agendas patterns across policy topics. In other words, gridlock (*Reformstau*) is conditional on policy area. Environmental as well as law-and-order topics are less affected than other policy topics by institutionally generated veto points. The previous literature overlooked this possibility because of its focus on veto-ridden policy areas. At a minimum, figure 8.3 suggests that other modes of interaction between the two chambers exist. Bräuninger and König (1999) might be a starting point for further inquiry. They show that the type of policy as well as the type of legislation (i.e., whether it is mandatory or not) determined upper-chamber approval of policy change during the late Kohl era. Since their study is restricted to a narrow time period and only two policy areas, it is an open question whether different legislative procedures or policy-specific features enable legislative activity despite substantial legislative roadblocks.

Ministerial Agenda Control

One theoretical and empirical problem in the study of ministerial influence is that newly elected governments regularly change the number and purpose of ministries. They often do so in order to highlight an important policy area on the governing agenda. By abolishing or establishing a ministry, governments essentially institutionalize government attention to a particular policy area and purposely reduce attention to others. For example, three differently con-figured ministries were responsible for health-care issues between 1977 and 2005; others just survived one legislative period. Despite this limitation, it is worth considering (1) how much a ministry is involved in each of the seven macrotopics of the legislative agenda and (2) how dominant certain ministries are in a specific topic area.

Figure 8.4 displays the issue shares for each ministry. For comparative purposes, it also shows laws based on international agreements. The ministries are placed on the y-axis and are ordered according to the degree of their legislative involvement. Among the most actively involved ministries are justice, finance, interior, and further back, work and social support, agriculture, and the three versions of the health ministry. At the bottom are several ministries that existed for one legislative period and were responsible for just one law, such as the developmental ministry.

A few ministries operate in one policy area; many spread across issues. As the plot indicates, ministries with a nearly exclusive focus on their desig-nated policy area include the environment, defense, agriculture, transporta-tion, and the two education-related ministries. The ministries for social work as well as justice are spread out across several policy areas. For example, roughly half of all legislative involvement of the justice ministry is within the

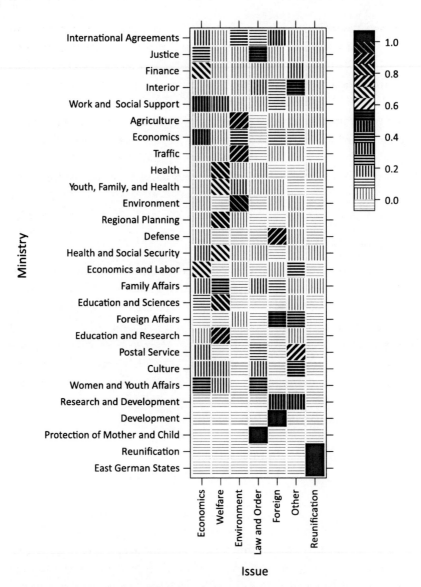

Figure 8.4. The German legislative agenda, international agreement, and ministerial responsibility

Note: The y-axis displays all German ministries ordered by the number of laws they were responsible for (top to bottom). The x-axis lists the seven macrotopics. The shape of the squares indicates the issue shares for each ministry. Darker squares indicate that a given ministry concentrates on a particular topic. Issue shares are in percentages across the seven macrotopics ($N = 3138$).

law-and-order policy field, and the other half is spread across the remaining six issue areas. An inspection of each macrotopic suggests that numerous ministries participate in the areas of economic management and welfare, while law and order is more or less exclusively managed by the interior and the family affairs ministry.

This inquiry indicates that hardly any ministry has an exclusive focus on a single policy dimension; this is especially true of some of the ministries that carry out central government functions, such as the justice, foreign affairs, finance, and interior ministries. In addition, nearly the same sets of ministries continuously occupy a substantive space on the legislative agenda. All told, this suggests that ministries do not just concentrate on their jurisdiction; instead, ministerial involvement occurs across policy topics. This finding indicates that the theoretical logic for ministerial dominance does not capture how ministries actually shape the legislative agenda. Instead, ministerial involvement across policy domains hints that policy change regularly originates outside the "natural habitat" of a specific issue. Legislative agendas might be dynamic because individual ministries are able to bring an issue to the collective attention, break up existing policy subsystems, and thereby gain control over this issue. In addition, core ministries, such as justice and finance, are the priced assets of coalition bargaining exactly for this reason: they can operate across all policy issues.

Conclusions

This chapter explores the content and dynamics of the legislative policy agenda in Germany. Even when the policy space is summarized by just seven large policy topics, major ebbs and flows of particular policy issues become apparent for the time period between 1977 and 2005. This is true for relative large policy areas, such as the economy, as well as small items, such as government operations. In addition, the pace of policy issues varies across topics. For example, law and order slowly emerged on the legislative agenda after the mid-1990s, while environmental concerns rapidly and sporadically burst to the forefront.

The examination of historical transformations and institutional structures in the context of legislative agendas delivers two lessons. First, institutional features and partisan control of government do not shape the legislative agenda equally across issue domains. To highlight some important findings: core ministries are involved in several policy domains, opposition control of the Bundesrat does not stymie legislation on environmental and law-and-order issues, and partisan differences are largely confined to economic issues. Second, straightforward theoretical expectations regarding the impact of reunification, partisanship, and ministerial agenda control cannot be substantiated. Consequently, more nuanced explanatory models of legislative politics need to be developed that incorporate policy issues more clearly.

For the broader literature on German politics, this chapter delivers two insights. First, the episodic rise and fall of legislative issues contradicts the notion of incremental, deliberative policy-making depicted in the classic literature on German politics. Instead of policy-making of the "middle way," the German legislative agenda rather can be described as "policy of the many ways." Despite opposition control of the Bundesrat and low governmental turnover, German legislators regularly and abruptly become active in different policy domains. This transformation results in a dynamic legislative agenda. Second, the findings of the chapter suggest that the scholarly debate about whether competitive or consensual features dominate in German politics is likely to be domain specific. While the impact of institutional configurations is apparent for economic and welfare issues, the environment, law and order, and foreign affairs appear more consensus driven. At the minimum, the apparent differences in policy domains call for future examinations of policy domain–specific institutions.

Notes

1. I would like to thank all those involved in the Comparative Policy Agendas project, especially Christoffer Green-Pedersen and Stefaan Walgrave for putting this edition together. Sarah Sophie Fleming, Joey Hawker, and Monika Wyrzykowska provided outstanding research assistance and are by now experts on the fine details of German legislative issues. More information about the German Policy Agendas Project can be found at http://gpa.uni.kn.

9   Strong Devolution but No Increasing
Issue Divergence: Evolving
Issue Priorities of the Belgian
Political Parties, 1987–2010

Stefaan Walgrave, Brandon Zicha, Anne Hardy,
Jeroen Joly, and Tobias Van Assche

ON 6 DECEMBER 2011 THE FIRST ELIO DI RUPO GOVERNMENT WAS
sworn in after several formateurs, mediatiors, and negotiators had at-
tempted to form a federal government after the elections of June 2010. The
country remained 541 days without a government of full powers, before a
classic tripartite of socialists, Christian democrats, and liberals from both
the Flemish and the French communities reached a government agreement.
Earlier, in December 2010, Belgium had broken the European record for the
longest period of government formation, and on 16 February 2011 it also
broke the world record—till then held by Iraq. The immediate reason for the
Belgian stalemate was not a mystery: deep political disagreement between
the two major language communities. The Dutch-speaking Flemish parties
did not want to form a government without a comprehensive agreement on a
major state reform that would shift more jurisdictions and fiscal autonomy to
the regions, while the French-speaking parties did not favor large changes to
the institutional status quo. The crisis exemplified the apparently increasing
tensions along the ethnic-linguistic cleavage. Belgium has had a long history
of linguistic conflicts, but the political crises in 2010 and 2011, observers
agree, was the worst to date. The country's very sustainability has become
a topic of debate among political analysts and scholars alike (Swenden and
Jans 2006).

The fact that devolution and state-reform issues blocked government
formation in 2010–11 is a reflection of a long-standing linguistic conflict—
not just about devolution, but about many issues that fall under the jurisdiction of the national government (and of the regional governments, for
that matter). The recurring incongruities form the major argument used by
the Flemings, who claim more competences for the regions, supposed to be

more internally homogeneous in their priorities and goals. Flemish parties state that it has become increasingly difficult to strike a national compromise between Flemish-speakers and Francophones because the two groups care about different issues; furthermore, even when they care about the same issues, they have different opinions on how to solve them. In this chapter we examine the first part of this contention. We examine to what extent the policy priorities of political actors from both regions differ and whether this has increased over time. It is a common diagnosis in Belgium that Flemings and Francophones have grown apart in terms of issue prioritization. Flemings, for example, are said to care more about crime, while Francophones prioritize bread-and-butter issues. Flemings allegedly have typical right-wing issue priorities (e.g., immigration), whereas Francophones prefer traditional left-wing issues (e.g., unemployment). Communities, according to frequent claims by pundits and politicians, have developed large differences in what they consider to be important and which problems should be tackled first. This growing issue divergence is believed to contribute to the increasing dysfunction at the national governance level, because the fight for priorities dominates the national arena and prevents the national government from acting decisively and crafting clear and effective policies.

This chapter deals with the alleged large and increasing differences in issue priorities of both communities. The agenda-setting approach and the available agenda evidence on Belgium allow us—for the first time—to tackle empirically whether Flemish and Francophone political actors put forward different issues. We focus on two main questions: (1) to what extent do Flemish and Francophone political actors (parties) hold different issue priorities; and (2) has the divergence in issue priorities increased over time? More concretely, we examine to what degree political parties have grown more divergent *across* the language communities relative to changes *within* these communities.

To address these questions we rely on two types of longitudinal evidence. First, we examine the issue attention in the party manifestos of all the main Flemish and Francophone parties from 1987 to 2007. Second, we categorize all oral questions asked in the lower chamber of the federal Parliament by the main parliamentary parties, again both Flemish and Francophone, from 1987 to 2007. We then calculate issue-overlap scores to assess how large the issue divergence is between the different parties, and whether issue overlap between Flemish and Francophone parties is systematically lower than among parties of the same linguistic camp. Finally, we also check whether cross-linguistic issue-overlap scores have increased or decreased over time.

Belgian Politics: Two Political Systems in One

Belgium is a bipolar federal state (much of the discussion below is based on Deschouwer 2009). After the major state reform of 1993, the country officially became a federal state, although many of the reforms were not put into force until 1995. The country consists of two large language communities: Dutch-speaking Flanders in the north (60% of the population) and French-speaking Wallonia in the south (30% of the population). Close to the German border there is a third, very small, German-speaking community. Central is the capital of Brussels, officially bilingual but in fact largely French-speaking (10% of the Belgian population). Each community has its own regional government and parliament. The national Parliament and government still exert a lot of power and hold many competences. All the Flemish parties (some more than others) want some remaining national competences to be shifted to the regional level. Most Francophone parties are very hesitant about this matter and do not want the federal level to lose more jurisdiction.

The former Belgian bilingual unitary political parties split along language lines into Flemish and Francophone versions of the prior "parent" party as early as the 1960s and 1970s. As a consequence, Belgium has two socialist parties, two Christian-democratic parties, two liberal parties, two green parties and so on. These parties are entirely separate: each has its own structure, organization, and policy program. Each competes in elections in its own community and does not address the population on the other side of the language border. The media too are split into two separate systems. Hence, there are basically two independent political systems in Belgium that come together, or clash, at the federal level. Linguistic tensions flare up regularly, because both regional interests have to be reconciled at the national level.

The period under study here, 1987–2010, covers an epoch in which the Belgian state was fundamentally reformed from a unitary into a federal state. There had been two state reforms before, in 1970 and 1980, but three successive state reforms leading to more competences for the regions took place within the time frame of our study: in 1988, 1993, and 2003. The 1993 reform was probably the most thorough of them all: it provided Belgium with its federal structure and installed separate elections for the regional institutions.

Owing partly to this ongoing process of devolution in which both communities gradually developed their own institutions with separate elections, parliaments, and governments; with political parties growing further apart; and with ever more distinct media systems, we expect to find increasing issue divergence over time, particularly after major state reforms. Hence, Flemish and Francophone parties should gradually drift apart over time. It is important to note that increasing issue divergence can be the consequence as well as the cause of the ongoing process of devolution in Belgium.

There are also a number of other reasons why we expect to find great, and growing, issue divergence in the Belgian federation. Major socioeconomic differences are expected to entail different socioeconomic problems and, thus, differences in the perceived urgency of certain problems. The Flemish region is more affluent than Wallonia and Brussels in almost every respect. Flanders has lower levels of unemployment, lower poverty rates, better schools, and so on. We expect this to affect the priority of these problems and lead to a decreasing issue overlap between Flemish and Francophone parties. The signals they get from their respective constituencies about the severity and urgency of problems differ, and we expect them to emphasize these problems in different ways.

Also, the mere fact that there are two separate political arenas is likely to lead to a centripetal political competition. Indeed, political competitors tend to closely observe each other's issue priorities and emulate them (for Belgium, see Vliegenthart, Walgrave, and Meppelink 2011). Hence, because the two party systems are completely separated, this may lead to internal dynamics that could diminish the congruence between them. For example, once a party on one side of the language border addresses an issue successfully, chances are high that other, competing parties in the same arena will start emulating this party's strategy and incorporate this new issue into their discourse, leading to a high degree of issue overlap between competing parties. The parties in the other political arena have little incentive to mimic the behavior of the innovator, because it is not threatening their market share. As a consequence, the new issue will be widely addressed in one political system while neglected altogether in the other. This is what may have happened with the breakthrough of the anti-immigrant party Vlaams Blok (now Vlaams Belang) in the 1990s. The other Flemish parties, under pressure because of Vlaams Belang's successive electoral victories, also started devoting more attention to the immigration issue. In French-speaking Belgium, however, the (anti)immigration discourse remained marginal, as there was no successful "first adopter."

Issue Divergence between Party Elites: Consequences and Origins

Why is some degree of issue overlap important, and why is issue divergence a problem? Issue overlap is important because political attention is inevitably in short supply. According to the original political agenda–setting claim, each political system has to solve the difficult problem of determining which issues deserve political attention. The societal problems requiring political attention are infinite. However, political actors' time, energy, motivation, and money are all scarce. That is why Jones and Baumgartner argue that the decision to devote attention to a given issue and not take other issues into account is the single most important policy process determining all other subsequent policy-making and decision-making steps (Jones and Baumgartner 2005). Hence, when different elites address different issues, when they decide to focus on one issue rather than on another, this has important consequences for the kinds of decisions that are reached and even whether decisions are reached in the first place. When priorities differ, actors are talking across, not to, each other. A minimum amount of issue overlap is simply a precondition for decision making. The political conflict shifts from the question of which solutions fix which problems to the question of which problems should be addressed in the first place.

The general idea that some amount of issue overlap between elites is necessary for a political system to be able to reach decisions and function properly is even more applicable to strongly divided, consociational democracies than to majoritarian democracies. In his classic work, Lijphart (1999) claims that divided societies resort to consociational mechanisms to overcome their divisions. These arrangements involve all kinds of institutional mechanisms through which power is spread over different actors and by which minorities are granted veto power. The Belgian federal state is a prime example of such accommodating structures that protect the minority, in this case the French-speakers, against the will of the Flemish majority. As a consequence, at the federal level it is impossible for the Flemish to impose their agenda on the French-speaking parties. Because the constitution guarantees that half of the ministers in the national government are to come from Francophone parties, they can at all times block any governmental decision at the national level. The whole Belgian system is permeated with such checks and balances, making it impossible for any majority to simply overrule a minority and impose its issues. Hence, owing to this constitutional design, Flemish and Francophone parties *have* to agree on the national governmental policy agenda; otherwise, policy is simply impossible.

Consociationalism, though, not only implies structural and constitutional brakes on majority will but also involves a certain political culture of negotiation among elites who seek consensus and are prepared to accommodate in order to overcome rift and conflict. In consociational systems, elite consensus is said to be a crucial asset (Lijphart 1975). It is partly the consociational behavior of the elites, and not only the consociational structures, that keeps strongly divided countries together. We believe that addressing the same issues, and thus a certain level of issue overlap, may be one of the cornerstones of elite consensus in divided states. That elites are prepared, and publicly announce this preparedness, to talk about issues that "the other side" considers important is the first step to accommodation and compromise. The complete opposite of the centrum-seeking accommodating behavior of typical consociational elites is the neglect of the issues the other side deems important and the exclusive focus on the issues only the "own side" cares about. In that sense, we argue that a certain amount of issue overlap in Belgium would be evidence of the fact that consociationalism is still to some extent alive. If, in contrast, Belgian elites are increasingly talking about different issues, this would demonstrate that the common ground is crumbling and that elites have stopped caring about the same issues.

Therefore, gauging the amount of issue overlap between opposing political elites is a relevant undertaking in divided countries such as Belgium. Some degree of issue overlap is important for divided countries: it may be the glue that keeps the country together, showing that elites across the divide still have a consensus about what issues they should deal with collectively. Issue overlap determines the extent to which extent collective decision making is still, if at all, possible. We suggest that if we find very limited, and over time decreasing, overlap between the issue priorities of Flemish and Francophone elites, this would threaten the core of the Belgian state and challenge the consociational consensus.

We define "political elites" in this chapter as being the political parties on both sides of the language border. We examine party manifestos and parties' behavior in Parliament. Belgium is widely considered to be a partitocracy, an extreme case of party government: more than in most other countries, it is the political parties in Belgium that decide about policies and keep a firm grasp of the entire state apparatus (Deschouwer, de Winter, and della Porta 1996). If the parties do not address the same issues, then the main institutions of government are likely to be internally divided. However, parties are not only relevant in the case of partitocratic Belgium. In fact, the key argument made in the seminal work of Filippov and colleagues on federalism is that in any federal system political parties are the key actors leading to sustainment of the federal compromise (Filippov, Ordeshook, and Shvetsova 2004). Each federal arrangement has redistributive effects, meaning that there are always incentives to renegotiate the constitutional equilibrium. Some parties representing regional interests will unavoidably have votes and power to gain when they challenge the status quo and ask for more autonomy and less solidarity with other regions. That is why the stability of federations, Filippov and colleagues claim, critically depends on mechanisms and stimuli that keep these omnipresent centrifugal tendencies among political parties in check. In short: it is parties' behavior that decides whether a federal system survives or collapses.

Note that we do not claim that if parties on both sides of the language border were to effectively address the same issues (issue overlap), the Belgian federation would be out of the danger zone and its continued existence guaranteed. Addressing the same issues is one thing; adhering to the same policy solutions to solve the problems is something entirely different. There is a difference between the prioritization of attention and the preferred solution—although they are closely related, according to the theories on selective emphasis (Budge and Farlie 1983) and issue ownership (Petrocik 1996) of political parties. As Sigelman and Buell (2004) argue, even if parties talk about the same issues, they can still opt for different solutions, remain very vague about their preferred solution, or even attack an opponents' point of view while talking about a common issue. Yet, we maintain that some level of issue overlap is a key factor in keeping decentralized systems together.

Data and Methods

To assess the level of issue overlap between the two main Belgian communities and track potential changes in overlap through time, we drew on extensive data from party manifestos and parliamentary questions over more than two decades (1987–2010). These data yield a representative picture of the issues that Flemish and Francophone political parties care about in the period under study.

All Belgian party manifestos drafted for general elections in 1987, 1991, 1995, 1999, 2003, and 2007 were coded on their issue content, sentence per sentence, following the basic methodology devised by the Comparative Manifesto Project (Budge et al. 2001) and later adapted by Zicha and Guinaudeau (2009). Belgium's party system was already strongly fragmented in the 1980s, with seven Flemish (Christelijke Volkspartij [CVP], later Christen-Democratisch en Vlaams [CD&V]; Socialistische Partij [SP], later Socialistische Partij Anders [Sp.a]; Vlaamse Liberalen en Democraten [VLD], later Open VLD; Volksunie [VU], later Nieuw-Vlaamse Alliantie [N-VA]; Vlaams Blok [VB], later Vlaams Belang [VB]; and Anders Gaan Leven (Agalev) [later Groen!]) and four Francophone (Parti Social-Crétien [PSC], later Centre Démocrate Humaniste [CDH]; Parti Socialiste [PS]; Parti Réformateur Libéral [PRL], later Mouvement Réformateur [MR]; and Ecolo) parties. Both party systems are parallel with Christian democrats (CD&V and CDH), social democrats (Sp.a and PS), liberals (VLD and MR), and greens (Groen! and Ecolo) on both sides of the language border. Additionally, in Flanders there is a strong Flemish nationalist party (N-VA) and a right-wing populist party (VB). In total, for the ten parties and the six elections, we issue coded 190,480 (quasi)sentences.

Regarding the parliamentary activities, we focused on oral questions and interpellations of the parties in the 1987–2010 time frame. Both activities target government and require oral answers in Parliament from a cabinet minister. Questions and interpellations may criticize governmental policy or lack thereof but can also contain simple requests for information. Government MPs are also engaged in these activities in Belgium, but opposition MPs are far more active when it comes to oral questions and interpellations (Vliegenthart and Walgrave 2011). Questions and interpellations can be considered representative for the symbolic parliamentary agenda: they often do not entail tangible consequences, their aim being foremost to communicate to the public. Drawing upon official parliamentary records and using the parliamentary thesaurus, we produced a dataset containing 48,469 parliamentary actions for the whole period on a weekly basis.

In each case we examined the complete agenda—or at least, as complete an agenda as we could reasonably consider. We coded each dataset using the codebook of the Comparative Agendas Project (see appendix), which is based on Baumgartner and Jones's (1993 and 2009) original U.S. codebook containing 250 specific codes. We rely only on issue saliency and do not get into the framing, direction, or tone of the issue attention on the different agendas, but we code issues in great detail. These detailed codes are then aggregated into twenty-two major issue codes.

To calculate issue overlap, we use the measure developed by Sigelman and Buell (2004), illustrated in equation 1. The overlap score lies between 0 and 100 and indicates the percentage agreement in the attention profile of each party pair. The maximum score (100) means that the two parties have a 100% identical distribution of attention; the minimum score refers to the complete absence of any overlap. The score is calculated by summing the absolute differences in the percentage of attention dedicated to each policy topic across all policy topics. In our coding scheme there are twenty-two topics. Dividing this sum by 2 calibrates the measure to be between 0 and 100, while subtracting the result from 100 translates this measure of difference to one of similarity or percentage of overlap.

Equation 1. Sigelman and Buell's (2004) Issue Overlap Score

$$100 - \frac{\left(\sum_{i=1}^{22} |P_1 - P_2| \right)}{2} = Issue\ Overlap$$

Issue Overlap across Parties over Time

We examined the degree of issue overlap—issue convergence or divergence—among parties across the language border in Belgium. Are the Flemish and the Francophone political systems two distinct systems in terms of issue priorities? To assess the amount of overlap, or absence thereof, *between* both communities' issue priorities, we need a benchmark. Therefore, we considered the issue overlap between the actors *within* a given community as the relevant comparison. When there was less issue overlap between actors across communities than within communities, we were able to state that the issue priorities of the two main Belgian regions were diverging.

Overlap can be calculated on different aggregation levels: years, months, and weeks. Indeed, different parties may devote attention to the same issues in Parliament when we take a longer average period (months or years) into account, or they may, even in the same week, devote attention to the same issues. These different aggregation levels are relevant. True issue overlap not only implies that two actors devote roughly an equal amount of attention to the same issue over time but that they do so at roughly the same time (see also Risse and van de Steeg 2003). Indeed, when Flemish parties strongly focus on, say, the unemployment issue in month A and the Francophone parties mainly address the environmental issue in that same month, and then both do exactly the opposite in month B, the issue overlap on an higher aggregate level may still be high. Yet, it is clear that both actors, in a given month, give diverging signals about what is important and what is not. Therefore, we valued the correlation at a lower level of aggregation as a better measure of politically relevant issue overlap than at a higher level of aggregation. Do actors on both sides of the language border bother about the same issue simultaneously?

We started with the party manifestos, for which the temporal aggregation is less of an issue, as we can only compare the once-every-four-years issue priorities of the parties. Do parties address the same issues in their manifestos for the same elections? Figure 9.1 contains three issue-overlap scores: (1) the average issue-overlap scores among Flemish parties (thin line), (2) the average issue-overlap scores among French-speaking parties (broken line), and (3) the average issue-overlap scores between Flemish and Francophone parties (thick line).

The issue overlap between party manifestos in Belgium scores on average around 70%; Belgian parties tend to address a fair number of similar issues during the campaign. They do not talk past each other all the time, as some

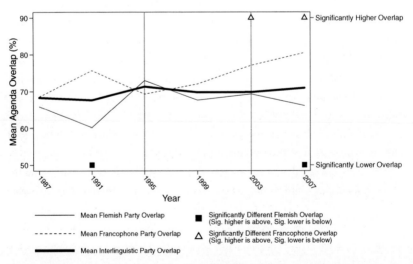

Figure 9.1. Issue overlap (%) between Flemish and Francophone party manifestos over time (six elections from 1987 to 2007)

of the issue-ownership literature suggests (Budge and Farlie 1983). Although parties propose, or are expected to propose, deliberately different programs, they all deal with more or less the same issues.

There are some slight differences in issue overlap across—as compared to within—language communities, but these differences are small. In 2003 and 2007 the Francophone parties on average overlapped statistically significantly more with each other than they did with Flemish parties (based on a two-sample unpaired comparison of means using the standard t-test). In 1991 and 2007 the Flemish parties overlapped significantly less among each other than they did with their Francophone compatriots. On the whole this suggests that, on average, Flemish parties are not addressing a larger number of different issues than Francophone parties do, and vice versa. Thus, although the electoral arenas are clearly separate, parties north and south of the language border do not have strongly divergent issue priorities.

The issue overlap between the parties on the Flemish side seems to be slightly smaller than among the parties on the French side: intra-Flemish overlap scores are usually lower than intra-Francophone scores. The average overlap among Flemish parties is 67%, compared to 74% among Francophone parties and 70% across the language border. The differences between the aggregate intraregional overlap scores and the interregional overlap score are not significant. It makes sense that the Flemish party system is more issue diverse because it is more fragmented, with some niche (N-VA) or even pariah (VB) parties, which may display systematically less issue overlap with the other parties. The French-speaking party system, with fewer parties, seems more integrated, with higher degrees of issue overlap. If we remove these two Flemish parties, for which no prominent equivalent exists among the French-speaking parties, we see that the significantly lower overlap in 1991 and 2007 among the Flemish parties disappears. The rest of the results, however, do not change.

Most important, figure 9.1 suggests that there is no tendency whatsoever toward increasing issue divergence over time. The interregion overlap line follows both intraregion lines closely. The data do not suggest that there was any structural break after state reforms. After reforms—in 1993–95, when Belgium officially became a federal state, and in 2003—the issue overlap between the parties in both regions did not become systematically lower than before. Both reforms are marked with a vertical line in the graph. There simply is no trend in the data. Although Belgium has gone through a substantial process of devolution, with many competences being shifted to the regions, and an increasingly federal constitutional structure with separate regional institutions, including their own elections, we do not observe that the two regional party systems drift apart through time. They are not becoming more different over time, but keep choosing similar issues to prioritize in federal institutions.

A possible explanation for the finding of stable interregional overlap in party manifestos may be that, precisely because of the evacuation of former national competences to the regions, the few remaining national competences are consistently covered in the party manifestos generated for the national elections. Hence, decreasing diversity of the national party manifestos may have led to a consistent issue overlap across the language border. However, this explanation does not hold. If anything, the issue diversity of the party manifesto over time increased rather than decreased. Most national party manifestos are more diverse, addressing more different issues in an equal proportion, in the last manifesto in 2007 compared to the first manifesto in 1987.

Another possible reason for the lasting interregional overlap may be that parties on both sides of the language border specifically address the issue of state reform and devolution more over time. This could lead to a consistent overlap precisely because the devolution issue has become more central to both party systems. Yet, this explanation is also not warranted by the facts. Among Francophone and Flemish parties alike, attention to the broad issue of government operations, of which the sub-issue of state reform takes a substantial share, has over the years gone down rather than up. Moreover, we systematically observed different issue emphasis between Flemish and Francophone parties on only a handful of issues: throughout the research period, Flemish parties cared more about the transportation issue and less about education. However, that was the only consistent difference.

A better explanation for the lasting overlap in issue priorities among language communities is that even in a split-party system, there are parties belonging to the same ideological party family on both sides of the language border. Perhaps these "sister" parties assure that parties on both sides continue to address the same issues. There is some evidence pointing in this direction. The average issue overlap between ideologically similar parties is, in fact, rather high. Of the twenty-four interregional issue-overlap scores between pairs of parties, the overlap scores among the ideologically similar traditional parties (CD&V-CDH, Sp.a-PS, and VLD-MR) are among the highest. These three combinations are each among the top seven of the highest

scores (the highest interregional overlap being between both Christian democratic parties, CD&V and CDH, at 79%). Thus, parties on both sides of the
language border sharing the same ideology—formerly united parties—refer
more to similar issues than the other parties. Hence, the party manifestos do
not reveal a particularly large issue divergence across the language border,
nor do they suggest that issue divergence is increasing over time. Parties
differ, of course, and place emphasis on different issues. Yet, the linguistic
differences are not the main fault line; ideological differences seem to be
more important.

We now turn to our second measure of overlap between parties' priorities:
the oral questions parties ask in the weekly parliamentary question time. It
may be that parties' manifesto pledges do not drift apart through time, but
their actions in Parliament do. We calculated similar issue-overlap scores for
questions. Figure 9.2 shows the overlap on a yearly level, and figure 9.3 on
a monthly level. Again we show three issue-overlap scores: among Flemish
parties, among French-speaking parties, and between Flemish parties and
Francophone parties.

The data on parliamentary questioning largely confirm, and reinforce,
the conclusions made from the analysis of the party manifestos. The average
overlap between the topics parties address in Parliament is slightly lower
but similarly high (around 66%) if we consider entire years (fig. 9.2). On a
monthly basis, the average issue overlap is lower (around 45%), as expected.
This means that overall parties address the same issues in Parliament but,
at a given point in time, their attention to issues is less concordant, sharing
priorities that overlap only a little less than half of the time (fig. 9.3).

Both the yearly and monthly figures confirm, as with the party manifestos,
that there are no structural differences between Flemish and Francophone
parties. The issue-overlap lines are very close to each other and run almost
parallel through the entire research period. The differences across linguistic
lines are not larger than among Flemish and Francophone parties at the
yearly level; this is evidenced by the presence of just a handful of indicators of
significance at the bottom and top of figure 9.2. However, the monthly scores
in figure 9.3 show that Flemish parties often have significantly higher average
overlap with each other than with their Francophone counterparts (see the
numerous dots at the top of the figure), although any trend in this direction
was broken in the early 2000s, when the average difference in overlap among
Flemish parties, compared to the overlap between Flemish and Francophone
parties, largely disappears. So, the interregional overlap *grew* and the differ-

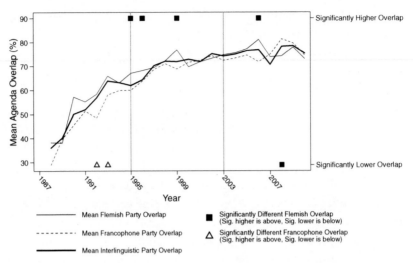

Figure 9.2. Issue overlap (%) between Flemish and Francophone parliamentary questions (yearly, 1987–2010)

ences with the intraregional overlap decreased over time, which goes directly against the idea that issue divergence between Flemish and Francophone parties would have grown.

Thus, there is no tendency toward increasing cross-regional issue divergence over time. During the twenty-three years of observation, which encompassed a number of substantial state reforms (marked with a vertical line on the graph), we did not observe a drifting apart of the parties in Parliament. On the contrary, both figure 9.2 and figure 9.3 suggest the exact opposite: there is a clear tendency toward more issue overlap over time. Both the monthly and the yearly data show that there has been a visible increase toward a higher degree of average issue overlap from 1995 onward. In the 2000s the upward trend seems to stabilize, but the overall picture points toward more rather than less integration of the Belgian party system, both within and between linguistic communities. Drawing on the monthly data, we tested whether 1995—the year in which the most important state reform was implemented—represent a structural break in the series. The trend in 1987–1994 compared to that in 1995–2010 proved to be significantly different. Yet, in contrast to what the issue-divergence thesis holds, the state reform of 1993–95 led to a structural *increase* in issue overlap between linguistic communities.

Again, the increased overlap between different-language parties is not due to a rising common interest in the issue of state reform itself, nor is it

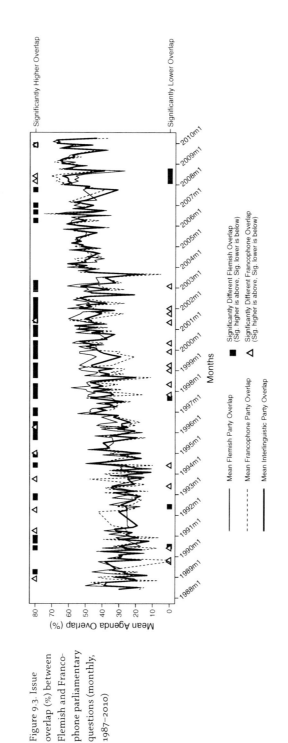

Figure 9.3: Issue overlap (%) between Flemish and Franco-phone parliamentary questions (monthly, 1987–2010)

Mean Agenda Overlap (%)

Months

Significantly Higher Overlap

Significantly Lower Overlap

——— Mean Flemish Party Overlap

– – – Mean Francophone Party Overlap

——— Mean Interlinguistic Party Overlap

■ Significantly Different Flemish Overlap
(Sig. higher is above. Sig. lower is below)

△ Significantly Different Francophone Overlap
(Sig. higher is above. Sig. lower is below)

caused by decreasing diversity as a consequence of a narrower federal issue agenda. Also, in parliamentary questioning, attention to the state-reform issue declined over the years, for both Flemish- and French-speaking parties. Moreover, there is no tendency toward less issue diversity in questions posed by Flemish and Francophone parties. Additionally, for none of the twenty-two issues do we see consistently higher levels of attention among Flemish than among Francophone parties, or vice versa. For all issues, in some years the Flemish parties devote more attention to them while in other years it was the Francophone parties.

Again, more detailed evidence taking pairs of parties into account suggests that ideological siblings across the language border tend, more than other pairs of parties, to address similar issues in Parliament. At the yearly aggregation level, the average cross-linguistic issue overlap score is 66%. The ideological sister parties display relatively high levels of issue overlap. The highest degree of overlap is between both liberal parties, MR and VLD (75%). Also, both socialist parties (70%) and both Christian democratic parties (66%) have relatively high issue-overlap scores.

To wrap up: has the issue overlap between Flemish and Francophone political actors decreased over time? Have we witnessed a gradual disintegration of the Belgian political system as both language communities have become preoccupied with different issues? The evidence presented does not support that claim. On the contrary: party manifestos of Flemish and Francophone parties have not drifted apart in terms of the issues they address. In parliamentary questioning, in contrast, the parliamentary parties on both sides of the language border have come considerably closer over time, discussing the same issues even more than before.

Discussion

Contrary to conventional wisdom in Belgian politics, we did not find diminishing interregional overlap in priorities among political actors in Belgium. Flemish and Francophone parties do not drift apart and do not systematically address dissimilar issues. But why? Why would both party systems keep addressing the same issues when they were becoming increasingly separated over time? We see a number of potential explanations. These are only suggestive, as we cannot test them empirically.

First, the fact that parties and members of Parliament institutionally still belong to the same system limits their ability to drift apart. National MPs' questions and manifestos for the national elections are naturally limited in issue scope precisely because they are institutionally embedded in a national system. For example, it would not make sense to ask questions about education in the Belgian national Parliament, as this is a competence of the communities and there is no national minister of education to be addressed. The same applies to party manifestos: why propose policy measures that are not relevant to the elections at stake? Chaqués-Bonafont and Palau developed a similar argument when examining the level of issue divergence of different Spanish regions. They concluded that changes in jurisdiction affected the issues receiving legislative attention by the autonomous regions and by the Spanish state (Chaqués-Bonafont and Palau 2011b). Hence, the division of competences between the national and regional levels limits the scope of issues that can be raised in the national Parliament and leads to continuing issue overlap. To test this idea, we need similar issue-attention data from both regional parliaments (which we do not have). In other words: institutional constraints prevent parties from addressing dissimilar issues.

Second, if politics is about solving real problems, then there is no a priori reason to expect that these problems would be very different in two adjacent regions in the heart of Europe. Policy-agenda scholars argue that agendas and issue attention are driven by the intrusion of new, or old and updated, information. Studies show that shifts in government composition, from a left-wing to a right-wing government for example, do not necessarily translate to changes in policy priorities (see chapter 2 in this volume, for example). As the problems to be solved stay the same, so does governments' attention to issues. Other policy studies show that, even in very different political systems, such as those of Denmark and the United States, the same issues catch political actors' attention around the same time (Green-Pedersen and Wilkerson 2006). This suggests that, even across different countries, governments are forced to devote attention to the same issues, because problems and challenges are universal and tend to arise at more or less the same time in different nations. Flemish and Francophone actors in Belgium may not drift apart in considering their issue priorities because the real-world problems these actors have to deal with are similar in both regions.

Finally, we presented evidence suggesting that the fact that party systems on both sides of the cultural border contain ideologically related parties puts a brake on issue divergence. The party systems may be separated, with parties competing only in their own regions, but they are still largely similar. Both party systems contain socialist, Christian democratic, liberal, and green parties. In Flanders, these traditional parties are complemented by substantial Flemish nationalist and right-wing populist parties. The former sibling parties do not systematically collaborate, nor do they have a privileged relationship. Yet, owing to similar ideologies, they put forward similar issues, address comparable topics in their manifestos, and cover the same issues in Parliament.

Conclusions

The research question this chapter started with was a double one: (1) to what extent do Flemish and Francophone political parties hold different issue priorities; and (2) has the divergence in issue priorities increased over time? The answers we provided are pretty straightforward. Flemish and Francophone parties hold different issue priorities, to some extent, but these differences are not greater than the differences within the Flemish and the Francophone parties. The overall picture is one of considerable issue overlap. Regarding the evolution over time, issue overlap has not decreased. In their manifestos, parties have not drifted apart over issues, and in their parliamentary questioning parties increasingly addressed the same issues, both across and within the language communities. Hence, we see no signs of a disintegrating party system, at least not when considered from the perspective of issue priority. Our findings directly challenge the idea that the blockade and stalemate in the Belgian system is due to diverging issue priorities. We see no signs of diminishing issue integration of the Belgian system during the last two decades; hence, the ongoing crisis in Belgium was not due to increasing priority differences on the two sides of the language border.

This conclusion does not imply that the conflict between the two language communities in Belgium is imaginary or purely symbolic, or that there are no real political differences between both regions. It only implies that political elites in Belgium still share common ground, in that they tended to, and still do, prioritize similar issues. The basic precondition for elite consensus and accommodation is thus present. Moreover, our quest, drawing on the agenda-setting approach, has proven to be useful and allows us to exclude one potential explanation for the Belgian crisis. Our agenda-setting approach, focusing on issues and on attention to issues, sheds new light on the crucial conflict dimension and structuring feature of a country such as Belgium. Drawing on agenda setting, we have empirically demonstrated that some of the most common claims about the Belgian system—that Flemings and Francophones, owing to economic and cultural differences, have different issue priorities—does not hold. The Belgian federation may be blocked and bogged down, but, as far as we can tell, diverging issue priorities did not cause this gridlock.

If not a matter of policy priorities, then what is Belgium's key political problem? We leave it to others to tackle this question empirically, but we suspect that the solutions proposed by political actors on both sides of the language border to solve the largely common problems may be increasingly divergent and contradictory. It requires another study and another design to test this preference-based and positional hypothesis regarding the Belgian stalemate. Also, the fact that the different traditional cleavages in Belgian politics, and especially the language conflict and the classic left-right socioeconomic divide, seem to converge to some extent—with right-wing Flemings against left-wing Francophones—exacerbates the conflict. In other words, the traditionally mitigating mechanism of cross-cutting cleavages dividing the elites seems in several ways to be withering.

One could go a step further and even reverse the argument by claiming that exactly *because* both communities care about the same issues, they cannot compromise with and accommodate each other. In fact, we can assume that it is more difficult for parties to give in on issues they have prioritized. When on both sides of the language border parties have publicly and explicitly adopted contradictory positions in their party manifestos and in their parliamentary discourse, it is more difficult to compromise afterward. This is what seems to have happened after the 2010 elections: before the elections, parties both north and south stressed that enacting (Flemish) or blocking (Francophone) a major state reform was an absolute priority. They addressed the same issue—state reform—but adopted diametrically opposite positions. Hence, we suggest that issue overlap could be both a precondition for accommodation and compromise—this is what we took as point of departure here—and a hindrance to accommodation.

The findings presented here may also be relevant beyond the Belgian case. Belgium is not a unique case, but it can be considered an example of a linguistically divided nation going through successive phases of devolution. Many federal and confederal countries are witnessing similar conflicts regarding centralization and decentralization. We believe that analyses similar to those conducted in this chapter may be useful in understanding centrifugal or centripetal tendencies in these other countries and in generalizing beyond the Belgian context.

10   The Impact of Party Policy Priorities on Italian Lawmaking from the First to the Second Republic, 1983–2006

Enrico Borghetto, Marcello Carammia, and Francesco Zucchini

O N 8 MAY 2001, ON THE VERGE OF ITALIAN ELECTIONS, THE CENTER-right coalition leader and media tycoon Silvio Berlusconi signed a contract with "his" voters during a popular television talk show. The contract listed five general policy pledges and a provision whereby he would resign from politics at the end of his mandate if at least four of the points were not fulfilled. From a symbolic viewpoint, this was a pathbreaking event in postwar Italian history: media exposure strengthened to an unprecedented level the linkage between campaign pledges, policy actions by the elected executive, and the threat of electoral sanction (in this case self-inflicted).

The rhetorical stratagem of the contract fit rather conveniently with the emergence of bipolar competition in Italy after the 1994 elections and marked the enormous distance between the new political system and the logic underlying the so-called First Republic, when real alternation in government was not an option.[1] At that time parliamentary majorities—and their common programmatic platforms—were formed only *after* elections through prolonged negotiations between the omnipresent Democrazia Cristiana (Christian Democrats [DC]), their centrist allies (and their respective social partners), and, after 1963, the Partito Socialista Italiano (Italian Socialist Party [PSI]). Given the low level of effective political competition, the threat of an electoral sanction did not appear very credible, thereby weakening the strategic importance of elections as a mechanism of direct accountability between elected officials and citizens.

The political consequences of the early-1990s Italian transition from a pivotal to an alternational party system have dominated scholarly discussions since then (see, e.g., Bull and Rhodes 2007; Zucchini 2011a). This chapter contributes to the debate by focusing on a hitherto neglected issue: is there evidence that the new alternation system brought about greater congruence between the policy priorities declared during election campaigns by the political parties that get into government after elections and the policy priorities included in the government legislation?

This should be the case according to mandate theory (Klingemann, Hoffer-bert, and Budge 1994; Budge et al. 2001; McDonald and Budge 2005). In its classic version, mandate theory expects utility-maximizing governing parties to stick as close as possible to election promises to avoid retaliation by disappointed voters at the next elections. A number of conditions have to be met for a mandate to exist, although, arguably, a crucial one is the existence of the political conditions for government alternation. If these conditions are in place, the content of party manifestos should be a good predictor of the distribution of legislative activity across policy sectors during a mandate.

The policy-agenda approach challenges this view by bringing to the fore the importance of information alongside the traditional focus on preferences. The effects of the Italian transition for the congruence between party and legislative priorities should be less remarkable than is expected by party-mandate theory. This is first of all the consequence of the intrusion of issues in the government agenda that were not expected at the time the manifesto was drafted. Second, it derives from the persistence of cognitive and institutional frictions across the two periods. In particular, the presence of fragmented multiparty coalitions (Chiaramonte 2007) and a relatively equal distribution of power between the legislative and executive branches (De Micheli and Verzichelli 2004) still constrain the legislative agenda-setting power in the hands of Italian governments and their capacity to implement their programmatic platforms.

Our study builds on these two theoretical approaches to analyze whether and how, other factors being relatively unchanged, after the introduction of alternation in office the programmatic priorities laid out in the manifestos of winning coalitions (party agendas) are reflected more in the policy priorities of laws adopted once that coalition enters government (the legislative agenda). Answering this question is important for understanding the effects of Italian transition on one fundamental pillar of any democratic system: government responsiveness to the electoral mandate. Given the importance of the question, existing research has already devoted attention to this issue, mostly by evaluating the rate of pledge fulfillment for a few Second Republic governments (Moury 2011; Newell 2000). This chapter adopts a different approach, building its analysis on an original dataset that permits us to investigate the congruence between the distribution of issue attention in manifestos and legislative outputs across a span of twenty-three years (1983–2006). Rather than evaluating whether and how the policy content of party manifestos is faithfully carried out in the laws, our design, which is both longitudinal and cross-sectional, allows us to measure diachronically the similarity of policy attention between the two agendas.

We first set the stage for the analysis by discussing existing theories about the relationship between party policy priorities and the legislative agenda, and how they can be applied to the analysis of the Italian transition. We then make our expectations explicit and illustrate the data and methods used to test them empirically. Finally, we show and discuss our findings and draw our conclusions.

Government Alternation and the Mandate Theory

MANDATE AND AGENDA-SETTING THEORY

The party-mandate theory revolves essentially around the role of elections in a democracy. More precisely, it focuses on the way and extent to which political institutions translate voter preferences into collective choices. According to this theory, political parties play a fundamental role in democracy because "they alone tie representatives to a particular set of past and promised policies on which voters can make an informed choice in the elections" (Budge and Hofferbert 1990, 113). Parties compete in elections by presenting voters with different policy options. Political parties generally produce written documents—"party manifestos"—spelling out their own electoral platforms. Voters are informed about the policy profiles of each party and, after comparing them, give their vote to the party that is closer to their preferences. The winner tries to run government in line with the policy pledges made before the election, because it is on the basis of those pledges that it was elected in the first place. Ultimately, failure to fulfill its mandate would reduce the odds of its being reelected. The party-mandate theory presumes that political preferences are fixed during the election campaign and that the legislative agenda is mainly affected by the agenda of party manifestos. Voting is assumed to be retrospective. According to party-mandate theory for elected politicians, being faithful to the preferences of the citizens who elected them is necessary and equivalent to being accountable to the preferences of the citizens who will vote next time.

Policy-agenda scholars propose a different account of the relationship between electoral priorities and legislative policy agendas. According to this theoretical perspective, even if governing parties wanted to stick to the policy priorities spelled out during election campaigns, a number of factors would limit their capacity to do so. First, political systems are information-rich environments: incoming information about policy problems and ways to deal with them, coming from outside and/or from within the political system, continuously reshapes actors' preferences and policy priorities (Jones and Baumgartner 2005). At the time party platforms are drafted, a government cannot anticipate every problem it will encounter. Moreover, one of the main roles of a political opposition is to draw attention to problems and solutions that are not on the majority agenda (Green-Pedersen and Mortensen 2010).

Cognitive and institutional frictions make the translation of policy inputs (party platform priorities) into policy outputs (legislative production) less than efficient (Jones and Baumgartner 2005). Cognitive frictions emerge from the limited capacity of political actors to simultaneously attend to the virtually endless number of competing issues demanding their attention. Governing this complexity requires a constant prioritization of political issues. This limited issue-attention capacity is evident in the content of party manifestos, which are by definition incomplete (for reasons of space, minor issues have to be set aside; De Winter 2004, 36) and biased toward distinctive policy topics (in line with the ideological positions of their drafters; Walgrave and Nuytemans 2009).

Like all policy-making activities, the process of drafting party platforms and subsequently translating them into legislative outputs incurs transaction and decision-making costs. This phenomenon, which is captured by the concept of institutional friction, may be the consequence of a number of factors such as the requirement of supermajorities, presidential or courts' vetoes, or weak executive agenda-setting powers. Importantly, frictions do not lead to constant policy gridlock, but rather to a pattern of extreme stability and occasional bursts of change, as described in the punctuated-equilibrium model of policy change (Baumgartner and Jones 1993). In sum, political preferences are, according to the policy-agenda approach, continuously reshaped; the party manifestos agenda is only one of those that affect the content of legislative outputs; and elected officials are constantly sniffing the political environment in search of the smoke of hot policy issues.

What is relevant to our argument is that, in their radical versions, mandate and agenda-setting theories lead to different expectations about the impact of alternation on the congruence of party program with policy. Mandate theory predicts that in the Second Republic, government coalition platforms will be taken as policy templates for legislative choices. Conversely, agenda-setting theory predicts that ruling coalitions will be generally inefficient in translating the policy input incorporated in party manifestos into legislative responses. Certain issues mentioned in party platforms will be more or less neglected by the legislator, others will receive a disproportionate amount of attention, and little or no change will be observable from one type of party-system dynamics to another.

Political, institutional, and cognitive variables are strictly interconnected and play different roles in the two approaches. Cross-country comparative designs are less appropriate in disentangling their reciprocal interaction. In principle, all these factors can vary when different countries are compared. Conversely, a longitudinal study of a single country should allow better control for the effect of cognitive variables. In this respect, the Italian case is very promising. After the shocks of the late 1980s and early 1990s, the Italian political system moved from a blocked political system with no alternation in power (1948–94) to a system where alternation became the rule: no coalition was reconfirmed in power at any of the five elections held between 1996 and 2013. If we assume that the role of information and cognitive frictions is relatively constant in policy-making, then the Italian case allows us to test interesting hypotheses about the way institutional and political factors affect the capacity of political parties to transform election agendas into legislative priorities, and the incentives to do so in the first place. We look at whether and how changes in the format (number and identity of parties and coalitions) and dynamics (relationships between and within coalitions) of the party system, culminating in the passage from monopoly to alternation in power, affect the relation between party election agendas, on the one hand, and legislative agendas, on the other.

MANDATES AND ALTERNATION IN ITALY

For mandate theory to work, all parties should be legitimate candidates for a position in government. Italy stands out among other parliamentary democracies because for most of its republican history this condition was lacking. Imagine a country where all political players know that no government will be possible without a party (DC), and many of them also believe that no government will be possible with two other parties that are labeled "anti-system": the second-largest party, Partito Comunista Italiano (Italian Communist Party [PCI]), and the neofascist party, Movimento Sociale Italiano

(Italian Social Movement [MSI]). Imagine also that both beliefs are always confirmed by electoral results as well as by postelectoral coalitions. In other words, imagine a country where governing parties are always the same and are supposed to be the same, election after election, no matter how many cabinets are formed and broken during a legislature (Galli 2000). This is a description of the Italian First Republic, where the DC, as the party of relative majority, stayed permanently in office for more than forty-five years in alliance with small center-right and center-left parties.[2]

This status quo did not imply that there were no substantive rivalries within the governing coalition and between parliamentary party groups and ministers. The proportional electoral system compelled parties to maintain distinct identities, especially after the mid-1970s and the increase of electoral volatility and fragmentation. The main policy lines of the governing coalition were generally agreed upon after the elections, when coalition parties could count their votes and negotiate agreements (mainly on the distribution of government portfolios) far from the spotlight of public attention (Verzichelli and Cotta 2003).

At the beginning of the 1990s, a combination of long-term structural factors and specific contingencies brought about the unexpected implosion of the party system (see, e.g., Newell 2000): the fall of the Berlin wall, the mismanagement of the state budget, the financial crisis, and the delegitimization of the party system after the *mani pulite* investigation. The change affected not only the identity and internal composition of political parties, but also the structure of the party system itself. With the change of electoral rules in 1993 from a proportional to a mixed electoral system, and above all with the 1996 general elections and the installation of a center-left government following a center-right government, Italy seems to have taken the path toward competitive democracy.

The change is unquestionable if one looks at electoral outcomes: since the mid-1990s, two center-left coalitions (1996 and 2006) alternated with two center-right coalitions (2001 and 2008). At least on the surface, this change implied a relative simplification of the system, which shifted from a tripolar format to a competition between two preelectoral coalitions headed by two leaders (the candidates of each coalition to the position of premier). Coalition agreements then took the form of large preelectoral "coalition manifestos," spelling out policy pledges as in typical majoritarian democracies. More important, with alternation of government a genuine possibility, the link between the political fortune of the governing majority and the implementation of policy programs has been strengthened, at least in the political discourse.

Yet despite the institutionalization of a bipolar logic in the electoral arena, other elements still make this link weak and prevent the development of a clear party program-policy nexus even in the Second Republic. First, party fragmentation has thrived under the umbrella of coalitions—indeed, it even increased with respect to the First Republic—as shown by the recurrent shifts in alliances and the aggregation and/or separation of new party groups (Chiaramonte 2007). Because of the dispersion of power within ruling coalitions, government initiatives in Parliament are often hampered by the vetoes of allies. Thus important policies, sometimes solemnly promised in the coalition platform, are often sacrificed on the altar of coalition stability (see, e.g., D'Alimonte and Bartolini 2002). Second, the system of coalition management is not as efficient as in similar systems elsewhere, and despite an increase in government agenda-setting powers beginning in the late 1980s (Zucchini 2011b), the "stickiness" of the legislative process for executive-sponsored bills remains a trademark of Italian politics (Capano and Giuliani 2001; De Micheli and Verzichelli 2004). Third, the growing agenda-setting power of mass media (reinforced by the rise of Berlusconi; see, e.g., Ginsborg 2005) may have made the political agenda more volatile, diverting politicians' attention from their electoral promises.

Data and Methods

Academic research has developed several methods to assess the overlap between party and legislative agendas. Each operationalization entails gains and losses in terms of validity and reliability (Pétry and Collette 2009). This study moves from an approach that was developed by scholars associated with the Comparative Manifesto Project (CMP) and applied both in comparative (Klingemann, Hofferbert, and Budge 1994) and single-country studies (Budge and Hofferbert 1990; Hofferbert and Budge 1992). In its original version, the CMP method correlated variations in the thematic emphases of party platforms in specific policy domains to the proportion of central governmental expenditures on corresponding policy areas.

We adopt a correlational design too, but depart from the CMP in the way both party and legislative agendas are operationalized (see appendix for details). In particular, we focus on legislative production, rather than budget expenditures, as a measure of the policy output. We thus seek to take the best from what is recognized as a major contribution to the study of comparative politics and public policy,[3] and at the same time adopt the Comparative Agendas Project (CAP) coding techniques, which allow us to compare systematically the policy content of party manifestos and laws. To code the content of party platforms we broke down the text into sentences (or "quasi-sentences" in the case of sentences containing more than one policy reference) and assigned each sentence a policy code.[4] As regards legislative agendas, all analyses were run on a dataset including laws (except for delegating laws) and legislative decrees drawn from the Italian Lawmaking Archive (Borghetto et al. 2012). The set of laws and legislative decrees composing the legislative agenda have been coded at the document level—that is, each law or decree has been assigned to a single policy topic.

Party and legislative agendas were coded based on the Italian version of the CAP coding scheme (Borghetto and Carammia 2010), consisting of a taxonomy of about 240 policy topics aggregated into twenty-one broad policy areas (see appendix).[5] We calculated correlations at the subtopic rather than at the major topic level. The major topic level is very general and may obscure differences among different manifestos and legislative agendas. Because laws vary greatly in length, we consider the overall number of words for each subtopic rather than the number of laws.[6] The time span studied covers more than twenty years.

As shown in Table 10.1, six parliamentary terms alternated in the period 1983–2006. The three terms shown at the top of the table are the last First Republic terms. Combined, the ninth and tenth term lasted nine years (1983–92), during which seven governments alternated. All governments were supported by the *pentapartito* (consisting of the DC, PSI, PRI, PSDI, and PLI) except the last one, which was not supported by the PRI.[7] The eleventh term was a highly turbulent one in which two governments alternated, both supported by the DC, PSI, PLI, and PSDI. This parliamentary term, which experienced the economic and political turmoil that led to the end of the First Republic, lasted only two years.

The Second Republic was opened by another unstable parliamentary term: the twelfth legislature (1994–96). A coalition between the new Berlusconi's Forza Italia Party, Lega Nord, MSI, and other minor centrist allies won the elections. However, the first Berlusconi government was overturned after less than one year, followed by the "caretaker" government of Lamberto

Table 10.1. Legislative terms and party coalitions in Italy, 1983–2006

Legislative term	Election year	Majority (seats in the lower chamber)
Ninth	1983	DC (32.9 %)
		PSI (11.4 %)
		PRI (5.1 %)
		PSDI (4.1 %)
		PLI (2.9 %)
Tenth	1987	DC (34.3 %)
		PSI (14.3 %)
		PRI (3.7 %)
		PSDI (2.9 %)
		PLI (2.1 %)
Eleventh	1992	DC (28.4 %)
		PSI (14.4 %)
		PSDI (2.7 %)
		PLI (2.4 %)
Twelfth	1994	FI (30 %)
		LN (32 %)
		CCD (8 %)
		AN (30 %)
Thirteenth	1996	Ulivo (46 %)
		RC (5.5 %)
Fourteenth	2001	CDL (58 %)

Dini, which, against all odds, survived for another year. The 1996 elections saw the victory of the center-left "Olive Tree" coalition that, with the external support of Partito della Rifondazione Comunista (Communist Refoundation Party [PRC]), gave life to the first Romano Prodi government.[8] After two and a half years the PRC withdrew its support to the government. Following the breakdown of the Prodi government, the PRC split into two formations, one of which supported the three governments (the first and second Massimo D'Alema governments and the second Giuliano Amato government) that brought the term to its end. The 2001 elections were won by the center-right coalition of the Casa della Libertà (House of Freedoms [CdL]), including by and large the same parties that had supported the first Berlusconi government. Significantly, this coalition governed again for a full parliamentary term (2001–6), during which two Berlusconi governments alternated.

Summing up, the period under observation covers six legislative terms (the nineteenth through the fourteenth), three from the First Republic and three from the Second Republic. The "central" legislatures in this series (the eleventh and twelfth) were anomalous in several respects, as shown by their short duration and by the presence of "caretaker" governments. In order not to bias the analysis, we do not include them in our study. Instead, we focus on four "long" legislative terms, two from the First Republic (the ninth and tenth, covering the period 1983–92) and two from the Second Republic (the thirteenth and fourteenth, covering the period 1996–2006).

Findings: The Correlation between Party and Legislative Agendas between the First and the Second Republic

This section illustrates the empirical findings of our analysis. We begin by observing correlation scores between the policy content of party manifestos, on the one hand, and legislative outputs, on the other. We then control for the policy content of legislation issued during previous legislative terms in order to understand how much of the correlation still holds once we take legislative inertia into account. We next observe those topics that systematically receive higher (or lower) amounts of attention in laws than in party manifestos. We call such differences the "legislative gap" and analyze them in aggregated figures to see whether and how they are affected by the passage from the First to the Second Republic.

THE CORRELATION BETWEEN PARTY PRIORITIES AND LEGISLATIVE AGENDAS IN THE FIRST AND SECOND REPUBLICS

According to party-mandate theory, we should expect to find an overall high correlation between party and legislative policy priorities during the legislatures of the Second Republic when the political system is characterized by government alternation. The risk of being replaced in government should be a powerful incentive for political parties to seriously consider the legislative implementation of electoral promises.

All Italian legislative terms were characterized by multiparty governments. During the First Republic (the ninth and tenth legislature) preelectoral agreements were not stipulated, whereas they became standard practice in the Second Republic. This is an important difference, for it makes the documents of the two periods not perfectly comparable. In principle, coalition manifestos of the Second Republic should be more binding because they are stipulated by coalition members under the eye of the electorate. Conversely, coalition agendas in the First Republic were the outcome of undisclosed postelectoral bargaining between its members, reiterated throughout the course of the legislature.

In order to correlate coalition priorities to legislative outputs, we first had to "reconstruct" First Republic coalition agreements. Because each reconstruction can only be an approximation, this chapter uses three different methods to aggregate party agendas. We considered:(1) only the manifesto of the main and median party of the coalition; (2) the sum of policy priorities of all parties that support the government, considering single manifestos as equally important (coalition agenda); and (3) the manifestos of all government parties, weighted for their relevance in terms of parliamentary seats (weighted coalition agenda). Different hypotheses about the decision-making process inside the cabinet and in the Parliament underlie these three different operationalizations. The median party–mandate thesis (McDonald and Budge 2005) posits that the median party controls the government policy agenda. According to veto players theory (Tsebelis 2002), we would expect all government parties to have the same influence on the government agenda. Finally, the weighted measure follows demands by other scholars to relax the expectation of equal relevance of large and small parties (Strøm 2000).[9]

As regards our central questions—how strong the relationship between party and legislative agendas is, and whether the passage to the Second Republic makes the relationship stronger—the data point to mixed evidence. The overall level of correlation between party and legislative agendas is significant,[10] yet not very strong, with the highest correlation (observed for the center-right coalition of the fourteenth legislative term) reaching a level of 0.53. However, party priorities and legislative outputs are much more strongly correlated in the Second than in the First Republic: the highest correlation observed during the First Republic is lower than the lowest correlation found for the Second Republic. During the First Republic, correlations ranged from 0.17 (for the manifesto of the DC in the ninth legislative term) to 0.38 (for the weighted coalition agenda of the tenth legislative term). During the Second Republic, correlations ranged between 0.41 (for the weighted agenda of the center-left coalition governing during the thirteenth legislative term) to 0.53 (for the coalition agenda of the center-right Berlusconi governments of the fourteenth term). The longitudinal variation in our correlation indexes is more clearly evident when we average the different measures of party agendas for each legislative term. The increase is steady although not dramatic, moving from 0.23 and 0.34 respectively in the ninth and tenth term of the First Republic to 0.46 and 0.53 in the thirteenth and fourteenth term.

Findings are also mixed with regard to the different measures of coalition agendas. Figure 10.1 shows that in two out of the three legislative terms where we observe such differences, the correlation with the legislative agenda is stronger for those measures of party agendas that take into account the role of bigger coalition parties. This is the case for the Christian Democracy during the tenth legislative term, and for the Olive Tree (a coalition rather than a party, whose priorities we can observe separately from those of the smaller "external" ally, the PRC) during the thirteenth legislative term. During these terms the median-party agenda is almost as relevant as the weighted coalition agenda, whereas the correlation with legislative outputs decreases if the unweighted coalition agenda is taken into account. Consistent with the median party–mandate theory, this finding seems to point to a stronger role of the bigger actor within the coalition. Yet things look different in the case of the ninth legislative term, where smaller coalition parties seemed to have a much stronger role in setting legislative priorities consistent with their agendas. The limited number of observations does not permit us to explain this difference, which deserves further analysis.

Overall, the analysis of total correlations lends partial support to mandate theory: the difference we find between the First and Second Republics suggests that a mandate effect exists, but it is not as strong as might have been expected. Correlation scores are significant, yet the "congruence between promise and performance" that we find is far from "remarkable" (Klingemann, Hofferbert, and Budge 1994, 2). In this respect, our findings are also consistent with the prediction of policy-agenda theory of an imperfect match between election priorities and legislative agendas. Despite the magnitude of changes in the Italian party system, the intervention of cognitive and institutional frictions and the emergence of unforeseen problems still determine a lack of proportion between the attention allocated to certain issues before elections and at the decision-making stage.

Admittedly, total correlations between party and legislative agendas may hide a number of factors distinct from the electoral party platforms, which are also likely to affect the distribution of attention among policy areas in the lawmaking process. These factors include information about problems that were unexpected at the time manifestos were drafted, low-politics issues that do not normally enter party manifestos, changes in the law due to successful lobbying by interest groups, old programs that need to be renewed, compelling problems that require attention no matter the party in office, and so on.

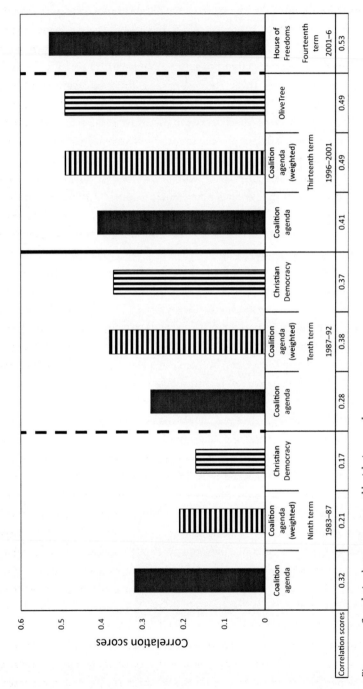

Correlation scores	Coalition agenda	Coalition agenda (weighted)	Christian Democracy	Coalition agenda	Coalition agenda (weighted)	Christian Democracy	Coalition agenda	Coalition agenda (weighted)	OliveTree	House of Freedoms
		Ninth term			Tenth term			Thirteenth term		Fourteenth term
		1983–87			1987–92			1996–2001		2001–6
	0.32	0.21	0.17	0.28	0.38	0.37	0.41	0.49	0.49	0.53

Figure 10.1. Correlation between party and legislative agendas

Note: The continuous vertical line separates the First and Second Republics.

To uncover factors unrelated to party manifestos that are likely to affect their relationship with legislative outputs, we controlled our correlations for the policy content of legislative agendas in earlier legislatures. This way we aim at depurating relationships from nonparty and nonelectoral factors. Therefore, we checked correlations between party and legislative agenda for the tenth legislative term by controlling for the legislative agenda of the ninth term; correlations for the thirteenth term controlling for the legislative agenda of the tenth term; and correlations for the fourteenth term controlling for the legislative agendas of the thirteenth.

Table 10.2 shows (1) total correlations between party and legislative agendas, (2) the same correlations controlling for the policy structure of earlier legislation, and (3) the difference between the two—in other words, the net effect of the control variable on total correlations. All correlation scores drop once earlier legislative agendas are taken into account, yet this decrease does not affect all legislatures in the same way. First of all, we observe a more marked decrease during the First Republic tenth term than during Second Republic terms. The partial correlations for the tenth term go down to levels ranging between 0.15 and 0.23, and the statistical significance of the relationships is also affected.

Overall, scores decrease less with respect to Second Republic terms, suggesting a stronger net correlation between party and legislative agendas. The relationship is significantly stronger in the case of the center-right Berlusconi governments of the fourteenth term, which points to a stronger net party effect but also to a more decisive departure from policy priorities of earlier center-left legislation. This finding is consistent with the turn toward a more majoritarian confrontation between majority and opposition in the Italian Second Republic: once they get into government, center-right and center-left coalitions are willing—and to some extent able—to enforce distinctive policy priorities in legislative agendas in a way that coheres better with their party programs than it was during the First Republic. What we see is not only a stronger, though still limited, correspondence between party and legislative agendas; but also a more marked change between the laws made by competing coalitions that alternate in government—and the two are probably related.

Therefore, even if the impact of nonparty and nonelectoral factors is nonnegligible, it seems more relevant when the party system dynamics are not characterized by government alternation. In sum, the evidence of a structural

Table 10.2. Correlations between party and legislative agendas controlling for the legislative priorities of earlier legislatures

Legislative term	Control variable	Party agenda	Correlation between party agendas and legislative agendas		
			Total correlation	Controlled correlation	Difference
Tenth (1987–92)	Legislative agenda, ninth term	Christian Democracy	0.37***	0.23**	−0.13 (−35%)
		Coalition agenda	0.28***	0.15*	−0.11 (−39%)
		Coalition agenda (weighted)	0.38***	0.22**	−0.14 (−37%)
Thirteenth (1996–2001)	Legislative agenda, tenth term	Olive Tree	0.49***	0.33***	−0.16 (−33%)
		Coalition Agenda (Olive Tree/Communists)	0.49***	0.33***	−0.16 (−33%)
		Coalition Agenda (Olive Tree/Communists—weighted)	0.41***	0.27***	−0.14 (−34%)
Fourteenth (2001–06)	Legislative agenda, thirteenth term	House of Freedom	0.53***	0.42***	−0.09 (−17%)

* Significant at the 0.05 level.

** Significant at the 0.01 level.

*** Significant at the 0.001 level.

break between First and Second Republic terms is strengthened: government alternation has made the agendas of winning party coalitions more similar to their legislative agendas.

UNKEPT PROMISES AND UNPROMISED LAWS

The distribution of attention among different policy sectors seems increasingly similar between party manifestos and law production. Yet we do not know exactly how this phenomenon takes place. Do the same unchanged "electoral" issues enjoy more legislative consideration in the Second than in the First Republic? Or are new promises just more easily kept by legislators than old ones? And, more generally, does the Italian Parliament systematically overlook the same issues while always "overlegislating" in favor of the same groups? To answer these questions we calculated the differences between attention in election manifestos and attention in legislative production for each policy sector. We call this measure "legislative gap." A positive legislative gap indicates that the Parliament disregarded an issue that was given more relevance by the coalition during the election campaign. A negative value means that the level of attention exhibited by the Parliament would not be justified by the electoral manifestos. For instance, during the 1987 election the issue of employment training and workforce development attracted 1.4% of the attention in the manifestos of the Olive Tree coalition, but only 0.2% of the attention in the legislative agenda of the thirteenth legislature. The legislative gap was thus equal to 1.2. During the same legislature the issue of government employee benefits and civil service received significant attention from legislative bodies (3.5%), while it was practically ignored in electoral platforms (0.1%). The legislative gap in this case was −3.4.

We need to take a further step. By correlating the values of the legislative gap in a legislature with those observed in the following legislature, we can gain a better understanding of those policy sectors on which the political system is stably (un)able to legislate, and about the stability (or otherwise) of these patterns.[11]

As Table 10.3 shows, legislative gaps are quite strongly and significantly correlated during the legislatures of the First Republic (the ninth and tenth legislatures). Indeed, the structure of the gaps of the ninth legislature seems quite similar to the structure of the thirteenth legislature. However, the most striking results regard the low correlation between the thirteenth and fourteenth legislatures: what was overlooked or overemphasized in legislative activity in one Parliament has almost no correlation to what was overlooked or overemphasized in the other. In spite of the temporal distance, the legislative gaps of the First Republic are more fully correlated with the legislative gaps of the fourteenth legislature than with those of the thirteenth legislature. This finding strengthens the above argument about the effect of political change in Italy: the alternation in government that took place between the thirteenth and fourteenth legislatures deeply differentiated the structure of party and legislative agendas in the two legislatures.

Table 10.3. Legislative gap by legislature: correlations

	Legislative gap, tenth term	Legislative gap, thirteenth term	Legislative gap, fourteenth term
Legislative gap, ninth term	0.58***	0.40***	0.26***
Legislative gap, tenth term		0.25***	0.24***
Legislative gap, thirteenth term			0.11*

* Significant at the 0.05 level.

** Significant at the 0.01 level.

*** Significant at the 0.001 level.

Conclusions

This chapter presents a longitudinal analysis of the correlation between party priorities and legislative outputs in Italy between 1983 and 2006. It analyzes whether the systemic change culminating in the introduction of alternation in government that occurred between the First and Second Republics affected the correspondence between the priorities declared by political parties in their party manifestos and their legislative choices once they entered government. We contend that the case of Italy offers a quasi-experimental context, not easily found elsewhere, for studying the effect of the introduction of alternation in government on the party program-to-policy link while other structural factors can be assumed to be relatively constant. We cast different expectations based on two partly competing theoretical frameworks. According to mandate theory, one should expect a significant increase in correlation between party and legislative agendas when government alternation becomes a feature of the political system. Conversely, a policy-agenda approach would suggest that political parties have more limited control over the legislative agenda, so that a weak relationship between party and legislative priorities should be observed both in the First and Second Republics.

The evidence we found is in fact mixed and suggests moderating the most radical readings of both party-mandate theory and policy-agenda approaches. We observed a low correlation between party manifestos and legislative agendas during the First Republic, which is consistent with both theories. The introduction of alternation had some effect on the transposition of manifesto priorities into legislative outputs: consistent with party mandate theory, the relationship became stronger—not strong enough, however, to be considered a "test of democracy." At best, no more than half of the policy priorities of party manifestos were translated into legislative agendas. The introduction of government alternation created the conditions for the mandate effect to work, yet the adaptation of legislative priorities to electoral platforms is still subject to multiple frictions, as predicted by agenda-setting theory.

Our findings suggest that some aspects of the two theories ought to be integrated rather than directly opposed to each other. Agenda-setting theory provides the general background for understanding the loose relationship connecting party and legislative agendas. Mandate theory, in turn, explains how and why alternation in government increases the significance of party programs. Moreover, alternation accounts for another important phenomenon: even though party and coalitional platforms are poor predictors of legislative agendas throughout the period we consider, legislators overlooked or paid disproportionate attention to different policy issues across Second Republic legislatures; this does not hold for the legislatures of the First Republic. In other words, the introduction of alternation in the political system does not remove policy frictions, but affects the distribution of attention to issues that reflect the ideology of the current majority. Clearly, the fulfillment of the mandate is only one of the factors considered by office-seeking politicians.

So far we have considered the collapse of the Italian First Republic and the birth of an alternational party system as exogenous; at a more general level of analysis, we may take this abrupt institutional innovation as strictly connected to the long phase of political inertia that preceded it. The case of Italy suggests that a deep mismatch between policy programs and output might be considered one contributing factor in the erosion of the system in the first place. Policy dynamics take place in an institutional environment that is periodically reshaped by those dynamics. This is evidence that, beyond a certain threshold, the level of policy friction affects the pace and magnitude not only of policy change, but also of institutional change.

Notes

1. Remarkably, since 2001 most Italian governments have featured a minister without portfolio who is officially in charge of implementing the government program.

2. The DC coalition partners were the Partito Liberale Italiano (Italian Liberal Party [PLI]), the Partito Repubblicano Italiano (Italian Republican Party [PRI]), the Italian Social Democratic Party (Partito Socialista Democratico Italiano [PSDI]), and, from 1963, the PSI.

3. See in particular the growing body of literature on pledge fulfillment originating from the approach elaborated by Royed (1996), which looks at specific party pledges and determines how many pledges have been redeemed.

4. For both manifestos and legislation, the coding activities were carried out by two different coders and then cross-checked under the supervision of one of the authors. Note that sentences that could not be fitted into any of the topics available were categorized as "uncoded," which includes on average 10% of coded items and never exceeds 20%.

5. More information about the Italian Policy Agendas Project can be found at http://italianpolicyagendas.weebly.com/. The authors wish to acknowledge the financial support of the Italian Ministry of Education and Research, Project Prin 2009TPW4NL_002, "Institutions and Agenda-Setting: Actors, Time, and Information." Enrico Borghetto acknowledges the financial support of the Fundação para a Ciência e a Tecnologia (FCT, Government of Portugal, SFRH/BPD/89968/2012).

6. Because the frequency of zero values in some topics could affect the correlation re-

182 BORGHETTO, CARAMMIA, AND ZUCCHINI

sults, we created an additional dataset from which we excluded policy issues to which no attention was devoted in party manifestos or legislation. The results are not substantially different and are available on request. See appendix for more details on our technical and methodological choices.

7. Note that we do not include the PRI manifesto in the analysis because of the poor quality of the only document available (a newspaper interview with the Republican leader Giovanni Spadolini, without any reference to policy priorities). We computed the scores of the coalition agenda weighted for the share of parliamentary seats owned by each party considering all parties and excluding PRI. Because differences were not appreciable, we used the first procedure to compute coalition agendas in the X term.

8. With regard to the Second Republic, data about disaggregated party priorities within coalitions are only available for the thirteenth legislative term—when the PRC issued a manifesto that differed from the Ulivo's (the latter actually being a coalition manifesto in itself)—because the center-right CDL only issued a coalition manifesto before the elections for the fourteenth legislative term.

9. During the thirteenth legislative term, however, the PRC presented a separate manifesto from the rest of the center-left coalition, though it provided external support to the government. To control for its influence, we computed correlations for the whole (weighted and unweighted) coalition agenda, as well as for the Olive Tree coalition alone (all center-left parties, excluding the PRC). Since, according to veto players theory, only government parties have agenda-setting prerogatives, the measure that considers only the preelectoral coalition's manifesto fits the veto players theory better. Conversely, the other measures that also consider the other nongovernment party are more in line with Strøm's recommendation (2000).

10. All correlations are statistically significant at least at the 0.05 level.

11. Once again, we do not take into account the short legislatures that characterize the transition between the First and Second Republic (eleventh and twelfth legislature).

11   Policy Promises and Governmental Activities in Spain

Laura Chaqués Bonafont, Anna M. Palau, and Luz M. Muñoz Marquez

F ROM 1982 TO 2012 SPAIN EXPERIENCED ITS LONGEST PERIOD OF democratic stability ever. The victory of the Partido Socialista Obrero Español (Spanish Socialist Workers' Party [PSOE]) in the 1982 general elections symbolized the consolidation of a democratic parliamentary monarchy, which follows most of the characteristics that Lijphart attributes to majoritarian democracies. Democratization has parallelled a process of political decentralization, which, after more than forty years of an authoritarian regime, represents a radical change in the territorial distribution of power in Spain, from a highly centralized country under Francoism to one of the most decentralized countries in Europe (Linz and Stepan 1996; Colomer 1999). This process has occurred gradually as a result of intense and controversial political negotiation between national and regional political forces and parallels a process of political delegation of authority to the European Union (EU).

The successful transition to democracy completely transformed the role of the state in the economy and the provision of welfare. Spanish public expenditures grew fast—from 20% of GDP in the mid-1970s to almost 50% in 1993—particularly for the support of new social programs (Boix 2006). In the mid-1990s Spain was already what Esping-Andersen (1999) categorizes as a corporatist welfare state, its welfare spending about 90% that of other European countries. These changes took place following a gradual process. The majority governments of Felipe González (1982–93) developed the welfare state and a program of industrial reconversion and economic modernization, based on a major tax reform and the construction of basic infrastructures. During the 1990s welfare issues lost some of their dominant position in the governmental agenda to economic liberalization and privatization policies aimed at fostering economic competitiveness. Once the PSOE won the elections in 2004, welfare- and rights-related issues captured increasing attention from the Spanish government.

After 1982 there were important changes in the pattern of issue prioritization by the Spanish government. The questions we pose here are whether policy dynamics occur following the programmatic commitments of the governing political parties as expressed in the party manifestos, and to what extent changes in the implementation of policy promises are explained by institutional factors, mainly the type of government and issue jurisdiction. The underlying assumption is that the correspondence between policy commitments and policy outputs varies across types of governments and policy subsystems depending on whether issue jurisdiction is shared with the regional governments (e.g., welfare-state issues such as health or education) or the EU (e.g., environmental issues) and whether the incumbent government has the majority of seats in the Spanish Parliament. The capacity or willingness of the Spanish government to respond to the electoral promises defined in the party manifesto is expected to be lower for issues with shared jurisdiction such as health or social policy, for which policy makers are better able to blame each other for inaction in the context of a multilevel system of government. By the same token, we expect that correspondence will be lower under minority governments, when the incumbent government is forced to adopt (or abandon) some policy priorities that were not directly emphasized in the party manifesto.

These questions have been addressed from different perspectives. The party-mandate theory (Budge and Hofferbert 1990; Klingemann, Hofferbert, and Budge 1994) highlights the importance of partisan government for policy-making. According to this view, political parties clearly announce their policy priorities for the next legislature in their party manifestos during the electoral campaign and present to voters alternative policy agendas that they promise to enact if they are elected (Gunther and Montero 2009). The ability of the incumbent government to keep policy promises depends on institutional factors—mainly, whether or not there is a majority government. By contrast, Maravall (1999) argues that policy makers are not inextricably tied to policy promises, among other things because the incumbent government can manipulate information to its advantage, limiting the capacity of citizens to assess whether the government is pursuing their interests and whether it should be rewarded in the next election (Maravall 1999, 192).

The agenda-setting approach goes beyond policy preferences to offer an alternative explanation of how and why certain issues enter the Spanish political agenda (Baumgartner, Jones, and Wilkerson 2011). According to this view, the policy process should be seen as an essentially disorderly and unplanned one in which party preferences are just one of the variables to be taken into account to explain policy outcomes (Jones and Baumgartner 2005; Walgrave, Varone, and Dumont 2006; Green-Pedersen 2007; Baumgartner, Jones, and Wilkerson 2011; John, Bevan, and Jennings 2011). Correspondence between mandates and policy outcomes is not expected, and issue attention is driven not only by party preferences and institutional factors, but also by new information and unexpected circumstances or events, such as spikes in unemployment or a terrorist attack. By analyzing the implementation of policy promises using the lens of the agenda-setting approach, we contribute to the analysis of how democracy has worked in Spain for the past several decades.

Our research is based on several comprehensive databases about party manifestos, speeches of the Presidente del Gobierno (prime minister), bills, and laws passed between 1982 and 2008. These databases have been created by the Spanish Policy Agendas Project (www.ub.edu/spanishpolicyagendas) following the methodology of the Comparative Agendas Project (CAP; www.comparativeagendas.info). The first section of the chapter defines the hypothesis according to existing literature. In doing so, we rely on existing analyses of mandate responsiveness, mainly the salience theory of the party manifestos project, and the agenda-setting approach. The second section describes our data and the coding method. The third explains the connection between institutional factors—type of government and institutional friction—and mandate responsiveness. The fourth is devoted to the analysis of external factors and to an explanation of why mandate responsibility declines over time.[1]

Policy Dynamics and Mandates

Spatial theories of party behavior hold that in a representative democracy there should be some congruence between the promises and the policies of the governing parties such that they avoid electoral reprisals (Downs 1957). From this perspective, political conflicts are related to policy positions (i.e., which goals should be achieved), and it is assumed that the capacity to maximize the number of votes depends on whether the political party is able to respond to voters' positions on different issues. In contrast, the saliency perspective suggests that political parties compete less by taking opposing sides of an issue and more by selecting their own particular issues (Budge and McKay 1994; Petrocik 1996; Green-Pedersen 2006; Walgrave, Vliegenthart, and Zicha 2010).

The party-mandate theory (Budge and Hofferbert 1990; Klingemann, Hofferbert, and Budge 1994) departs from the idea that political parties give more salience to issues on which they seem more capable of offering an efficient policy solution; instead, political parties respond to the electorate's preferences by giving more salience to the issues they "own" (Klingemann, Hofferbert, and Budge 1994; Green-Pedersen 2006). Electoral promises are identified more by issue salience than by voters and party positions on issues, and it is assumed that the incumbent government is bound to the electoral promises made in party manifestos during the legislative session (Budge and McKay 1994; Thome 1999, 570). Incumbent governments will try to fulfill the ideas and promises contained in the party manifesto as a means to gain reelection and to avoid the political costs associated with the lack of implementation of policy promises.

But the fulfillment of this task varies depending on institutional arrangements, mainly the type of government. According to the party-mandate approach, in countries like the Netherlands, with its long tradition of coalition governments, the ability of governments to translate promises into action will be lower than in a majoritarian democracy like Spain. The institutional structure of the Spanish political system generates a bias toward the formation of stable, single-party governments, the overrepresentation of big parties (the Partido Popular [People's Party; PP]) and PSOE always account for more than 80% of the seats of the lower chamber), and the executive's domination of the legislative process (Lijphart 1999). There is a prevailing position of the executive before the Spanish Parliament, which results in a greater capacity to implement policy promises, especially when the incumbent political party is governing with the majority of seats under the mandate of a majority (Sánchez Cuenca and Mújica 2006).

Several research projects have tested these ideas about the link between institutional factors and mandate responsiveness. The results provided by Budge and Hofferbert (1990), and Klingemann, Hofferbert, and Budge (1994), and Budge et al. (2001) indicate that policy priorities articulated in the party manifestos during national elections are actually reflected in the subsequent budgetary decisions of national governments, especially when the government is a majority government, with some exceptions such as Belgium. Stimson, MacKuen, and Erikson (1995) and Walgrave, Varone, and

Dumont (2006) also demonstrate that legislative activities are affected by electoral promises. Following this line of research, we expect that minority governments have more difficulty in fulfilling political promises, as defined in the party manifesto, than do majority governments.

The link between issue prioritization in the party manifestos and policy outputs will never be perfect, mainly because political parties are unable to fully predict policy priorities for the next legislature. According to the agenda-setting approach, the policy process should be seen as an essentially disorderly and unplanned process in which party preferences are only one of the variables to be taken into account to explain policy outcomes (Baumgartner and Jones 1993 and 2009).Variations in the implementation of policy promises do not follow a defined pattern—a greater or lesser ability to fulfill electoral promises according to the type of government—but a more erratic trend linked to external factors. Unexpected circumstances explain why governments might abandon their electoral promises during the legislature, adapting policy to new conditions in order to pursue the citizenry's best interests. Issue prioritization varies across legislatures in response to external events or new ideas that draw attention to an issue that was not necessarily taken into account by the incumbent government when defining its party manifestos (Baumgartner, Jones, and Wilkerson 2011). The fact that policy makers do not respond to electoral promises is linked not to the idea of self-interest, as Ferejohn (1999) would suggest, but to bounded rationality (Manin, Przeworski, and Stokes 1999; Jones 2001).

In order to analyze the importance of external events and new information we compare the correspondence between party manifestos and two type of speeches: the *discurso del candidato a la Presidencia del Gobierno* (*discurso de investidura* [investiture speech]; the speech that the candidate for Presidente del Gobierno gives to seek the confidence of Parliament) and the *discurso del Presidente del Gobierno sobre el Estado de la Nación* (the Presidente del Gobierno's state-of-the-nation speech).[2] We should expect greater correspondence between the first speech and the party manifesto than for the rest of speeches, among other things because the time lag is almost nonexistent— the speech must be given within two months after an election, and the candidate has to pass a final vote to become Presidente del Gobierno. Any discrepancies between the promises highlighted during the political campaign will be widely publicized by the media and political parties, generating a situation of political discontent. The state-of-the-nation speech is an annual speech in which the Presidente del Gobierno informs the Parliament about policy priorities as well as the evolution and implementation of the initial political program. While giving this speech, the Presidente del Gobierno pays particular attention not only to the issues defined in the party manifesto (as expected in the investiture speech), but also to new events that have become important to the political agenda (Chaqués-Bonafont et al. 2008). As the legislature moves forward, the correspondence between promises and speeches follows a random pattern depending on these new ideas and information. Accordingly, we expect the correspondence between electoral promises and speeches to be larger in the first (investiture) speech than in speeches later in the legislature.

Finally, we examine whether correspondence between electoral promises and policy outputs varies across policy issues depending on the level of political decentralization. From the transition to democracy to the present, Spain has gradually become a multilevel system of governance (Hooghe, Marks, and Schakel 2008). From 1986, the EU has gained increasing capacity to define issue priorities on the Spanish legislative agenda, especially for issues related to the single market and the environment (Palau and Chaqués-Bonafont 2012; Brouard, Costa, and Köning 2012). By the same token, the national government has lost some of its political authority over the formulation and implementation of some issues, especially welfare issues such as health, education, or and social policy, which have gradually been increasingly delegated to regional governments (Chaqués-Bonafont and Palau 2011b). Despite this, party manifestos are more and more fragmented across issues (Walgrave and Nuytemans 2009), and political parties continue to pay attention to issues with shared jurisdiction, putting forward policy proposals whose implementation basically depends on agreement with regional governments or the EU.

According to Anderson (2006), Aguilar and Sánchez-Cuenca (2008), and Soroka and Wlezien (2010), political parties follow this strategy in a context in which the costs of not implementing policy promises are especially low. In a multilevel system of government the attribution of responsibilities is less clearly defined, and citizens have less precise knowledge about which government is politically accountable for each policy area (Gunther and Montero 2009; Chaqués-Bonafont and Palau 2011a). The assignation of responsibility for policy outcomes is increasingly complex, and different levels of government tend to engage in a process of shifting blame and taking credit (Anderson 2006; Soroka and Wlezien 2010). As a consequence, policy makers keep paying attention to these issues in the party manifestos, regardless of their ideological positions, in order to respond to the wishes and concerns of the electorate, knowing that in the case of inaction they can always blame the EU or the regions—such as left-wing political parties blaming the EU for the privatization of public services following the creation of the European Monetary Union (EMU), or conservative political parties blaming the regions for not implementing policy promises to reduce public expenditures related to health care. According to this argument, we would expect correspondence between electoral promises and laws to be lower for those issues with shared jurisdiction than for issues that remain under the sole authority of the national government.

Methodology

To study mandate responsiveness, we have created several longitudinal databases containing information about party manifestos, laws, bills, and speeches for the period of 1982–2007. These datasets have been coded manually by two coders according to the methodology of the Comparative Agendas Project (CAP)—19 major topics and categories and 247 subcategories (see appendix). The party manifestos database includes seven manifestos, one for each general election held in Spain in the period 1982–2007, coded at the quasi-sentence level, resulting in 12,628 entries. As in many other countries, in Spain party manifestos are unified documents approved by a political party that contain policy pronouncements made during an electoral campaign. The average length of the manifestos is 1,804 quasi-sentences, but there are important differences across time. Overall, José Luis Rodríguez Zapatero's (PSOE, 2004–12) manifestos were longer than José Aznar's (PP, 1996–2004)—3,272 quasi-sentences compared to 2,071. and José María Aznar's manifestos were longer than González's (PSOE, 1982–96)—1,303 quasi-sentences. The laws database contains 1,509 entries, with information about all types of laws (ordinary and organic laws, legislative decrees, and decree laws) passed between 1982 and 2007. The bills database contains 1,640 entries also for the period 1982–2007, and the speeches database contains 8,582 entries (quasi-sentences), including information about two types of speeches—the state-of-the-nation speech and the investiture speech, both given by the Presidente del Gobierno.

Correspondence in issue attention between party manifestos and laws, bills, and speeches was analyzed using correlation analysis. Because of the different temporal structure of the time series—party manifestos can be measured only once every four years, for instance[3]—the correlations between party manifestos and laws, bills, and speeches have been calculated in three ways.

1. At the legislature level: calculating the percentage of attention by code and legislature for the laws, bills, and speeches and correlating them with the percentages of attention by code of the party manifestos. Legislature correlations allow us to analyze mandate responsiveness at the aggregate level, taking into account the policy output of the whole mandate.
2. At the annual level: duplicating the issue-attention proportion of the party manifestos for all the years corresponding to the same legislature and correlating them with the annual percentage of attention of laws, bills, and speeches. In this way we analyze whether the implementation of policy promises varies over the years.
3. At the topic level: correlating the percentage of attention by topic in each series.

Issue Attention and Mandates

Issue attention has changed following different patterns across policy venues (fig. 11.1). First, economic issues always capture an important share of the legislative agenda (45% of the laws) and to a lesser extent of the party manifestos (30%) and speeches (25%).[4] During the first socialist governments under González's mandate (1982–96), attention to the economy was related to economic crises (especially unemployment, which in 1982 was above 20%), the modernization of Spanish industry, the construction of basic infrastructures, and reform of the tax system, all of which were completely underdeveloped after forty years of Francoism. The PP's (1996–2004) attention to the economy is more connected to the privatization of public services and deregulation and liberalization of economic sectors—especially telecommunications and energy—and to the convergence criteria of the EMU. Finally, after the PSOE won the 2004 elections, attention to economic issues became less important, although the Spanish model of economic growth was coming to an end, as the economic crisis of the late 2000s highlights. During his first term Rodríguez Zapatero did not engage in major economic reforms, focusing his attention instead on welfare and rights issues.

Overall, attention to welfare issues is particularly high in the party manifestos (34%), especially from the mid-1990s, while only 15% of the laws and

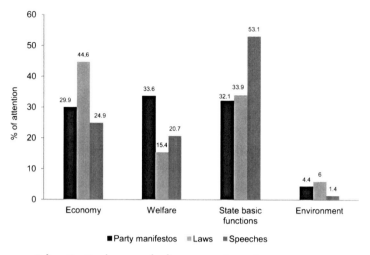

Figure 11.1. Policy attention by area and policy venue, 1982–2008

21% of the speeches are related to welfare issues. Still, attention to welfare in the legislative agenda is quite constant for the whole period, while in the case of speeches and party manifestos attention increased from 1982 to 2007. González led the construction of the Spanish welfare state, focusing on the universalization of education and health-care policies and on the reform of the social security system, going beyond most of the reforms made by the Unión de Centro Democrático (Union of the Democratic Center [UCD]) governments during the political transition. Aznar and Rodríguez Zapatero also devoted their attention to welfare, but with quite different goals: the PP focused on the privatization of social services, especially health, while the socialist governments beginning in 2004 paid special attention to expanding social-protection spending, increasing the benefits of the disabled and elderly.

Finally, the state's basic functions always capture most of the attention of the speeches of the Presidente del Gobierno (or prime minister) and almost the same amount of attention of party manifestos and the legislative agenda (32%), and in all cases there is a reduction of the level of attention, which is especially important in the case of speeches (from 60% in 1982 to 50% in 2007) and laws (from 42% to 30%). Issues related to government operations, defense, and foreign affairs were especially important in Felipe González's first term (1982–86). This is explained by the entry into NATO,[5] the fight against terrorism by the Euskadi Ta Askatasuna (ETA), the first wave of transfer of competencies to the Comunidades Autónomas (regional governments [CCAA]), and the entry into the EU (then the European Economic Community) in 1986. In contrast, during González's last term, attention to governmental issues increased as a result of scandals and political corruption (especially highlighted in speeches) and increasing political decentralization toward the CCAA as a result of a second-wave transfer of issue jurisdiction in the early 1990s. Attention to state functions was also important for Aznar and Zapatero, but for quite different purposes: while the PP talked about the professionalization of the armed forces, entering the war in Iraq, and reform of public administration, Rodríguez Zapatero talked about ending the military intervention in Iraq and about right-wing issues such as immigration, abortion, and same-sex marriage.

Electoral Promises and Governmental Activities

According to our first hypothesis, the ability of Spanish governments to fulfill electoral promises as defined in party manifestos should be lower under minority governments. From the first general elections of 1977 to the present there has always been a single stable party in government, though that has oscillated from minority to absolute-majority governments. The UCD led the process of democratic transition to a democracy under a minority government, and once the process was completed in 1982, there was always a winning party, the PSOE or PP, that defined the political agenda and implemented its policy program for the whole term. The PSOE governed for almost twenty-two years, with a majority of seats in the Congreso de los Diputados (lower chamber) for more than ten years (1982–93), while the PP governed from 1996 to 2004, with a majority of seats during its second and last term. Minority governments were always supported by conservative nationalist parties (the Convergència i Unió [Convergence and Union; CiU], the Partido Nacionalista Vasco [Basque Nationalist Party; PNV], and/or the Coalición Canaria [Canarian Coalition; CC]), with the exception of the PSOE beginning in 2004, which has governed with the support of the Izquierda Unida (United Left [IU]) and the nationalist Esquerra Republicana de Catalunya (Republican Left of Catalonia [ERC]).

To analyze whether the capacity of different governments to fulfill electoral promises is related to the type of government, we have limited the comparison to four legislatures—two under the majority government of the PSOE (1989–93) and the PP (2000–4), and two under the minority government of the PSOE (1993–95) and the PP (1996–99). In this way we control for party ideology and avoid the methodological problems related to the larger number of years of majority governments. As figure 11.2 illustrates, there are almost no differences between the socialist majority and minority governments: the correlation between the party manifesto and the legislation passed in the Spanish Parliament is 0.4 when the PSOE is governing with the majority of seats and decreases to 0.38 when the PSOE is governing under a minority The case of the PP gives even less support to the minority-majority government hypothesis because the correlation between electoral promises and laws is higher under a PP minority government (0.5) than under a PP majority government (0.3).

The same is true for government bills: the correlation is practically the same when the PSOE is governing with the minority or majority of seats of the Spanish Parliament; when the PP is governing with the majority of seats, correspondence always declines. Aznar feels more confident about departing from his initial political program and implementing policy proposals that were always implicitly connected to the PP but never explicitly mentioned in the party manifesto. Actually, once the PP wins the majority of seats of the Spanish Parliament and regional political parties lose their pivotal position in government formation, there is a radical shift in national-regional government relations oriented toward limiting the process of political decentralization. This policy position is clearly illustrated by the increasing political conflicts and divergences on agenda priorities between the national government and some CCAA, especially the Basque country under the government of Juan José Ibarretxe (Chaqués-Bonafont and Palau 2011b).

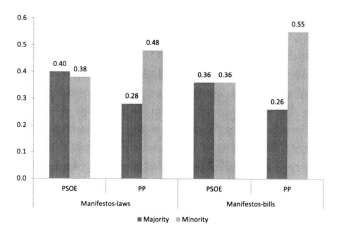

Figure 11.2. Mandate responsiveness and type of government, 1982–2008

Overall, these results do not permit a definitive conclusion about the impact of minority-majority governments on mandate responsiveness in Spain. Rather, our results support the second hypothesis, about the impact of external factors and sudden changes on the implementation of policy promises as defined in the party manifestos (Jones 2001; Jones and Baumgartner 2005). From 1982 to the present, the governments of González, Aznar, and Rodríguez Zapatero had to deal with unexpected circumstances and crises that were quite difficult to predict in a party manifesto. The mad cow disease scandal, the Prestige oil spill, the Iraq War, and the terrorist attack on Madrid in 2004 are examples of unforeseen situations that the conservative governments of the PP had to face from 1996. By the same token, in the early 1990s the socialist government had to deal with a deep economic crisis, rising unemployment, and corruption scandals, some of which were difficult to forecast.

Uncertainty and unpredictability are related not only to focusing events but also to the (in)accessibility of information about available public resources (Stokes 2001). Once the winning political party enters office, it realizes the economic situation and the public resources available to carry out its political program and may decide to redefine its policy priorities accordingly. This is exactly one of the arguments González made to explain why one of his key electoral promises in 1982 (the creation of 800,000 new jobs) was impossible to achieve during the first socialist legislature. The PSOE's calculation was based on existing public information about the public deficit that did not correspond with actual indicators, forcing the PSOE to redefine its policy goals just after winning the elections (Maravall 1999).

One way to analyze whether misinformation and unpredictable conditions help to explain the failure to implement policy promises is to test whether the correspondence between electoral promises and policy outcomes is especially large during the first (investiture) speech compared to the rest of the speeches during the term. The investiture speech should take place within two months after elections, which limits the possibility of justifying deviations from the original party manifesto owing to unforeseen conditions and external events. For the rest of the speeches, we expect the Presidente del Gobierno to explain the fulfillment of initial policy goals, lay out plans for further implementation of policy promises, and respond to unexpected situations. Our results support this hypothesis. As figure 11.3 illustrates, the correlation between speeches and manifestos is higher during election years and follows a random pattern as the legislature moves forward.

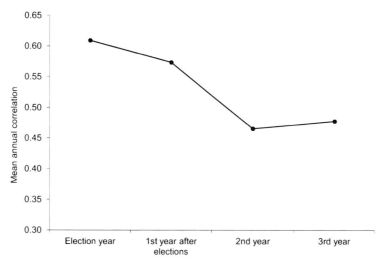

Figure 11.3. Differences in mandate responsiveness across the legislature (speeches and party manifestos), 1982–2008

Mandate Responsiveness in a Multilevel System of Governance

The analysis presented so far illustrates that mandate responsiveness declined over time, following a gradual trend from 1982 to the present. As figure 11.4 highlights, there is increasing divergence between electoral promises and policy outputs. The correlation between party manifestos and laws during González's first socialist government was quite high (0.63), especially compared with Aznar's second legislature (2000–4) (a correlation of 0.21) and Rodríguez Zapatero's first legislature (2004–8) (0.31). This decline could be related to the gradual process of political decentralization toward the CCAA and the EU, which led to the consolidation of a multilevel system of governance. In this context we expect that correspondence between political promises and policy outcomes should be higher for issues without shared jurisdiction, such as defense or foreign affairs.

Tables 11.1 and 11.2 summarize the results. As expected, correlation is especially high for issues without shared jurisdiction such as defense, rights, government, research and development, and economic issues. For issues with shared jurisdiction, such as education, agriculture, environment, or health care, correspondence is lower. The differences are especially high in the case of education, which has captured an increasing share of attention in the party manifesto (an average of 12.5%) even though it is a highly decen-

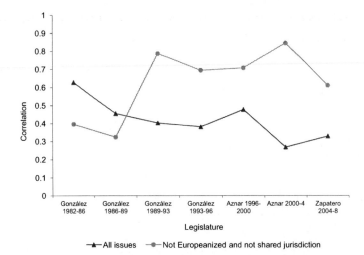

Figure 11.4. Legislature correlation between party manifestos and laws, 1982–2008

Table 11.1. Mean annual correlation between party manifestos and laws by code: shared vs. not-shared competences, 1982–2008

Issue	Jurisdiction*	Mean correlation	
Defense	Not shared	0.72	
Rights	Not shared	0.66	
Commerce and banking	Not shared	0.51	
Science and technology	Not shared	0.28	
Government	Not shared	0.28	
Water	Not shared	0.15	Mean not shared:
Economy	Not shared	0.17	0.15
Transportation	Not shared	0.09	
Energy	Not shared	0.08	
Foreign trade	Not shared	−0.14	
Foreign affairs	Not shared	−0.14	
Labor	Not shared	−0.50	
Housing	Shared	0.34	
Social policy	Shared	0.22	
Health	Shared	−0.16	
Environment	Shared	−0.34	Mean shared:
Justice and law	Shared	−0.33	−0.17
Agriculture	Shared	−0.44	
Education	Shared	−0.50	

Note: The asterisk (*) refers to the distribution of competences between the Comunidades Autónomas (regional governments) and the national government.

tralized issue. One reason for this mismatch between promises and policy outcomes may be that more than 54% of Spanish citizens still think that education policy is mainly under the jurisdiction of the central government (Lago and Lago 2011). Even though most of the implementation of education policy is controlled by the regional governments, the national government

Table 11.2. Correlation between laws and party manifestos by code and percentage of Europeanized legislation, 1982–2008

Issue	% of Europeanized legislation	Mean correlation	
Agriculture	63	−0.54	
Environment	63	−0.46	
Science and technology	59	0.19	Mean
Economy	56	0.11	Europeanized:*
Foreign trade	56	0.11	−0.05
Energy	52	−0.16	
Industrial policy	50	0.41	
Health	33	−0.03	
Labor	26	−0.51	
Government	26	0.28	
Social policy	25	0.62	
Foreign affairs	25	−0.23	
Education	22	−0.58	Mean
Transportation	22	−0.07	non-Europeanized:
Water	20	0.14	0.10
Rights	20	0.64	
Justice and law	12	−0.47	
Housing	11	0.7	
Defense	2	0.73	

* If the percentage of Europeanized legislation is ≥50%

continues to pay attention to the issue, which results in a lower rate of mandate responsiveness.

The analysis of Europeanization illustrates that for those issues that are more Europeanized,[6] such as agriculture, the environment, or energy, there is, as expected, a lower correlation between laws and party manifestos (table 11.2). For less Europeanized issues, such as defense or rights, we observe a higher correlation between laws and party manifestos. This supports the hypothesis that the greater the delegation of political authority to the EU, the lower the correspondence between laws and party manifestos. A comparison of the PSOE (1982–95) and PP (1996–2004) governments lends further support to this hypothesis. Beginning in 1996 there is less and less correlation between mandates and legislative output for issues that are more Europeanized or more decentralized to the CCAA.

In short, these results indicate that mandate responsiveness varies across issues: the more jurisdiction is delegated away from the national government, the less correspondence we find between promises, as defined in the party manifesto, and policy outcomes. These variations are also important for explaining why mandate responsiveness declined steadily from 1982 to 2008. Our results indicate increasing divergence between party manifestos and policy outputs and a clear trend toward less correspondence. Actually, for issues without shared jurisdiction and a low level of Europeanization (defense, rights, labor, government affairs, transportation, and foreign affairs), the correspondence between mandates and policy outputs is not declining, which further supports this idea (fig. 11.4).

In our view this is explained by a major political transformation, namely the consolidation of a multilevel system of governance and how this process has taken place in Spain. In this context, political parties continue to pay attention in their party manifestos to issues that are important for their electoral purposes but out of their jurisdiction while they are in government. Political parties do not refuse to highlight the relevance of issues such as education or health care in their party manifestos, although some of the problems related to these welfare issues have over time been transferred to the CCAA. By the same token, an important part of the legislative agenda has been devoted to issues related to the EU (such as the transposition of directives on agriculture or the environment), which are not necessarily highlighted in the party manifesto. The result is an increasing decline in mandate responsiveness, with important variations across issues depending on the level of political decentralization upward to the EU or downward to the CCAA.

Conclusions

The analysis of mandate responsiveness in Spain from an agenda-setting perspective demonstrates that issue attention is driven not only by party preferences and institutional factors but also by new information and sudden changes in circumstances. The results we present here illustrate the importance of such external factors as unemployment peaks, food safety scandals, or terrorist attacks on changes in the implementation of mandates from the early 1980s to the present. The ability of the governments of the PSOE and the PP to fulfill electoral promises follows a random trend after the Presidente del Gobierno's first speech independently of whether the incumbent government has the majority of seats in the Congress of Deputies; this is partly explained by the impossibility of predicting the importance of issues like the war in Iraq while defining the party manifesto.

We have argued that institutional factors such as the type of government are not especially relevant for explaining political parties' ability to fulfill electoral promises. The party-mandate theory applies only when the PSOE is governing with a minority of seats in the Spanish Parliament. On the contrary, our results indicate that changes in the implementation of electoral promises are closely related to the consolidation of a multilevel system of governance. Mandate responsiveness varies across issues depending on the level of political decentralization. The more authority is delegated to the EU and/or the CCAA, the less correspondence there is between promises as defined in the party manifesto and policy actions by the incumbent government at the national level.

These variations in mandate responsiveness across issues are important in explaining declines in mandate responsiveness across time. The capacity of the Spanish government to respond to electoral promises declines over time, a situation connected to the consolidation of a multilevel system of governance. During national electoral campaigns, political parties continue to pay attention to issues with shared jurisdiction and to introduce policy proposals whose implementation depends mainly on regional authorities. As a result, there is an increasing mismatch between policy promises and legislative outputs for issues with shared jurisdiction such as education and agriculture, while mandate responsiveness follows a random pattern across time for issues without shared jurisdiction, such as defense or foreign affairs.

The question for future research is whether this means a decline in the quality of democracy in Spain. The ability of the incumbent government to justify changes to initial promises and to avoid being punished by voters for not keeping policy promises could increase in a multilevel system of government in which the limits of political jurisdiction are blurring and the possibilities of blame shifting increase over time. Our results indicate that the decline in mandate responsiveness is directly connected to issues whose jurisdiction has been gradually delegated to supranational or subnational institutions. Still, further research should be developed to test whether this increasing mismatch is the result of a rational calculation of political parties that continue to pay attention to issues they own in order to reap the electoral rewards from a misinformed electorate or of the changing role of party manifestos as an instrument to predict policy output.

Notes

1. We would like to thank the reviewers of previous versions of this chapter and the rest of the members of the Spanish Policy Agendas Project. The research for this paper is an output of the project CSO2009-09397 (Ministerio de Ciencia e Innovación) and SGR 536 (AGAUR). More information about the Spanish Policy Agendas Project can be found at www.ub.edu/spanishpolicyagendas.

2. The proposed candidate (designated by the king after consultation with the representatives designated by each parliamentary group with representation in the Spanish congress) has to submit to the house of representatives the political program of the government he intends to form.

3. The constitution defines a maximum period of four years for each legislature, but the Presidente del Gobierno may call for new elections before that period. All the legislatures have lasted four years, with the exception of the first (1979–82), the third (1986–89), and the fifth (1993–96), for different reasons. The first case was directly connected with political instability and the coup d'état in 1981; the second is the result of a rational calculation of González's second government aimed at winning elections again by absolute majority in a political and economic context that was becoming increasingly less favorable to the socialist government. In 1995 González called for new elections in a context of political scandals that led to the victory of the PP.

4. In order to better describe some of the characteristics of Spanish politics we have created four main categories of topics: issues related to the economy, state functions, the welfare state, and the environment. To organize the topics in this way allows us to have a more complete understanding of the relevance of these issues across time (e.g., the evolution of the welfare state from an important intervention in the 1980s at the national level to an increasing decentralization toward regional governments beginning in the 1990s).

5. The entry into NATO was promoted by the UCD's last government in 1981. The PSOE took a strongly belligerent position against this decision, introducing as one of its policy promises the derogation of the international treaty concerning the entry into NATO. A few months later, once in office, the PSOE called for a referendum, taking a clear pro-NATO position, which completely contradicted its initial position as defined in the party manifesto. This generated one of the most controversial policy decisions in the democratic period.

6. Europeanization has been measured by considering the percentage of laws with EU content, that is, laws that are directly linked with a binding EU regulatory act (directives, regulations, decisions, European Court of Justice decisions, and treaty provisions). For more information see Brouard, Costa, and Köning 2012; see also Palau and Chaqués-Bonafont 2012 for the Spanish case.

12 Diffusion of Policy Attention in Canada: Evidence from Speeches from the Throne, 1960–2008

Martial Foucault and Éric Montpetit

THE CANADIAN FEDERATION IS OFTEN PRAISED FOR ITS DECEN-tralized nature. It is said that such decentralization enables different provincial and regional communities to live peacefully under the same political system (Montpetit 2006). Scholars have paid much attention to Canadian federalism by investigating vertical relations between the federal government and provinces but have ignored horizontal relations (i.e., those between provinces). This pattern is not surprising: different forms of federalism in Canada have stressed the content of institutional arrangements and the policy-making process through negotiation and deliberation among the members of the executive branches of federal and provincial governments. However, with the evolving nature of Canadian federalism comes a transfer of competencies to provinces, which presents a new puzzle for intergovernmental relations. Not only have the provinces received more autonomy in implementing education, health, and environment policies, but they have also developed a large variety of official and unofficial horizontal arrangements. Consequently, it remains to be seen to what extent provinces define policy priorities and elaborate policies by taking into account what neighboring provinces have done and/or what the federal government allows them to do.

Within the latest developments in the public-policy literature, theories of policy diffusion have become popular and shed light on diffusion processes in public policy. In addition to political scientists, political economists and sociologists have also been paying more attention to policy-diffusion processes, without necessarily identifying them as such. In particular, this can be seen in the fiscal federalism literature, since it examines the impact of jurisdictions' tax and fiscal choices on other jurisdictions. This avenue of research underlines two important considerations: space and time. Space is important in a federal system because vertical strategic interactions occur between the center and the local jurisdictions, along with horizontal strategic interactions that arise when jurisdictions compete among themselves (Boadway and Shah 2009). And time is important in a federal system because the reaction of a local government can be based on a neighboring jurisdiction's decisions or derived from either rational or limited rational expectations (Besley and Case 1995). Although we do not ignore such developments in the literature, our argument is not directly linked to the behavior of political actors in a federal system. Instead, we focus on how the prioritization of attention in a federation entails a certain dynamic within political institutions and shapes policy-diffusion processes. Since around 2000 political scientists have revitalized policy-diffusion studies through the use of either new empirical tools, such as history-event analysis and dyad analysis (Shipan and Volden 2008), or new datasets (Nicholson-Crotty 2009; Krause 2011). Nonetheless, these approaches share a common goal: understanding why and how some governments at either the local or the national level adopt new policies. Three main avenues of research have been identified: (1) the influence of neighboring jurisdictions' decisions through a mechanism of learning or competition (Shipan and Volden 2006 and 2008); (2) regional patterns of policy adoption (Walker 1969); and (3) the role of institutions (i.e., intergovernmental relations) as disseminators of policies (Dolowitz and Marsh 1996; Weyland 2005; Gilardi 2010). However, little attention has been paid to the salience of policy issues and their potential diffusion in a federal context. For example, Soroka (2002) focuses only on the dynamics of agenda setting in Canada at the federal level. This argument seems to be particularly relevant when analyzing federal systems as decentralized as Canada's. The long tradition of decentralization in Canada offers not only a case for a laboratory of democracy but also an intriguing institutional framework for observing the propensity of provincial and federal governments to compete with or coerce each other.

In other words, we are more concerned with the emergence of issues in a decentralized system where each provincial government attempts to define its policy agenda, regardless of what the other provinces are doing. To improve our understanding of how policy priorities are distributed within subnational governments and federal governments, we propose to analyze a unique dataset based on 445 Speeches from the Throne delivered in each Canadian province, as well as in the federal Parliament, from 1960 to 2009.

In this chapter, our main theoretical objective is to combine the agenda-setting literature with policy-diffusion theories in an attempt to highlight policy patterns in Canada over the longest period ever empirically tested for this case. We focus on the nature of diffusion that may occur during this period of transformation in Canadian federalism and ask to what extent regional and federal governments' agendas influence each other by comparing the magnitude of change (or stability) in attention paid to policy issues.

The first section offers an overview of Canadian politics since the early 1960s to better specify expectations about the diffusion of policy attention in an evolving federation. The second section briefly discusses the main mechanisms of policy diffusion that have influenced political actors in order to analyze policy attention across provincial governments over the past fifty years. We describe in the third and fourth sections our testable hypotheses and data, respectively. In the fifth section we present our results before concluding and discussing the next steps of a research agenda on policy diffusion with agenda-setting data for Canada.

Norms of Canadian Federalism

John and Jennings (2010, 565) argue that political scientists have described postwar British politics as "club government," controlled at the summit by a "policy-making elite" that promotes "a closed and secretive style of government," unresponsive to interest groups and changes in public opinion. Perhaps unsurprisingly, this image could just as well describe postwar Canadian politics. Canada inherited Westminster-style legislative institutions whereby single-party governments controlled the legislative agenda. Thanks to cabinet governments, policy-making has been the purview of the prime minister, who is surrounded by a closed circle of ministers and high-ranking civil servants (Savoie 1999 and 2008). However, unlike the United Kingdom, Canada is a federal country in which a constitutional division of legislative responsibilities between the federal and provincial governments prevails. Moreover, the Canadian Senate does not provide for provincial representation, distinguishing the country from other federations such as Germany, Switzerland, and the United States. Instead, Canada's upper house is modeled after the British House of Lords and has only a limited legislative role. The combination of federalism and cabinet governments at both levels has led to the development of intense intergovernmental relations outside of formal institutions. These intergovernmental relations have become one of the most distinctive features of Canadian politics in the postwar period (Smiley 1987).

The Constitution Act of 1867 confers on the provinces exclusive jurisdiction over social policy, which includes health and education. Several exclusive federal jurisdictions are related to the economy, such as banking, interprovincial trade, and fishery. Federal jurisdictions also include criminal justice, defense, and international affairs. Agriculture and immigration are the only two jurisdictions shared between the two levels of government. Before 1982 only two minor constitutional amendments altered this division of powers: the first one transferred unemployment to the federal government in 1940 and the second one transferred pensions to the federal government in 1951 (Rice and Prince 2000, 74).

As long as federal and provincial interventions were limited (up until World War II), Canadian federalism was consistent with so-called watertight-compartments federalism, whereby each level of government was confined to policies strictly within its constitutional jurisdictions (Bakvis and Skogstad 2002, 7). Thanks to this form of federalism, Canadian politics was similar to British secretive politics, only with multiple club governments: one at the federal level and one in each province.

With government expansion, intergovernmental relations came to play a prominent role. After World War II, intellectuals and the political elite agreed that the provinces, acting alone, would not be able to develop welfare policies as efficiently as most industrialized countries (Rice and Prince 2000). Consequently, policy makers in several provinces began displaying a flexible attitude toward the constitutional division of powers, accepting federal intervention and national standards in social policy. More specifically, the immediate postwar period was characterized by the development of several shared-cost and other forms of joint programs between the federal and provincial governments (Barker 1988). Intergovernmental meetings of politicians and high-ranking civil servants presided over the development of these programs. No longer divided among multiple government clubs, policy in postwar Canada has often been developed by a "cartel" of government clubs (Breton 1988). Since then intergovernmental meetings of all sorts have featured prominently in the study of Canadian politics (Bakvis and Skogstad 2002, 9).

Canadian scholars have developed several typologies and concepts to describe the evolution of Canadian federalism. Cameron and Simeon (2002) distinguish between cooperative federalism (1950–1968), executive federalism (1969–1991), and collaborative federalism (1992–present). Cooperative federalism is associated with stable and discrete intergovernmental relations dominated by civil servants. Executive federalism refers to publicized inter-governmental relations, dominated by come-and-go politicians. Collabora-tive federalism is closely associated with visible performance management and the objective of reducing intergovernmental conflicts. Some scholars prefer to speak in terms of a period of province building, beginning in the mid-1960s, which followed a period of Canadian state building (Black and Cairns 1966; Young, Faucher, and Blais 1984). While Canadian state building involved the intervention of the federal government in the development of a Canadian welfare state, province building involves the promotion by pro-vincial governments of their distinctive resource-based economies. Other scholars simply rely on a dichotomy between an early period characterized by cooperative intergovernmental relations and a more competitive later period.

Theoretical Background

MECHANISMS OF POLICY DIFFUSION

The diffusion of policy attention in federal systems is related to two perspec-tives on federalism. The first insists on the autonomy of the decentralized units of federal arrangements, while the second focuses on policy coordina-tion among the various governments of the federation.

Proponents of the first perspective argue that federated units have op-portunities for experimentation on a small scale as well as opportunities to diffuse their innovations. Containing policy change within the territory of one or a few federated units limits the cost of each experiment, thereby in-creasing the possibilities for experimentation. With these increased possibili-ties also come increased chances not only of innovation, but also of eventual nationwide policy change. Even scholars who do not believe in the reality of such a quasi-natural selection process sometimes admit that federal systems offer more venues to those who press for policy change than unitary states. When federal policy makers refuse to embrace change, whether innovative or not, advocates for change can always try to convince subnational policy makers (Constantelos 2010).

Proponents of the second perspective stress the interdependence of governmental action within modern federal states. They argue that experi-mentation with policy change is never achieved on a completely autono-mous basis by federated units, given the complex policy context of modern states. Because policy decisions in one sector can have important effects on the policies of another, federations can no longer function with watertight divisions of responsibilities. Modern federations have intergovernmental forums within which federated units and the federal government coordinate their policy decisions. In fact, some scholars argue that these forums have become the center of policy decisions in several federations, including Canada. Certainly discussions and negotiations taking place among policy makers within these forums enable the transmission of information about policy experience, thereby allowing policy makers to focus their attention on certain topics.

The literature on policy diffusion emphasizes various mechanisms through which diffusion occurs (see Shipan and Volden 2008). Our goal is not to test which mechanism of policy diffusion is most prominent in the Canadian federation. We do not have the relevant data needed to carry out an empirical analysis of the nature and intensity of policy diffusion in Canada. Since we are concerned only with the diffusion of policy attention, we make use of theories of policy diffusion in order to look at the extent to which such a process of diffusion may be applied to policy attention. In this perspective, a quick review of these mechanisms may be useful to highlight the plausibility of diffusion in a federal context.

A first mechanism—the learning or efficiency process—rests on policy makers' rational behavior of collecting information on the experiences of other governments prior to committing themselves to new policies. From this policy makers learn about inefficient policies to avoid and about efficient ones to follow. Given the relative economic and social similarities among federated units, this learning mechanism should be common in federations.

A second mechanism, called either mimicking, imitation, or isomorphism, emphasizes legitimacy rather than efficiency. It refers to what economists call a reaction function in a Stackelberg game, in which a leader and a follower compete with each other. Simply put, a government decides to adopt the policy implemented by a reputable neighbor in order to avoid being sanctioned by public opinion or its electorate for failing to adopt the policy. This mechanism assumes reputational discrepancies between the borrowing and the lending governments. Size is an example of a reputation-related discrepancy: politicians from smaller jurisdictions risk sanctions if they do not imitate the larger ones. Such discrepancies are common among federated units of federations.

A third mechanism—coercive process—is likely to occur in a federal system where vertical relations between the center and subnational governments are a source of conflict. In situations of conflict, governments will mobilize their resources to coerce rival governments to adopting policies that they would not otherwise adopt. For example, in Canada, Ottawa has frequently resorted to its so-called spending power to force provinces to adopt policies that they might not have favored as their first choice. But this mechanism is not necessarily a one-way street. Successful experimentation in one province might encourage policy makers to press the center to resort to coercion to diffuse similar policies across the federation.

Once again, the goal of this chapter is not to assess the prevalence of one or the other of these mechanisms in the Canadian federation. In fact, these mechanisms are not mutually exclusive; they can operate simultaneously and with differing degrees of intensity in federal countries.

ISSUE ATTENTION

The empirical study behind this chapter is linked to the agenda-setting and issue-attention literature. Particularly relevant are Baumgartner and Jones (1993 and 2009; see also Jones and Baumgartner 2005) whose approach, applied mainly to the American agenda, rests on the analysis of thousands of issue data in several institutional venues (bills, laws, parliamentary questions, hearings, budget, party manifestos, public-opinion polls asking what the most important problem is, etc.). The data have been used to document the spread of leptokurtic distributions of attention to policy issues across venues. These distributions, it has been argued, support the argument that government is unable to react proportionally to the large quantity of problems it has to face and information it has to process.

This chapter uses data collected according to the method originally devised by Baumgartner and Jones in order to analyze the diffusion of attention to policy issues rather than the proportionality of reaction to policy problems. Therefore, the distribution of the data within venues is less a concern in this chapter than correlations across jurisdictions.

In fact, the method derived from Jones and Baumgartner's approach consists of measuring policy actors' attention to main policy topics (and sometimes related subtopics). We assume that attention provides useful information on the variance of the intensity with which policy makers work on different or similar policy issues. Where diffusion is most important, policy makers should work on the same issues with similar intensity, hence this chapter's focus on space and time correlations. Before presenting theoretical expectations for the Canadian case, two methodological warnings are necessary. First, because we do not strictly test a theory of policy diffusion, we have not looked at some temporal reactions between levels of government by including lagged variables of policy attention. Moreover, such a design would have supposed that every Speech from the Throne be delivered at the same time (month or year). That is not the case, as reported in the fourth section. Second, Canadian federalism is often scrutinized through vertical relations. Our argument here consists in going further by testing the existence of both vertical and horizontal relations, mostly in terms of simultaneous interactions that could suggest diffusion of attention as a transferring mechanism from one government to another.

Expectations

Given current knowledge on Canadian federalism, we expect various correlations across three distinct dimensions: time, policy sector, and territory. We begin this discussion with time.

As explained above, Canadian federalism has gone through different phases. Some scholars speak of transitions between cooperative federalism, competitive federalism, and collaborative federalism. Others insist on phases of province building, which took off in the 1960s. Whatever might be the most appropriate characterization, this literature points to the fact that there are important variations in Canadian federalism over time.

Thinking strictly in terms of correlations between the federal and provincial governments over decades, three specific time-related expectations arise from the literature. Whether scholars speak of cooperative federalism or province building to describe the 1960s, they agree that provincial and federal governments prioritize distinct issues. On the one hand, the depiction of federalism as cooperative in the 1960s rests on the recognition of complementarities between the two orders of government. Cooperative federalism was in fact premised on a division of labor whereby provinces have the constitutional and administrative capacities to implement typical welfare-state policies, while the federal government has the fiscal resources to provide funding for those policies (Simeon and Robinson 2009, 165). The shared-cost programs that stemmed from the recognition of complementarities involved some attention to typical welfare-state policy (e.g., health care) by the federal government, but Ottawa was primarily concerned with fiscal and budgetary issues (Barker 1988). Meanwhile, provinces were paying more attention to substantial welfare-state issues and state administration. On the other hand, scholars who speak of province building insist on the desire of provincial governments to become full-fledged states, autonomous from the federal government. Consequently, provincial governments in the 1960s were developing policies of their own choosing, as independently as possible of the preferences of the federal government. In other words, the literature leads us to expect a low correlation between provincial and federal issue attention in the 1960s.

Expectations are different for the 1970s. In fact, the 1970s witnessed growing competition between newly built modern provincial governments and the federal government. Once welfare-state policies were consolidated, provinces became interested in the control of their respective economies, resulting in increased attention to policy domains that had once been dominated by the federal government. Intergovernmental conflicts became increasingly frequent, with governments competing for policy space within the same domains. Therefore, in the 1970s correlations between provincial and federal issue attention should be stronger than in the 1960s.

Correlations, the literature further suggests, should be strongest in the phase of intergovernmental relations, beginning in the 1990s. Tired after many years of intergovernmental conflicts and related policy stalemates, policy makers across Canada started working toward ways to improve collaboration. The emergence of new policy issues, including environmental protection, public health, food safety, and international trade, was seen as an opportunity to leave behind fighting over jurisdictions and work collaboratively toward innovative solutions. By then new managerial tools such as performance evaluation had become popular and were used to focus collaboration on policy performance. According to some scholars, the policy results of these collaborative efforts were far from impressive (Simeon and Robinson 2009; Montpetit 2006). Nevertheless, they have doubtless encouraged the diffusion of policy attention across Canada. We certainly expect stronger correlations of attention between the federal government and provinces starting in the 1990s.

As suggested above, diffusion can occur through mechanisms that are more subtle than direct intergovernmental relations. Mimicking, for example, does not require direct discussions between the borrowing and the lending governments. However, everything else being equal, mimicking among provinces is more likely to occur in domains of provincial jurisdiction. In the classification of policy topics that we present in the data section below, there are three responsibilities in which provinces enjoy a large degree of autonomy: education, community development and housing, and local government administration. Correlations of provincial attention over these topics, therefore, are likely to be stronger than those in domains of exclusive federal jurisdiction such as defense, foreign affairs, and criminal justice. Naturally, correlations of attention between provinces in policy areas where both orders of government collaborate directly should be just as strong as correlations of attention between provincial and federal governments. In short, variations in correlation between governments from one topic to the next are plausible.

Lastly, the geographical size of Canada and its regional histories suggest territorial variations in correlations. In his seminal study of policy diffusion in the United States, Walker (1969) found regional clusters. In Canada, at least three territorial clusters of correlations are likely to be found. First, with their similar natural resources and economies, the western provinces are likely to be strongly correlated among themselves. Second, Quebec and Ontario, the two largest industrial provinces, both located in central Canada, should also yield strong correlations. Lastly, eastern Canadian provinces, all of which are relatively small and share a large coastal area, are also expected to be strongly correlated.

In the next section we turn to the empirical examination of these temporal, sectoral, and regional variations in correlations of issue attention among Canadian governments.

Data: Speeches from the Throne

At the beginning of each parliamentary session, Speeches from the Throne are read by the queen's representatives, the governor general at the federal level, and the lieutenant governors at the provincial level. The speeches, written by the close entourage of the prime minister and provincial premiers, announce the government's priorities. These speeches are similar to the State of the Union addresses in the United States. As John and Jennings (2010) argue, they can be more revealing of policy priorities than laws, as government policies frequently do not involve lawmaking.

As indicators of government priorities, they also present some shortcomings. They cannot be considered faithful reactions to all cabinet deliberations, nor can they be taken as indicative of specific policy formulations and implementations (John and Jennings 2010). A high-ranking Canadian public servant who has been involved in the preparation of Speeches from the Throne told the authors of this article that he views them as poor indicators of government priorities. They are like "Christmas trees" he said, with a little bit of something for everyone. Were this view correct we would have observed a wide spread in the attention given to issues, with little change over time. In contrast, we found that Speeches from the Throne frequently concentrate on a few issues, with large variations over time (Montpetit and Foucault 2012). Therefore, we adopt John and Jennings's (2010) view that a Speech from the Throne is a robust aggregate-level measure of policy-making attention.

Five closely supervised research assistants have coded all federal and provincial Speeches from the Throne between 1960 and 2009. A total of 445 speeches have been coded, with an intercoder reliability of 90% (based on a random selection of speeches). The coding was achieved using the codebook of the Comparative Agenda Project (CAP), with only minor adjustments to account for the specificity of Canadian politics.

The coding method requires the deconstruction of speeches into quasi-sentences. Most quasi-sentences are in fact full sentences, but sentences can be split when they contain more than one topic. Quasi-sentences are then distinguished between those that have and those that do not have political content. Quasi-sentences with political content are then associated with one of twenty-five topic codes. Again, a quasi-sentence has only one code for the main topic, but it can have subtopics. We do not use subtopics in this chapter.

In order to assess variations in correlations from policy sector to policy sector, we distinguished between topics of federal, provincial, or shared jurisdiction. Note that this classification does not perfectly match the formal constitutional division of powers; rather, it reflects our own assessment of the actual policy responsibilities of provincial and federal governments.

1. Federal responsibilities: banking, finance and domestic commerce; defense; foreign trade, international affairs and foreign aid; space, science, technology and communication
2. Provincial responsibilities: community development and housing issues; education; provincial and local government administration
3. Shared responsibilities: agriculture and forestry; civil rights; minority issues and multiculturalism; constitutional and national unity issues; culture and entertainment; energy; environment; fisheries; government operations; health; intergovernmental relations and trade; labor, employ-

Table 12.1. Descriptive statistics of Speeches from the Throne, 1960–2009

Jurisdiction	Number of speeches	Average number of quasi-sentences	Average policy content	Average level of issue attention	Average positive level of issue attention
Newfoundland	44	14474	0.908	11.698	14.841
Prince Edward Island	48	15359	0.872	10.692	14.820
Nova Scotia	38	8460	0.885	7.7252	9.957
New Brunswick	47	13978	0.916	9.9004	12.685
Quebec	29	7902	0.877	10.390	13.746
Ontario	37	10452	0.892	9.2843	12.303
Manitoba	34	7847	0.915	7.5811	10.594
Saskatchewan	36	7652	0.908	9.4729	11.789
Alberta	49	10120	0.886	7.1616	9.283
British Columbia	48	12362	0.861	8.1758	10.722
Federal	35	8147	0.833	7.5505	9.234

ment and immigration; law, crime, and family issues; the macroeconomy; Native (First Nations) affairs; public lands and water management; social welfare; transportation

All the details of the method can be found online at www.policyagendas. com. We have classified 116,753 observations (quasi-sentences) into twenty-five main categories. Table 12.1 provides a statistical summary of the data and the distribution of quasi-sentences according to both the main policy topics and the jurisdictions (ten provinces and the federal state). On average, about 90% of speeches have a political content, from which we built our measure of policy attention.

Results

EMPIRICAL METHODS

We study the diffusion of attention to policy by constructing a symmetrical correspondence matrix where each entry is the correlation between issue attention in jurisdiction i ($i = 1, \ldots, 11$) to jurisdiction j ($j = 1, \ldots, 11$) over the period 1960–2008. The basic idea remains to measure interactions between provinces themselves and between the federal and provincial governments to capture the intensity of policy attention. Following the method adopted by Jones, Larsen-Price, and Wilkerson (2009), we first construct a priority-by-time matrix, where each column is a policy-content topic (twenty-five in total) and each row is a year. Each cell in the matrix indicates the level of the attention dedicated to one of the twenty-five topics for each year. Next, we construct similar activity-by-time matrices, where each entry is the percentage of attention (i.e., the political content of each quasi-sentence) that is devoted to each one of these twenty-five issues in a given year (forty-nine years total). All in all, eleven matrices (ten provincial and one federal) were built, from which we performed a correlation analysis to ascertain whether provinces devote attention simultaneously to the same issue and comparatively with the federal government.

The correspondence matrix is the matrix of correlations formed by the priorities by time and activities by time matrices for our specific policymaking channel, that is, Speeches from the Throne. We then correlate the level of attention dedicated to one issue in province i with the level of attention to the same issue in province j (11 jurisdictions × 25 topics × 49 years). Before presenting the results, a methodological issue related to the type of correlation calculations must be pointed out and carefully addressed. Indeed, the first step consists in selecting an appropriate method for measuring the correlation of the series' bivariate. The data reveal huge variations across time and space, and, as expected after the creation of histograms for each variable, there was a significant nonnormal form to the data. Since the appropriate coefficient of correlation depends on the normality condition being satisfied, we performed a Shapiro-Wilk W-test for normality for each variable.[1] Not surprisingly, we had to reject the assumption of normal distribution for all variables. Consequently, the usual Pearson coefficient was not appropriate, so we chose to calculate the Spearman coefficient of correlation in order to respect the nonnormality condition. This method is far more relevant because it is suitable for use with the structure of our data. Let us not forget that our aim is to reveal the level of attention for each jurisdiction and for all issues, which implies aggregating the level of attention for all twenty-five topics and comparing the priorities for each topic analyzed independently. The same procedure has been applied to measuring attention according to specific time periods, geographical distribution, and kinds of responsibilities.

THE CORRELATES OF ATTENTION DIFFUSION

Our results are divided into three parts. The first objective was to ascertain whether correlations of attention to policy issues between provincial governments and the federal government vary according to the different phases of Canadian federalism. Figure 12.1 provides evidence suggesting that the temporal expectations presented above are correct. That is, correlations are weakest in the 1960s and strongest in the 1990s.

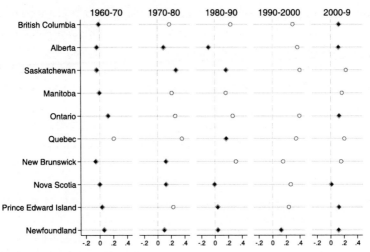

Note: o means significant Spearman's rho with p-value < 0.05

Figure 12.1. Correlation between provinces' policy attention and the federal government by decade

The graph on the left in figure 12.1 (1960–70) indicates that none of the provinces except Quebec had a pattern of policy attention similar to that of the federal government. The peculiar situation of Quebec might be explained by the determination of the provincial government during this decade to obtain additional powers from the federal government. Thus, Quebec experienced harsh intergovernmental disputes before any of the other provinces. Again, intergovernmental conflicts became more common in the 1970s.

The fourth graph in figure 12.1 shows strong correlations in the 1990s. In fact, the graph shows that the federal agenda is correlated with the agendas of eight out of nine provinces (we have data for only nine provinces because some data for Manitoba are missing). The desire to improve collaboration in the 1990s encouraged provincial and federal governments to pay attention to similar policy issues. The emergence of problems that did not neatly fit the constitutional division of jurisdictions (e.g., climate change, public health, food safety) combined with collaborative federalism to create common provincial and federal patterns of attention to policy issues. Throughout this entire period, Newfoundland stands out as a province that defines its agenda autonomously from the federal government.

Results are more ambiguous for the 1970s and 1980s, with Ontario and British Columbia seemingly most connected to federal priorities. Although stronger than in the 1970s and the 1980s, correlations for the 2000s are weaker than they were for the 1990s, suggesting that collaborative federalism was short-lived. Overall, figure 12.1 justifies examining time-related patterns of diffusion of policy attention.

We also spelled out above territorial expectations about policy diffusion. Following Walker (1969), we argued that three regional clusters of correlations are likely to occur in Canada: western, eastern, and central. Table 12.2 confirms the existence of these clusters. Correlations in the three gray zones of the table are generally higher than correlations outside of the zone, and they are particularly strong in the western cluster. Geographical proximity (perhaps in addition to social as well as economic proximity in the west) affects the diffusion of attention. Neighboring provinces appear to interact over policy issues among themselves more intensively than they interact with provinces located in the other regions of the country. However, these results must be interpreted with some caution: we found positive and significant correlations among all provinces, suggesting that interactions even among the provinces located farthest from each other also occur (British Columbia and Newfoundland). Correlations simply suggest that they occur with less intensity than among neighboring provinces. In any case, the shaded areas in table 12.2 leave little doubt about the existence of territorial differentiations of patterns of diffusion of policy attention.

One last intriguing observation about table 12.2 needs to be made: correlations between provinces are significantly stronger than correlations between the federal government and any of the provinces. The finding suggests that, over the entire period, so-called horizontal patterns of diffusion of attention have been stronger than vertical ones. Although our objective was not to test the prevalence of the various mechanisms of diffusion, this result may suggest that coercive mechanisms are less prevalent than mimicking and perhaps learning, if and only if the entire period is considered.

Lastly, we formulated expectations regarding variations of correlations from policy sector to policy sector according to the division of governmental responsibilities between the provinces and Ottawa. We expected weak correlations among the topics corresponding to mainly provincial and federal responsibilities and stronger correlations among the topics for which the two orders of government share responsibilities. Figure 12.2 provides evidence supporting our expectations, with one exception.

As expected, figure 12.2 fails to indicate a positive correlation between priorities announced in the Speeches from the Throne of any of the provinces and those of the federal government for issues that are mainly federal

Table 12.2. Correlation between Canadian jurisdictions' policy attention, 1960–2009

General agenda (size)	New-foundland	Prince Edward Island	Nova Scotia	New Brunswick	Quebec	Ontario	Saskatchewan	Manitoba	Alberta	British Columbia	Federal
Newfoundland		0.4923***	0.5080***	0.3946***	0.3458***	0.3225***	0.3842***	0.3973***	0.3920***	0.4489***	0.0832**
Prince Edward Island	0.4923***		0.5806***	0.4494***	0.3112***	0.4028***	0.4275***	0.4747***	0.4816***	0.4615***	0.1300***
Nova Scotia	0.5080***	0.5805***		0.4655***	0.2765***	0.4675***	0.4964***	0.5807***	0.5575***	0.5438***	0.0725*
New Brunswick	0.3946***	0.4494***	0.4655***		0.2621***	0.3770***	0.4385***	0.4236***	0.4374***	0.4490***	0.1168***
Quebec	0.3458***	0.3112***	0.2765***	0.2621***		0.4045***	0.3572***	0.3583***	0.3574***	0.3282***	0.2731***
Ontario	0.3225***	0.4028***	0.4675***	0.3770***	0.4045***		0.4774***	0.5344***	0.4411***	0.4392***	0.2069***
Saskatchewan	0.3842***	0.4275***	0.4964***	0.4385***	0.3572***	0.4774***		0.5743***	0.5731***	0.5278***	0.1282***
Manitoba	0.3973***	0.4747***	0.5807***	0.4236***	0.3583***	0.5344***	0.5743***		0.5907***	0.5333***	0.1722***
Alberta	0.3920***	0.4816***	0.5575***	0.4374***	0.3574***	0.4411***	0.5731***	0.5907***		0.5334***	0.0639*
British Columbia	0.4489***	0.4615***	0.5438***	0.4490***	0.3282***	0.4392***	0.5278***	0.5333***	0.5334***		0.1386***
Federal	0.0832**	0.1300***	0.0725*	0.1168***	0.2731***	0.2069***	0.1282***	0.1722***	0.0639*	0.1386***	

*p < 0.1.

**p < 0.05.

***p < 0.01.

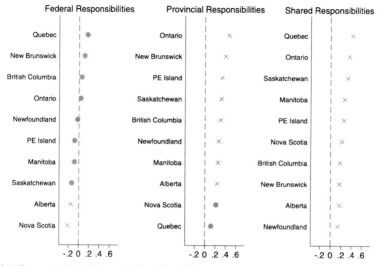

Note: X means significant Spearman's Rho with p<0.05

Figure 12.2. Correlation between provinces' policy attention and the federal government by responsibility, 1960-2009

competencies (banking, finance, domestic trade, defense, foreign affairs, international affairs, space, and science and technology). Significant signs in areas of federal responsibilities were found only for Nova Scotia and Alberta. However, the coefficients are negative, suggesting that the two provinces pay attention to federal responsibilities only when the federal government prefers to prioritize other policy issues.

In addition, the graph on the right in figure 12.2 is perfectly consistent with our expectations. In sectors for which both the provincial and federal governments share policy responsibilities (e.g., health, energy, culture, social welfare, and transportation), strong positive and significant correlations were found. This finding is consistent with our argument about collaborative federalism. Emerging problems that do not neatly fit the constitutional division of policy responsibilities encourage intergovernmental collaborative effort or joint problem solving. Rather than fighting over who should do what, governments pool their resources to find efficient solutions to these problems.

Unexpectedly, however, we found several instances of positive correlations between the provinces and the federal government in areas of provincial responsibilities. This finding echoes common complaints about interventions of the federal government in areas of provincial jurisdictions. Although the horizontal correlations in Table 12.2 are stronger than the vertical correlations, the latter are nonetheless statistically significant. Figure 12.2 adds evidence of the vertical transmission of attention by the federal government to the provinces. Our results, however, do not offer any conclusion about the precise mechanism through which this vertical diffusion occurs. It might occur through coercion, as those who complain about federal intrusions into provincial jurisdictions would suggest. Alternatively, it might occur through learning, although one might wonder why provinces learn from federal officials in their own areas of responsibilities while federal officials fail to learn anything from their provincial colleagues when devising policies of federal competencies.

Conclusions

As argued by Walgrave and Green-Pedersen in the introduction of this volume, institutions in a given political system may exert a significant influence on which issues will be attended to and which will not. Institutions impose rules of collaboration and competition. Political actors are embedded in these institutions, whose rules constrain the issues they can attend to. Institutions create "free" attention space that begs to be "filled," while at the same time they limit the amount of attention that can be paid to issues at any given time. In this chapter we demonstrated that the traditional question laid out by agenda-setting scholars—why policy agendas move on some issues and not on others—is particularly relevant in a federal context. We relied on an original dataset of Speeches from the Throne between 1960 and 2008 to show that intergovernmental relations in Canada generated attention to some issues, with important variations in three dimensions: time, space, and sector. Using the method of the CAP, we discussed policy attention in Canada along with theoretical expectations that emerge from the literature on policy diffusion and Canadian federalism. Our goal was not so much to measure the distribution of attention, but rather to examine correlations among the various governmental units of the Canadian federation and investigate the existence of horizontal relations in policy attention between provinces.

The data and correlation analysis led to three key conclusions. First, we found that the 1990s was the period during which both federal and provincial agendas were the most convergent. Second, we found territorial clusters of attention, with a particularly strong one in western Canada. Third, we found stronger correlations of attention between the federal and provincial levels in shared areas of responsibility than in exclusively federal ones. Unexpectedly, we found weaker but significant federal-provincial correlations in areas of exclusively provincial responsibilities. This latter finding invites further investigation into diffusion mechanisms such as learning, mimicking, and coercion. In fact, the partial evidence presented in this chapter does not enable us to draw any strong conclusions about the extent to which the federal government might coerce provinces to pay attention to topics that they would otherwise ignore.

Future research might compare the diffusion of attention in executive speeches (input) with the concrete fiscal outlays of governments (output). In a federal context, measuring the competitive versus cooperative forms of federalism once a combined measure of policy inputs and outputs is carried out might largely focus on both vertical and horizontal processes of policy diffusion. For instance, developments in spatial econometrics could enable us to ascertain the existence of mimicking behavior and then measure its intensity from one jurisdiction to another in a context of competitive federalism. On the other hand, cooperative intergovernmental relations could arise if the priorities of one jurisdiction appear to be (strategic) complements for those of other jurisdictions, including the federal government. This would be an illustration of promising avenues of future research on policy diffusion combined with agenda-setting literature.

Notes

1. Owing to limitations of space, we do not present the results from the Shapiro-Wilk test for normality in the appendix. However, all results can be obtained from the authors directly.

13 Conclusion: What It Takes to Turn Agenda Setting from an Approach into a Theory

Christoffer Green-Pedersen and Stefaan Walgrave

WE STARTED THIS BOOK WITH THE CONTENTION THAT THE agenda-setting approach potentially has a lot to offer to political science. The book was meant to show that it does. Did we succeed? Our key claim is that agenda setting—that is, political actors' distribution of attention to various political issues—is a fundamental and ubiquitous process in politics. Simply put: without agenda setting, decision making is unthinkable and impossible. Focusing on agenda setting enables political scientists to highlight key mechanisms and dynamics in political systems and thus to assess power in politics. It enables scholars to lay bare the streams of influence within and among political institutions in a polity. As stated famously by Bachrach and Baratz (1962), agenda setting is the second face of power. This has been widely recognized in political science but rarely if ever turned into an empirical research program.

The introduction further stated that political agenda setting is not just a perspective in policy studies but possibly a more general view of politics that is capable of tackling and comparing political systems in a new and informative way. Is this claim warranted by the facts? Is agenda setting really such a useful lens on politics? The case studies in this book demonstrate that political agenda setting applies far beyond the typical policy studies. None of the chapters deals with a specific policy area or is interested in the outcome of a particular decision-making process. Almost all incorporate evidence on entire agendas, including all possible issues, into an encompassing categorization. The studies are not interested in specific outcomes but in general patterns across issues. In addition, the actors and institutions whose agendas are examined are not the insiders and end-of-the-policy-cycle actors so typical of policy studies. Almost all the chapters deal in some way with political parties and elections, and thus with the issue preferences of actors at the beginning of the policy cycle. This focus on parties draws political agenda setting close to mainstream behavioral political science, where elections and parties form the core subject for many scholars. So it is safe to say that this volume effectively demonstrates that political agenda–setting theory is much more than a specific theory of policy-making.

The main contribution of political agenda setting is that it gives scholars an analytical instrument with which to investigate how issue attention on one agenda, or by one actor, does or does not affect the issue attention on another agenda or by another actor. Issues can be followed through the political system, and by observing many different issues evolving in a system over time, the agenda-setting approach lays bare the mechanism of power in a polity. By narrowing down the analysis to issue attention only and by discarding the meaning, framing, and direction of issues, agenda-setting theory generates a "tracer liquid" that can be injected into a polity and traced across institutions or time. In a sense, stripping issues of their meaning and just considering the bare issue generates a kind of standardized measure of politics. However, the flip side of the political agenda–setting perspective in this book is exactly the lack of research into the meaning of attention to issues. No one disagrees that this is a serious limitation, but we think this volume has shown that it is a helpful limitation since, based on our "tracer liquid," the authors were successful in offering new and compelling evidence regarding key features of their country's political system.

Political agenda setting not only offers an attractive lens through which to look at politics, it also draws attention to the role of information about real-world problems, to the issue preferences of political actors, and to the enabling and at the same time constraining role of institutions. The chapters confirm agenda setting's capacity to integrate many different political activities into a single analytical framework assessing the amount of attention devoted to a range of issues. Almost all chapters combine similar attention measures of very different political agendas. Drawing on the same unifying approach, the authors studied party manifestos, legislation, government speeches, parliamentary questions, bills, referendum outcomes, executive initiatives, parliamentary debates, and so on. Most of the chapters incorporate several agendas into a single analysis. From a purely analytical point of view, the volume attests to the integrating contribution of agenda-setting theory to the study of politics and political systems.

We also think that, in terms of substantive contributions, the agenda-setting approach lives up to the expectations set out at the start of the book. All chapters address landmark properties and/or key puzzles in the eleven countries. Some are about large-scale political change. For example, the German chapter deals with the agenda consequences of reunification in 1989, the Belgian chapter with the apparently irresistible devolution process that has been going on since the end of the 1970s. Others study more stable but no less important features of political systems. The UK chapter directly addresses the agenda correlates of the classic Westminster system, while the Swiss chapter focuses on this country's unique combination of direct and representative democracy.

The eleven country chapters were roughly divided into two groups. A first group of six chapters (the UK, the United States, France, Denmark, the Netherlands, and Switzerland) address the electoral-input side of politics—that is, parties and party competition, elections, government formation, and government priorities. The underlying research question unifying these chapters is how political actors set their priorities in a stable institutional environment. The second group of five chapters (Germany, Belgium, Italy, Spain, and Canada) addresses the output side and changing institutional structures. Again, political actors are at center stage, but the studies compare actors' priorities before and after major institutional change (devolution or reunification). The underlying question is whether institutional change leads political actors to revise their priorities.

It is impossible to summarize eleven country studies into just a few points, especially since the book is not set up as a comparative undertaking and each chapter focuses on a single country and a distinct puzzle regarding it. Yet, some common conclusions emerge from the two sections. Table 13.1 provides a rough summary of the findings. It shows that several chapters examine the translation of parties' issue priorities into government output and find that it is a murky and discontinuous process. Party priorities are only partially turned into policies or even policy priorities. That this seems to be the case also in the reputedly extremely accountable and mandate-driven UK system demonstrates that there is more to politics than the ideological preferences of parties. The U.S. analysis of legislative productivity makes a similar point: the content of the legislative agenda in the United States is virtually unrelated to the size of partisan majorities. The analysis of the French party manifestos broadens the finding, as it shows that parties, even before they start governing, address largely the same issues in their manifestos, with a lot of issue overlap—a finding that challenges the issue-ownership thesis. Thus, issue priority differences between parties and between governments in the same country over time are surprisingly small. Party priorities and

Table 13.1. Summary of main chapter findings

	Independent variable	Dependent variable	Outcome
Electoral cycle:			
UK	Government party change	Queen's Speeches + Acts of Parliament	Small effect for some issues only + smaller effect for laws than for speeches
US	Partisan majority	Legislative productivity and topics	Hardly any effect
France	Parties (ideology) and time	Issue-attention differences in party manifestos between right- and left-wing parties	More effect of time than of parties
Denmark	Elections + party system change	Parliamentary debates (party system agenda)	Weak effect, probably the other way around
Netherlands	Government agreement	Bills	Weak effect
Switzerland	Electoral breakthrough of radical challenger party	Attention of other parties to challenger party's issues (motions and popular initiatives)	Considerable effect (due to direct democracy)
Institutional change:			
Germany	German unification	Legislative agenda	Weak and only temporary effect
Belgium	Devolution to decentralized federal system	Issue-attention differences in party manifestos and parliamentary questions among Dutch-speaking and French-speaking parties	No effect
Italy	Electoral system change (towards majoritarian)	Match between government party priorities and legislative output	Small effect
Spain	Installation of multilevel system by regionalization	Match between government party priorities and policy output (laws)	Small effect
Canada	Installation of "collaborative federalism: with mixed competences	Similarity in issue priorities of national vs. regional governments (Speeches from the Throne)	Small effect

government legislation do evolve, but they are not stable. They seem to be reactive to something—and if not (only) to deep-rooted ideological party preferences, then to what? The answer is as simple as it is elusive: parties and policies react to information about problems in the real world. Politics is the art of solving problems, and when new problems show up, political actors, irrespective of what they promised to do beforehand or what they would prefer to attend to, address the new problem.

This point stands out clearly in the Dutch case. In the Netherlands, coalition agreements are crucial for making governments work. From an agenda-setting perspective, the issues mentioned in a coalition agreement are the issue priorities of the participating parties. Therefore, in order to prevent destabilizing the coalition, they try to reach agreement before entering into it. The Dutch case shows how difficult this is. Politics is dynamic because real-world problems change, and the legislative agenda shows that the coalition cannot stick to the prioritization of attention laid out in the coalition agreement. This is a potential source of coalition instability.

The tricky thing is, however, that we are not able to truly measure this real world, at least not for all issues incorporated in pooled analyses. We can only assume that changing government and partisan priorities are the consequence of new, or newly discovered, problems. Agenda scholars have therefore coined the term "issue intrusion" (Jones and Baumgartner 2005, 55–90) to refer to the taking up over time of compelling new issues. This phrase does not imply that agenda setting is simply a matter of issues forcing themselves onto the agenda and agendas being simply a reflection of the development of real-world problems. Real-world problems and changes in them affect political agendas because actors actively try to take advantage of these developments and turn real-world developments into political issues. Agenda setting is a political process. Real-world problems matter because actors need and use them. How can you turn immigration into a major political issue without a significant number of immigrants, or make the economy a major issue if you have no deteriorating economic indicators to refer to?

Seeing real-world problems as the key cause of political change also implies that the strong focus on elections that characterizes much traditional comparative politics is too restricted. Not that elections and the possible election of a new government with different preferences is unimportant, but focusing too strongly on it has led to an extremely limited understanding of political dynamics. Real-world developments are not tied to elections, and the main political struggles over how to prioritize scarce attention and deal with real-world problems do not take place at election time. One could even claim the opposite and see elections and their results as the outcome of an earlier struggle over attention that took place in elections. An example is the landmark 2001 Danish elections, when the 1990s' struggle over attention to immigration culminated (see chapter 5).

Several chapters address the dynamics of issue intrusion with a focus on party competition. For example, the French analysis shows that the traditional parties in France adopt the issues of their more extreme, and threateningly successful, competitors the Front National and the Green Party. The electoral successes of new radical parties taught them that issues such as the environment and immigration were important. Interestingly, the Danish case suggests that issue transfer goes not only from new niche parties to the traditional parties, but also the other way; by devoting attention to upcoming new issues, traditional parties provide fertile ground for their more extreme challengers. At the same time, they are capable of keeping issues such as European integration away from party competition, although the extremist challengers try to make the issue part of party competition (Green-Pedersen 2012). In other words, focusing on issues and attention to them does not imply less interest in politics, for instance party competition. But it does mean moving attention away from focusing solely on what parties do at election time to their ongoing competition related to issues—real-world problems—in routine political times.

These analyses show one of the key advantages of the agenda-setting approach, namely its ability to study issue dynamics. Questions about new political issues and new political parties have received considerable attention in studies of Western European politics, and the debate has mainly centered on whether new issues form part of a new cleavage in Western Europe (Kriesi et al. 2008). The findings vary, but the focus on possibly underlying new cleavages has reduced the focus on the dynamics of how new issues actually reach political agendas. New, so-called niche parties (Meguid 2005) are argued to play a crucial role, but few studies have really analyzed how they promote new issues and how they interact with established parties. The Swiss contribution is particularly interesting in this respect because it focuses on one of these new radical parties, the Swiss People's Party, and shows how it adopted a sharp issue profile especially employing the voter-centered typical Swiss venue of popular initiatives. Unlike other studies of this type of party, this chapter is able to trace the effort of such a new actor across different political venues.

The Swiss chapter, like the Danish and French chapters, also shows that party competition forces the other parties to react to issues put forward by successful competitors. Parties' issue priorities impact other parties' priorities through the party-system agenda: a hierarchy of issues addressed by the parties as a whole, forcing parties to talk about the same issues (Green-

Pedersen and Mortensen 2010). Remarkably, all these analyses suggest that party competition may not make parties more different as they try to occupy unique niches, but just the opposite: party competition makes parties more *alike* as they imitate one another and try to steal one another's issues.

Wrapping up the first section of this volume, the pervasive finding that parties' issue priorities are not very different and that, when they enter government, parties do not pursue systematically diverging agendas challenges the core idea of party government and mandate politics. It also challenges the idea that issue competition among political parties is just a matter of parties focusing on their preferred issues or the issues they own. This has been the typical point of departure for the idea of party competition as a matter of selective emphasis (Budge and Farlie 1983). In terms of issues addressed by government, the party in power does not seem to make much difference. This does not mean that parties do not compete intensively over which issues should dominate the agenda or that parties do not have preferred issues that they would like to dominate the agenda. However, they are constrained both because their competitors also want their preferred issues to dominate the agenda and because real-world developments matter.

In the second section of the volume, five chapters examine the extent to which grand institutional change leads to shifting priorities of political actors, again mainly parties and governments. Summary results are presented in the lower part of table 13.1. Overall, the results in this section are less clear and more mixed than those in the first section. Institutional change does lead in some instances to shifts in issue priorities, but these shifts are often small. For example, German reunification did not fundamentally change the issue content of the legislative output of German politics. Despite the massiveness and pervasiveness of the operation, the reunification of West and East Germany did not really, and definitely not resiliently, change the legislative priorities in the German Bundestag.

In Belgium, parties' priorities seem totally unaffected by the innate changes in the institutional setup of the Belgian polity. Belgian devolution is not caused by gradually disjointed issue priorities on both sides of the language border, and decentralization did not inspire Belgian parties to adopt gradually more diverging agendas. Actually, an agenda-setting and party-competition perspective may go some way toward explaining why Belgium has not yet broken down. State reform and separation are a political issue in Belgium and have to compete with many other political issues. The Belgian federation might be in danger if parties maintained a constant focus on the separation issue, but they do not. Many other issues attract party attention and thus push the separation issue aside.

The chapters on institutional change in Italy, Spain, and Canada suggest that it has some effect on the priorities of parties and of government, and on the link between them. The collapse of the Italian party system and the vital alteration of the electoral system did increase the match between party priorities and subsequent legislative output, but the change is small. The evolution from a proportional and gridlocked system to a straightforward two-block majoritarian system—a major institutional change—made only a small difference in terms of the congruence between promises and deeds. This conclusion is particularly striking considering that the match was very poor from the outset.

The Spanish chapter comes to similar conclusions. The installation of a full-fledged, multilevel system with extensive regionalization has to some extent affected the mandate responsiveness of the Spanish parties: there is less congruence between electoral promises in manifestos and the actual policy outputs after than before regionalization. But the difference is again small. The Canadian chapter seems to confirm the small-effects conclusion. Canadian federalism evolved from "watertight compartment federalism," with completely separated jurisdictions, to a form of collaborative federalism, with more mixed jurisdictions. This had consequences for the issue priorities of the Canadian government and the Canadian provinces: over time their issue priorities became more similar. The Canadian and the Spanish chapters thus both show the potential of an agenda-setting approach in terms of analyzing competition between different levels in a multilevel political system. The literature on multilevel governance or governments on different levels is booming, and the starting point is exactly that such political systems cannot be understood by viewing the different levels as clearly separated jurisdictions; they compete and interact. The chapters in this volume show the potential of analyzing this competition and interaction from an agenda-setting perspective.

Overall, the chapters that address the issue consequences of institutional change suggest that it is not institutions that primarily drive changes in issue priorities. Even when institutions change, priorities and pledge fulfillment are to some extent unaffected. The fact that the arena changes does not imply that actors bring other priorities to the fight. Together with the above observation that actor preferences are only part of the story of issue priorities, these results suggest, again, that changing real-world circumstances are crucial drivers of political change, especially in the long term. Institutions and preferences are often stable, but even when institutions change they do not affect to a defining extent the issues a political system processes. The moving target of politics is real-world problems.

These findings contribute to both the study of actors' priorities and to our knowledge of how actors react to institutional change. More important, many of the studies in this book generate counterintuitive evidence and bring new and often unexpected results to the table. Findings about devolution in Belgium, reunification in Germany, major landmark elections in Denmark, party government in the UK Westminster system, the limited success of the Swiss People's Party, change in the Italian electoral system, the absence of issue ownership in France, and the like all contradict conventional wisdom about these countries. The chapters offer innovative and exciting conclusions that throw new light on accepted facts. This corroborates the notion that agenda-setting theory is an independent and interesting approach to the functioning of entire political systems, and not just policy-making. Following issue attention over time, and thus studying political systems indirectly by means of how they deal with issues and not by focusing directly on the properties of the systems themselves, agenda setting offers fresh new ways of looking at well-known and established bits of knowledge about politics in general and specific political systems in particular.

The potential of political agenda setting as a general approach or theory of political systems is also reflected in the ability to engage in dialogue with many different literatures within political science. The agenda-setting studies included in this volume have implications for the literature on issue competition, party-system change, party mandates, policy diffusion, devolution, federalism, and multilevel governance, to mention just a few. Analyzing political systems from an agenda-setting approach thus offers new insights into a wide range of debates in political science.

An unresolved theoretical issue is the relationship between issue priorities and actors' substantial preferences. If agenda setting deals with the second face of power, what is its relationship with the first face of power—that is, the actual decisions, in a given direction, taken by political actors? For agenda-setting theory to develop into a full theory, the relationship between agenda setting and decision making must be spelled out in more theoretical detail. As mentioned in the introductory chapter, agenda-setting scholars have mainly dealt with incoming information as the driver of changes in political attention: as new (or renewed old) problems show up, responsible and responsive political actors have to address these and change their priorities, at least temporarily. The fact that a number of contributions in this volume conclude that, irrespective of their own preferences and ideological beliefs, actors simply take up the issues of the day and talk about the problems at hand underpins the strength of information and problems. Yet, it is hard to believe that actors' preferences would play no role at all; actors are not simply robots reacting to incoming information about the real world. This is evident in, for instance, the French, Danish, and Swiss contributions, which analyze party competition over new issues. In other words, additional work is needed to integrate agenda-setting theory's typical emphasis on information about issues with classic approaches to political actors as being driven by ideological or strategic preferences. Some studies within the agenda-setting framework that deal with this integration have theorized, and tested the notion, that issue attention is the effect of the interaction between incoming information about issues and the issue preferences of actors, arguing that preferences guide issue selection but information about issues can also trigger latent preferences (see, e.g., Vliegenthart et al. 2013). Only when such integration can be accomplished could political agenda setting develop from just an *approach* to politics into a real *theory* of politics.

Integration of the logic of issue priorities and the logic of issue preferences could also be achieved, of course, by starting with a theory based on actors' issue preferences rather than on their issue priorities. Tsebelis's (2002) veto-player theory is probably the most well-developed example of this type of theory, which focuses on actor preferences and on how institutions turn these preferences into output, making institutions the main cause of variation in political output. However, the advantage of an agenda-setting approach in terms of achieving such integration is that it starts with what is arguably the major source of political change or stability, namely evolutions and events in the real world. Approaches such as the veto-player theory are powerful because their focus on institutions and preferences makes them deductive. Their weakness is that they have little to say about political change, and it is difficult to integrate them with theories that have a more dynamic starting point. Elections seem to be the only source of political change that results in a new distribution of preferences, which would fit this model. However, the agenda-setting approach dealing with issue priorities can more easily be integrated with theories about actors' issue preferences, as it offers a more versatile starting point for an integrative theory. Such integration would help turn the agenda-setting approach into a truly general theory of politics instead of a partial approach focusing on issue attention and information processing.

One further element in such a general theory of politics would have to be an understanding of the role of the framing or meaning of issues. Once issues are on the agenda, political actors turn their attention to them. The original policy-agendas literature—expanded in studies from the mid-2000s onward (see Baumgartner, De Boef, and Boydstun 2008)—has given ample evidence of how important this question is, but it has to a large extent been lost in the most recent wave of agenda-setting studies, of which this volume provides examples.

Clearly the present volume is not the ultimate contribution of political agenda–setting theory to the study of political systems. It is meant as an illustration of how agenda setting is a powerful lens through which to see how political systems work. Although we contended that the agenda-setting approach is eminently suited for comparative research because the unit of analysis—attention to issues—can be compared straightforwardly across institutions and nations, the volume is not comparative in the cross-national sense. All country chapters focus on a single country and compare different institutions, actors, and agendas within that country. It is fair to say that the comparative perspective remains undeveloped in this book. The fact that we were able to compare the agendas of different institutions or actors, often over time, within a country proves that the agenda-setting approach has the potential to develop into a real comparative approach of political systems. What has been lacking so far is comparable data across nations. The country studies demonstrate that the evidence to start making sweeping comparisons of entire nations, across institutions and time, is gradually becoming available. Scholars of agenda-setting have started to produce comparative studies (see, e.g., Mortensen et al. 2011; Baumgartner, Breunig, et al. 2009; Green-Pedersen and Wolfe 2009; Vliegenhart and Walgrave 2011). This suggests that political agenda setting has the potential to become a fruitful approach not just to politics, but to comparative politics. Because it was our intention to take the first step here and show that the agenda-setting approach is a potent instrument whereby to analyze key features of individual political systems, we leave it to other publications to demonstrate that it has the potential to enhance our knowledge of political systems comparatively. We are confident about the potential.

Appendix:

Major Topics of the Comparative Policy Agendas Project

(SEE HTTP://WWW.POLICYAGENDAS.ORG. FOR THE FULL CODEBOOK)

1. Macroeconomy
2. Civil rights, minority issues, civil liberties
3. Health
4. Agriculture
5. Labor, employment, and immigration
6. Education
7. Environment
8. Energy
10. Transportation
12. Law, crime, and family issues
13. Social welfare
14. Community development and housing issues
15. Banking, finance, domestic commerce
16. Defense
17. Space, science, technology, communications
18. Foreign Trade
19. International affairs and foreign aid
20. Government operations
21. Public lands and water management

References

Adams, James. 2001. *Party Competition and Responsible Party Government: A Theory of Spatial Competition Based upon Insights from Behavioral Voting Research*. Ann Arbor: University of Michigan Press.

Adler, Scott E., and John D. Wilkerson. 2012. *Congress and the Politics of Problem-Solving*. Cambridge and New York: Cambridge University Press

Aguilar, Paloma, and Ignacio Sánchez-Cuenca. 2008. Performance or Representation? The Determinants of Voting in Complex Political Context. In *Controlling Governments, Voters, Institutions, and Accountability*, edited by José María Maravall and Ignacio Sánchez-Cuenca, 105–30. Cambridge: Cambridge University Press.

Albæk, Erik, Christoffer Green-Pedersen, and Lars T. Larsen. 2012. Moral Issues in Denmark: Policies without Politics. In *Morality Politics in Comparative Perspective*, edited by Isabelle Engeli, Christoffer Green-Pedersen, and Lars T. Larsen. 137–60, London Palgrave.

Andersen, Mikael S., and Michael W. Hansen. 1991. *Vandmiljøplanen: Fra handling til symbol*. Harlev: Niche.

Andersen, Robert, and Jocelyn A. J. Evans. 2003. Values, Cleavages and Party Choice in France, 1988–1995. *French Politics* 1 (1): 83–114.

Anderson, Cameron D. 2006. Economic Voting and Multilevel Governance: A Comparative Individual-Level Analysis. *American Journal of Political Science* 50 (2): 449–63.

Andeweg, Rudy B., and Jacques Thomassen, eds. 2011. *Van afspiegelen naar afrekenen?* Amsterdam: Amsterdam University Press:.

Andeweg, Rudy B., and Arco Timmermans. 2008. Conflict Management in Coalition Governance. In *Coalition Bargaining: The Democratic Life Cycle in Western Europe*, edited by Kaare Strøm, Wolfgang C. Müller, and Torbjorn Bergman. Oxford: Oxford University Press.

Arter, David. 1999a. Party System Change in Scandinavia since 1970: "Restricted Change" or "General Change." *West European Politics* 22 (3): 139–58.

Arter, David. 1999b. *Scandinavian Politics Today*. Manchester: Manchester University Press.

Axelrod, Robert M. 1970. *Conflict of Interest: A Theory of Divergent Goals with Applications to Politics*. Chicago: Markham.

Bachrach, Peter, and Morton Baratz. 1962. Two Faces of Power. *American Political Science Review* 56: 947–52.

Bakvis, Heman, and Grace Skogstad. 2002. *Canadian Federalism: Performance, Effectiveness, and Legitimacy*. Toronto: Oxford University Press.

Bara, Judith. 2005. A Question of Trust: Implementing Party Manifestos. *Parliamentary Affairs* 58 (3): 585–99.

Barker, Paul. 1988. The Development of Major Shared-Cost Programs in Canada. In *Perspectives on Canadian Federalism*, edited by R. D. Olling and M. W. Westmacott. Scarborough: Prentice-Hall Canada.

Baumgartner, Frank R., Christian Breunig, Christoffer Green-Pedersen, Bryan D. Jones, Peter B. Mortensen, Michiel Nuytemans, and Stefaan Walgrave. 2009. Punctuated Equilibrium in Comparative Perspective. *American Journal of Political Science* 53 (3): 603–20.

Baumgartner, Frank R., Sylvain Brouard, and Emiliano Grossman. 2009. Agenda-Setting Dynamics in France: Revisiting the "Partisan Hypothesis." *French Politics* 7 (2): 75–95.

Baumgartner, Frank R., Suzanna L. De Boef, and Amber E. Boydstun. 2008. *The Decline of the Death Penalty and the Discovery of Innocence*. Cambridge and New York: Cambridge University Press.

Baumgartner, Frank R., Martial Foucault, and Abel François. 2009. Public Budgeting in the French Fifth Republic: The End of "La République des partis"? *West European Politics* 32 (4): 404–22.

Baumgartner, Frank R., Christoffer Green-Pedersen, and Bryan Jones. 2006. Comparative Studies of Policy Agendas. *Journal of European Public Policy* 13 (7): 959–1132.

Baumgartner, Frank R., and Bryan D. Jones. 1993. *Agendas and Instability in American Politics*. Chicago: University of Chicago Press.

Baumgartner, Frank R., and Bryan D. Jones. 2002. *Policy Dynamics*. Chicago: University of Chicago Press.

Baumgartner, Frank R., and Bryan D. Jones. 2009. *Agendas and Instability in American Politics*. 2nd ed. Chicago: University of Chicago Press.

Baumgartner, Frank R., and Bryan D. Jones. 2013. *The Politics of Information*. Unpublished manuscript. Chapel Hill and Austin.

Baumgartner, Frank R., Bryan D. Jones, and John Wilkerson. 2011. Comparative Studies of Policy Dynamics. *Comparative Political Studies* 44(8): 947–72.

Benoit, Kenneth, and Michael Laver. 2006. *Party Policy in Modern Democracies*. London: Routledge.

Besley, Timothy, and Anne Case. 1995. Incumbent Behavior: Vote-Seeking, Tax-Setting, and Yardstick Competition. *American Economic Review* 85 (1): 25–45.

Bevan, Shaun, Peter John, and Will Jennings. 2011. Keeping Party Programmes on Track: The Transmission of the Policy Agendas of the Speech from the Throne to Acts of the UK Parliament. *European Political Science Review* 3 (3): 395–417.

Black, Edwin R., and Alan C. Cairns. 1966. A Different Perspective on Canadian Federalism. *Canadian Public Administration* 9 (1): 27–44.

Boadway, Robin, and Anwar Shah. 2009. *Fiscal Federalism, Principles and Practice of Multiorder Governance*. Cambridge: Cambridge University Press.

Boix, Carles. 2006. The Roots of Democracy. *Policy Review* 35 (135): 1–32.

Borghetto, Enrico, and Marcello Carammia. 2010. L'analisi comparata delle agenda politiche: il Comparative Agendas Project. *Rivista Italiana di Scienza Politica* 2010 (2): 301–15.

Borghetto, Enrico, Luigi Curini, Marco Giuliani, Alessandro Pellegata, and Francesco Zucchini. 2012. Italian Law-Making Archive: A New Tool for the Analysis of the Italian Legislative Process. *Rivista Italiana di Scienza Politica* 2012 (3): 481–501.

Bornschier, Simon, and Romain Lachat. 2009. The Evolution of the French Political Space and Party System. *West European Politics* 32 (2): 360–83.

Börzel, Tanja A. 2006. Europäisierung der deutschen Politik? In *Regieren in der Bundesrepublik Deutschland: Innen- und Außenpolitik seit 1949*, edited by Manfred G. Schmidt and Reimut Zohlnhöfer, 491–512. Wiesbaden: VS Verlag.

Bräuninger, Thomas, and Marc Debus. 2009. Legislative Agenda-Setting in Parliamentary Democracies. *European Journal of Political Research* 48 (6): 804–39.

Bräuninger, Thomas, and Thomas König. 1999. The Checks and Balances of Party Federalism: German Federal Government in a Divided Legislature. *European Journal of Political Research* 36 (2): 207–34.

Breeman, Gerard, and Arco Timmermans. 2009. *Codeboek Nederlands Agenda Project*. Wageningen: Wageningen University; Leiden: Leiden University.

Breeman, Gerard, and Arco Timmermans. 2012. Myths and Milestones: The Europeanization of the Legislative Agenda in the Netherlands. In Oliver Costa, Sylvain Brouard, and Thomas König (eds.), *The Europeanization of Domestic Legislatures: The Empirical Implications of the Delors' Myth in Nine Countries*, 151–72. New York: Springer.

Breeman, Gerard, David Lowery, Caelesta Poppelaars, Sandra Resodihardjo, Arco Timmermans, and Jouke de Vries. 2009. Political Attention in a Coalition System: Analyzing Queen's Speeches in the Netherlands, 1945–2007. *Acta Politica* 44 (1): 1–27.

Breton, Albert. 1988. Competition and Cooperation in the Canadian Federal System. In *Perspectives on Canadian Federalism*, edited by R. D. Olling and M. W. Westmacott, 285–88. Scarborough: Prentice-Hall Canada.

Breunig, Christian. 2011. Reduction, Stasis, and Expansion of Budgets in Advanced Democracies. *Comparative Political Studies* 44 (8): 1060–88.

Brouard, Sylvain, Andrew Appleton, and Amy Mazur. 2008. *The French Fifth Republic at Fifty? Beyond Stereotypes*. Basingstoke: Palgrave.

Brouard, Sylvain, Olivier Costa, and Thomas Köning, eds. 2012. *The Europeanization of Domestic Legislatures: The Empirical Implications of the Delors' Myth in Nine Countries*, 75–94. New York: Jon Springer.

Brouard, Sylvain, Emiliano Grossman, and Isabelle Guinaudeau. 2012. La compétition partisane française au prisme des priorités électorales. *Revue française de science politique* 62 (2): 255–76.

Brunner, Matthias, and Pascal Sciarini. 2002. L'opposition ouverture-traditions. In *Changements de valeurs et nouveaux clivages politiques en Suisse*, edited by Simon Hug and Pascal Sciarini, 29–93. Paris: L'Harmattan.

Budge, Ian, and Dennis Farlie, eds. 1983. *Explaining and Predicting Elections: Issue Effects and Party Strategies in Twenty-three Democracies*. London and Boston: Allen & Unwin.

Budge, Ian, and Dennis Farlie. 1983. Party Competition—Selective Emphasis or Direct Confrontation? An Alternative View with Data. In *West European Party Systems. Continuity and Change*, edited by Hans Daadler and Peter Mair, 267–305. London: Sage.

Budge, Ian, and Richard I. Hofferbert. 1990. Mandates and Policy Outputs: U.S. Party Platforms and Federal Expenditures. *American Political Science Review* 84 (1): 111–32.

Budge, Ian, and Hans Keman. 1990. *Parties and Democracy: Coalition Formation and Functioning in Twenty States*. Oxford: Oxford University Press

Budge, Ian, and David McKay. 1994. *Developing Democracy*. London: Sage Publications.

Budge, Ian, Hans-Dieter Klingemann, Andrea Volkens, and Judith Bara. 2001. *Mapping Policy Preferences: Estimates for Parties, Governments and Electors, 1945–1998*. Oxford: Oxford University Press.

Bull, Martin J., and Martin Rhodes. 2007. Introduction—Italy: A Contested Polity. *West European Politics* 30 (4): 657–69.

Burkhart, Simone. 2008. *Deutsche Bundesgesetzgebung 1972–2005*. Release 1.0.Vertrieb über GESIS Datenarchiv, ZA4569. www.gesis.org/ZA/index.htm.

Cameron, David, and Richard Simeon. 2002. Intergovernmental Relations in Canada: The Emergence of Collaborative Federalism. *Publius* 32 (2): 49–71.

Capano, Giliberto, and Marco Giuliani. 2001. Governing without Surviving? An Italian Paradox: Law-Making in Italy, 1987–2001. *Journal of Legislative Studies* 7 (4): 13–36.

Carmines, Edward G. 1991. The Logic of Party Alignments. *Journal of Theoretical Politics* 3 (1): 65–80.

Carmines, Edward G., and James A. Stimson. 1993. On the Evolution of Political Issues. In *Agenda Formation*, edited by William Riker, 151–68. Ann Arbor: University of Michigan Press.

Castles, Frank, ed. 1982. *The Impact of Parties Politics and Policies in Democratic Capitalist States*. London: Sage.

Chaqués-Bonafont, Laura, and Anna M. Palau. 2011a. Are Spanish Policy-Makers Responding to Citizens' Priorities? *West European Politics* 34 (4): 706–30.

Chaqués-Bonafont, Laura, and Anna M. Palau. 2011b. Comparing Law-Making Activities in a Quasi-Federal System of Government: The Case of Spain. *Comparative Political Studies* 44 (8): 1089–1119.

Chaqués-Bonafont, Laura, Anna M. Palau, Luz Muñoz, and John D. Wilkerson. 2008. Comparing Governmental Agendas: Evolution of the Prioritization of Issues in the USA and Spain. *IBEI Working Papers* 14, pp. 1–30.

Chiaramonte, Alessandro. 2007. Il nuovo sistema partitico italiano tra bipolarismo e frammentazione. In *Proporzionale ma non solo: le elezioni politiche del 2006*, edited by Roberto D'Alimonte and Alessandro Chiaramonte, 369–406. Bologna: Il Mulino.

Chiche, Jean, Brigitte Le Roux, Pascal Perrineau, and Henri Rouanet. 2000. L'espace politique des électeurs français à la fin des années 1990: Nouveaux et anciens clivages, hétérogénéité des électorats. *Revue française de science politique* 50 (3): 463–88.

Church, Clive H., and Adrian Vatter. 2009. Opposition in Consensual Switzerland: A Short but Significant Experiment. *Government and Opposition* 44 (4): 412–37.

Clinton, Joshua, and John Lapinski. 2006. Measuring Legislative Accomplishment, 1877–1994. *American Journal of Political Science* 50(1): 232–49.

Cobb, Roger W., and Charles D. Elder. 1983. *Participation in American Politics*. Baltimore: Johns Hopkins University Press.

Colomer, Josep María. 1999. *El arte de la manipulación política*. Barcelona: Anagrama.

Constantelos, John. 2010. Playing the Field: Federalism and the Politics of Venue Shopping in the United States and Canada. *Publius* 40 (3): 460–83.

Cowley, Phil. 2005. *The Rebels: How Blair Mislaid his Majority*. London: Politicos.

Curtice, John. 2010. So What Went Wrong with the Electoral System? The 2010 Election Result and the Debate about Electoral Reform. *Parliamentary Affairs* 63 (4): 623–38.

D'Alimonte, Roberto, and Stefano Bartolini, eds. 2002. *Maggioritario finalmente? La transizione elettorale, 1994–2001*. Bologna: Il Mulino.

Damgaard, Erik. 2008. Cabinet Termination in Western Europe. In *Coalition Bargaining: The Democratic Life Cycle in Western Europe*, edited by Kaare Strøm, Wolfgang C. Müller, and Torbjorn Bergman, 301–26. Oxford: Oxford University Press.

Damgaard, Erik, and Palle Svensson. 1989. Who Governs? Parties and Policies in Denmark. *European Journal of Political Research* 17 (6): 731–45.

Damore, David F. 2004. The Dynamics of Issue Ownership in Presidential Campaigns. *Political Research Quarterly* 57 (3): 391–97.

Damore, David F. 2005. Issue Convergence in Presidential Campaigns. *Political Behavior* 27 (1): 71–97.

De Micheli, Chiara, and Luca Verzichelli. 2004. *Il parlamento*. Bologna: Il Mulino.

De Winter, Lieven. 2004. Government Declarations and Law Production. In *Patterns of Parliamentary Behavior: Passage of Legislation across Western Europe*, edited by Herbert Döring and Mark Hallerberg, 35–51. Aldershot: Ashgate.

Dearing, James W., and Everett M. Rogers. 1996. *Agenda-Setting*. London: Sage.

Deschouwer, Kris. 2009. *The Politics of Belgium*. Houndsmills, Basingstoke: Palgrave.

Deschouwer, Kris, Lieven de Winter, and Donatella della Porta, eds. 1996. *Partitocracies between Crises and Reform*. Brussels: Politologish Instituut.

Dodd, Lawrence C. 1976. *Coalitions in Parliamentary Government*. Princeton: Princeton University Press.

Dolowitz, David P., and David Marsh. 1996. Who Learns What from Whom: A Review of the Policy Transfer Literature. *Political Studies* 44 (2): 343–57.

Döring, Herbert, and Mark Hallerberg, eds. 2004. *Patterns of Parliamentary Behaviour: Passage of Legislation across Western Europe*. Aldershot: Ashgate.

Downs, Anthony. 1957. *An Economic Theory of Democracy*. New York: Harper & Row.

Elklit, Jørgen, and Mogens N. Pedersen. 2003. Decembervalget 1973: 30 år efter. *Politica* 35 (4): 365–76.

Elmelund-Præstekær, Christian, Ulrik Kjær, and Jørgen Elklit. 2010. The Massive Stability of the Danish Multi-Party System. A Pyrrhic Victory? In *Political Parties and Democracy*, edited by Kay Lawson, 121–38. New York: Praeger.

Erikson, Robert, Michael MacKuen, and James Stimson. 2002. *The MacroPolity*. Cambridge: Cambridge University Press.

Esping-Andersen, Gøsta. 1999. *Social Foundations of Postindustrial Economies*. New York: Oxford University Press.

Ezrow, Lawrence. 2007. The Variance Matters: How Party Systems Represent the Preferences of Voters. *Journal of Politics* 69 (1): 182–92.

Farrall, Stephen, and Will Jennings. 2012. Policy Feedback and the Criminal Justice Agenda: an Analysis of the Economy, Crime Rates, Politics and Public Opinion in Post-war Britain. *Journal of Contemporary British History* 26 (4): 467–88.

Ferejohn, John. 1999. Accountability and Authority: Toward a Theory of Political Accountability. In *Democracy, Accountability and Representation*, edited by Adam Przeworski, Susan Stokes, and Bernard Manin, 131–54. Cambridge: Cambridge University Press.

Filippov, Mikhail, Peter Ordeshook, and Olga Shvetsova. 2004. *Designing Federalism: A Theory of Self-Sustainable Federal Institutions*. Cambridge: Cambridge University Press.

Galli, Giorgio. 2000. *I partiti politici italiani (1943–2000)*. Milan: Rizzoli.

Garrett, Geoffrey. 1998. *Partisan Politics in the Global Economy*. Cambridge: Cambridge University Press.

Gilardi, Fabrizio. 2010. Who Learns from What in Policy Diffusion Processes? *American Journal of Political Science* 54 (3): 650–66.

Ginsborg, Paul. 2005. *Silvio Berlusconi: Television, Power and Patrimony*. London and New York: Verso.

Giugni, Marco, and Pascal Sciarini. 2009. Polarisation et politisation en Suisse. In *Rapport social 2008*, edited by Christian Suter, Silvia Perrenoud, René Lévy, Ursina Kuhn, Dominique Joye, and Pascale Gazareth, 222–43. Zurich: Seismo.

Goul Andersen, Jørgen. 1990. Denmark: Environmental Conflict and the "Greening" of the Labour Movement. *Scandinavian Political Studies* 13 (2): 185–210.

Grande, Edgar. 2008. Globalizing West European Politics: The Change of Cleavage Structures, Parties, and Party Systems in Comparative Perspective. In *West European Politics in the Age of Globalization*, edited by Hanspeter Kriesi, Edgar Grande, Romain Lachat, Martin Dolezal, Simon Bornschier, and Timotheos Frey, 320–43. Cambridge: Cambridge University Press.

Green-Pedersen, Christoffer. 2001. Minority Governments and Party Politics: The Political and Institutional Background to the "Danish Miracle." *Journal of Public Policy* 21 (1): 63–80.

Green-Pedersen, Christoffer. 2005. *The Political Agenda in Denmark: Measurement and Trends since 1953*. Aarhus: Department of Political Science, Aarhus University.

Green-Pedersen, Christoffer. 2006. Long-Term Changes in Danish Party Politics: The Rise and Importance of Issue Competition. *Scandinavian Political Studies* 29 (3): 221–37.

Green-Pedersen, Christoffer. 2007. The Growing Importance of Issue Competition: The Changing Nature of Party Competition in Western Europe. *Political Studies* 55 (4): 608–28.

Green-Pedersen, Christoffer. 2012. A Giant Fast Asleep? Party Incentives and the Politicisation of European Integration. *Political Studies* 60 (1): 115–30.

Green-Pedersen, Christoffer, and Jesper Krogstrup. 2008. Immigration as a Political Issue in Denmark and Sweden: How Party Competition Shapes Political Agendas. *European Journal of Political Research* 47 (5): 610–34.

Green-Pedersen, Christoffer, and Peter B. Mortensen. 2009. Issue Competition and Election Campaigns: Avoidance *and* Engagement. Potsdam, ECPR Conference. http://www.agendasetting.dk /papers /uploaded /115201044905PM.pdf.

Green-Pedersen, Christoffer, and Peter B. Mortensen. 2010. Who Sets the Agenda and Who Responds to It in the Danish Parliament? *European Journal of Political Research* 49 (2): 257–81.

Green-Pedersen, Christoffer, and Asbjørn Skjæveland. 2008. Le Danemark. In *Les démocraties européennes*, edited by Jean-Michiel de Waele and Paul Magnette, 103–19. Paris: Armand Colin.

Green-Pedersen, Christoffer, and Rune Stubager. 2010. The Political Conditionality of Mass Media Influence: When Do Parties Follow Mass Media Attention? *British Journal of Political Science* 40 (3): 663–77.

Green-Pedersen, Christoffer, and Lisbeth H. Thomsen. 2005. Bloc Politics vs. Broad Cooperation: The Functioning of Danish Minority Parliamentarism. *The Journal of Legislative Studies* 11 (2): 153–69.

Green-Pedersen, Christoffer, and John Wilkerson. 2006. How Agenda-Setting Attributes Shape Politics: Problem Attention, Agenda Dynamics and Comparative Health Politics Developments in the U.S. and Denmark. *Journal of European Public Policy* 13 (7): 1039–52.

Green-Pedersen, Christoffer, and Michelle Wolfe. 2009. The Hare and the Tortoise Once Again: The Institutionalization of Environmental Attention in the US and Denmark. *Governance* 22 (4): 625–46.

Grossman, Emiliano, and Nicolas Sauger. 2009. French Political Institutions at Fifty (special issue). *West European Politics* 34 (4): 243–437.

Grossmann, Matt. 2013. The Variable Politics of the Policy Process: Issue Area Differences and Comparative Networks. *Journal of Politics* 75 (1): 65–79.

Grunberg, Gérard, and Florence Haegel. 2007. *La France vers le bipartisme ? La présidentialisation du PS et de l'UMP*. Paris: Presses de Sciences Po.

Grunberg, Gérard, and Etienne Schweissguth. 1997. Vers une tripartition de l'espace politique. In *L'électeur a ses raisons*, edited by Daniel Boy and Nonna Mayer, 179–218. Paris: Presses de Sciences Po.

Gunther, Richard, and José Ramón Montero. 2009. *The Politics of Spain*. Cambridge: Cambridge University Press.

Hansen, Martin Ejnar. 2008. Reconsidering the Party Distances and Dimensionality of the Danish Folketing. *Journal of Legislative Studies* 14 (3): 264–78.

Heller, William. B. 2001. Making Policy Stick: Why the Government Gets What It Wants in Multiparty Parliaments. *American Journal of Political Science* 45 (4): 780–98.

Helms, Ludger. 2004. Five Ways of Institutionalizing Political Opposition: Lessons from the Advanced Democracies. *Government and Opposition* 39 (1): 22–54.

Hibbs, Douglas. 1977. Political Parties and Macroeconomic Policy. *American Political Science Review* 71 (4): 1467–87.

Hill, Jeffrey, and Kenneth Williams. 1993. The Decline of Private Bills. *American Journal of Political Science* 37 (4): 1008–31.

Hindmoor, Andrew. 2004. *New Labour at the Centre: Constructing Political Space*. Oxford: Oxford University Press.

Hix, Simon, and Klaus H. Goetz. 2000. Introduction: European Integration and National Political Systems. *West European Politics* 23 (4): 1–26.

Hobolt, Sara B., and Robert Klemmensen. 2005. Responsive Government? Public Opinion and Government Policy Preferences in Britain and Denmark. *Political Studies* 53 (2): 379–402.

Hobolt, Sara B., and Robert Klemmensen. 2008. Government Responsiveness and Political Competition in Comparative Perspective. *Comparative Political Studies* 41 (3): 309–37.

Hofferbert, Richard I., and Ian Budge. 1992. The Party Mandate and the Westminster Model: Election Programmes and Government Spending in Britain, 1948–85. *British Journal of Political Science* 22(2): 151–82.

Hooghe, Liesbet, Gary Marks, and Arjan H. Schakel. 2008. Regional Authority in 42 Democracies, 1950–2006: A Measure and Five Hypotheses. *Regional and Federal Studies* 18 (2–3): 111–302.

Howell, William, Scott Adler, Charles Cameron, and Charles Rieman. 2000. Divided Government and the Legislative Productivity of Congress, 1945–94. *Legislative Studies Quarterly* 25(2): 285–312.

Hug, Simon. 2001. *Altering Party Systems*. Ann Arbor: University of Michigan Press.

Hug, Simon, and Alexandre Trechsel. 2002. Clivage et identification partisane. In *Changements de valeurs et nouveaux clivages politiques en Suisse*, edited by Simon Hug and Pascal Sciarini, 207–35. Paris: L'Harmattan.

Ignazi, Piero. 1992. The Silent Counter-Revolution: Hypotheses on the Emergence of Extreme Right-Wing Parties in Europe. *European Journal of Political Research* 22 (1): 3–34.

Jennings, Will, and Peter John. 2009. The Dynamics of Political Attention: Public Opinion and the Queen's Speech in the United Kingdom. *American Journal of Political Science* 53 (4): 838–54.

Jennings, Will, Shaun Bevan, Arco Timmermans, Gerard Breeman, Sylvain Brouard, Laura Chaques, Christoffer Green-Pedersen, Peter John, Peter B. Mortensen, and Anna Palau. 2011. Effects of the Core Functions of Government on the Diversity of Executive Agendas. *Comparative Political Studies* 44 (8): 1001–30.

John, Peter, and Will Jennings. 2010. Punctuations and Turning Points in British

Politics: The Policy Agenda of the Queen's Speech, 1940–2005. *British Journal of Political Science* 40 (3): 561–86.

John, Peter, Anthony Bertelli, Will Jennings, and Shaun Bevan. 2013. *Policy Agendas in British Politics*. Basingstoke: Palgrave.

John, Peter, Shaun Bevan, and Will Jennings. 2011. The Policy-Opinion Link and Institutional Change: The Policy Agenda of the United Kingdom and Scottish Parliaments, 1977–2008. *Journal of European Public Policy* 18 (7): 1052–1068.

Jones, Bryan D. 2001. *Politics and the Architecture of Choice*. Chicago: University of Chicago Press.

Jones, Bryan D., and Frank R. Baumgartner. 2005. *The Politics of Attention. How Government Prioritizes Problems*. Chicago: University of Chicago Press.

Jones, Bryan D., Heather Larsen-Price, and John Wilkerson. 2009. Representation and American Governing Institutions. *Journal of Politics* 71 (2): 277–90.

Jones, Bryan D., Frank R. Baumgartner, Christian Breunig, Christopher Wlezien, Stuart Soroka, Martial Foucault, Abel François, Christoffer Green-Pedersen, Peter John, Chris Koski, Peter B. Mortensen, Frédéric Varone, and Stefaan Walgrave. 2009. A General Empirical Law of Public Budgets: A Comparative Analysis. *American Journal of Political Science* 53 (4): 855–73.

Katzenstein, Peter. 1987. *Policy and Politics in West Germany: The Growth of a Semisovereign State*. Philadelphia: Temple University Press.

Kerr, Henry. 1978. The Structure of Opposition in the Swiss Parliament. *Legislative Studies Quarterly* 3 (1): 51–62.

Kingdon, John W. 1995. *Agendas, Alternatives, and Public Policies*. New York: HarperCollins.

Kitschelt, Herbert. 1995. *The Radical Right in Western Europe: A Comparative Analysis*. Ann Arbor: University of Michigan Press.

Kitschelt, Herbert. 2007. Party Systems. In *The Oxford Handbook of Comparative Politics*, edited by Carles Boix and Susan Stokes, 522–54. Oxford: Oxford University Press.

Klingemann, Hans-Dieter, Richard I. Hofferbert, and Ian Budge. 1994. *Parties, Policies and Democracy*. Boulder, CO: Westview Press.

Krause, Rachel M. 2011. Policy Innovation, Intergovernmental Relations, and the Adoption of Climate Protection Initiatives by U.S. Cities. *Journal of Urban Affairs* 33 (1): 45–60.

Kriesi, Hanspeter. 1998. *Le système politique suisse*. 2nd ed. Paris: Economica.

Kriesi, Hanspeter, and Pascal Sciarini. 2003. Opinion Stability and Change During an Electoral Campaign: Results from the 1999 Swiss Election Panel Study. *International Journal of Public Opinion Research* 15 (4): 431–53.

Kriesi, Hanspeter, and Alexander H. Trechsel. 2008. *The Politics of Switzerland: Continuity and Change in a Consensus Democracy*. Cambridge: Cambridge University Press.

Kriesi, Hanspeter, Edgar Grande, Romain Lachat, Martin Dolezal, Simon Bornschier, and Timotheus Frey. 2008. *West European Politics in the Age of Globalization*. Cambridge: Cambridge University Press.

Krutz, Glen. 2000. Getting Around Gridlock: The Effect of Omnibus Utilization on Legislative Productivity. *Legislative Studies Quarterly* 25 (4): 533–49.

Lachat, Romain. 2008a. The Impact of Party Polarization on Ideological Voting. *Electoral Studies* 27 (4): 687–98.

Lachat, Romain. 2008b. Switzerland: Another Case of Transformation Driven by an Established Party. In *West European Politics in the Age of Globalization*, edited by Hanspeter Kriesi, Edgar Grande, Romain Lachat, Martin Dolezal, Simon Bornschier, and Timotheos Frey, 130–53. Cambridge: Cambridge University Press.

Lago, Ignacio, and Santiago Lago. 2011. *Descentralización y control electoral de los gobiernos en España*. Barcelona: Institut d'Estudis Autonòmics.

Lapinski, John. 2008. Policy Substance and Performance in American Lawmaking, 1877–1994. *American Journal of Political Science* 52 (2): 235–51.

Laver, Michael, and Norman Schofield. 1990. *Multiparty Government: The Politics of Coalition in Europe*. Oxford: Oxford University Press.

Laver, Michael, and Kenneth A. Shepsle. 1996. *Making and Breaking Governments: Cabinets and Legislatures*. New York: Cambridge University Press.

Laver, Michael, Kenneth Benoit, and John Garry. 2003. Estimating the Policy Positions of Political Actors Using Words as Data. *American Political Science Review* 97 (2): 311–31.

Lehmbruch, Gerhard. 1990. Die improvisierte Vereinigung: die dritte deutsche Republik. *Leviathan* 18 (3): 462–86.

Lehmbruch, Gerhard. 2000. *Parteienwettbewerb im Bundesstaat: Regelsysteme und Spannungslagen im politischen System der Bundesrepublik Deutschland*. Wiesbaden: Westdeutscher Verlag.

Lehnert, Matthias, Eric Linhart, and Susumu Shikano. 2008. Never Say Never Again: Legislative Failure in German Bicameralism. *German Politics* 17 (3): 367–80.

Lijphart, Arend. 1975. *Politics of Accommodation: Pluralism and Democracy in the Netherlands*. Berkeley and Los Angeles: University of California Press.

Lijphart, Arend. 1979. Religious vs. Linguistic vs. Class Voting: The "Crucial Experiment" of Comparing Belgium, Canada, South Africa, and Switzerland. *American Political Science Review* 73 (4): 442–58.

Lijphart, Arend. 1999. *Patterns of Democracy: Government Forms and Performance in Thirty-six Countries*. New Haven: Yale University Press.

Linder, Wolf. 2007. Direct Democracy. In *Handbook of Swiss Politics/Handbuch der Schweizer Politik*, edited by Ulrich Klöti, Peter Knoepfel, Hanspeter Kriesi, Yannis Papadopoulos, and Pascal Sciarini, 101–20. Zurich: Verlag Neue Zürcher Zeitung.

Linz, Juan, and Alfred Stepan. 1996. *Problems of Democratic Transition and Consolidation: Southern Europe, South America, and Post-Communist Europe*. Baltimore: Johns Hopkins University Press.

Lipset, Seymour M., and Stein Rokkan. 1967. Cleavage Structures, Party Systems, and Voter Alignments. In *Consensus and Conflict: Essays in Political Sociology*, edited by Seymour M. Lipset, 1–64. New Brunswick: Transaction Books.

Luebbert, Gregory M. 1986. *Comparative Democracy*. New York: Columbia University Press.

Mair, Peter. 1997. *Party System Change*. Oxford: Clarendon Press.

Mair, Peter. 2006. Cleavages. In *Handbook of Party Politics*, edited by Richard Katz and William Crotty, 371–75. London: Sage.

Manin, Bernard, Adam Przeworski, and Susan C. Stokes. 1999. Elections and Representation. In *Democracy, Accountability and Representation*, edited by Adam Przeworski, Susan C. Stokes, and Bernard Manin, 29–54. Cambridge: Cambridge University Press.

Manow, Philip, and Simone Burkhart. 2007. Legislative Self-Restraint under Divided Government in Germany, 1976–2002. *Legislative Studies Quarterly* 32 (2): 167–91.

Maravall, José María. 1999. Accountability and Manipulation. In *Democracy, Accountability and Representation*, edited by Adam Przeworski, Susan C. Stokes, and Bernard Manin, 154–96. Cambridge: Cambridge University Press.

Martin, Lanny W. 2004. The Government Agenda in Parliamentary Democracies. *American Journal of Political Science* 48 (3): 445–61.

Martin, Lanny W., and Georg Vanberg. 2004. Policing the Bargain: Coalition Government and Parliamentary Scrutiny. *American Journal of Political Science* 48 (1): 13–27.

Martin, Lanny W., and Georg Vanberg. 2011. *Parliaments and Coalitions: The Role of Legislative Institutions in Multiparty Governance*. Oxford: Oxford University Press.

Mayhew, David. 1991. *Divided We Govern*. New Haven: Yale University Press.

Mazzoleni, Oscar. 2003. *Nationalisme et populisme en Suisse: La radicalisation de la "nouvelle" UDC*. Lausanne: Presses Polytechniques et Universitaires Romandes.

McDonald, Michael D., and Ian Budge. 2005. *Elections, Parties, Democracy: Conferring the Median Mandate*. Oxford: Oxford University Press.

Meguid, Bonnie M. 2005. The Role of Mainstream Party Strategy in Niche Party Success. *American Political Science Review* 99 (3): 347–59.

Meguid, Bonnie M. 2008. *Party Competition between Unequals: Strategies and Electoral Fortunes in Western Europe*. New York: Cambridge University Press.

Michelat, Guy, and Michel Simon. 2004. *Les ouvriers et la politique: permanence, ruptures, réalignements*. Paris: Presses de Sciences Po.

Montpetit, Éric. 2006. Declining Legitimacy and Canadian Federalism: An Examination of Policy-Making in Agriculture and Biomedicine. In *Continuity and Change in Canadian Politics*, edited by Michelmann Hans and Cristine de Clercy, 89–116. Toronto: University of Toronto Press.

Montpetit, Éric, and Martial Foucault. 2012. Canadian Federalism and Change in Policy Attention: A Comparison with the United Kingdom. *Canadian Journal of Political Science* 45 (3): 635–56.

Mortensen, Peter. 2009. Political Attention and Public Spending in the United States. *Policy Studies Journal* 37 (3): 435–55.

Mortensen, Peter B. 2006. *The Impact of Public Opinion on Public Policy*. Aarhus: Politica.

Mortensen, Peter B., Christoffer Green-Pedersen, Gerard Breeman, Will Jennings, Peter John, Arco Timmermans, Laura Chaques, and Anna Palau. 2011. Comparing Government Agendas: Executive Speeches in the Netherlands, United Kingdom and Denmark. *Comparative Political Studies* 44 (8): 973–1000.

Moury, Catherine. 2011. Italian Coalitions and Electoral Promises: Assessing the Democratic Performance of the Prodi I and Berlusconi II Governments. *Modern Italy* 16 (1): 35–50.

Moury, Catherine. 2012. *Coalition Government and Party Mandate: How Coalition Agreements Constrain Ministerial Action.* London: Routledge.

Moury, Catherine, and Arco Timmermans. 2008. Conflitto e accordo in governi di coalizione: Il caso Italia. *Rivista italiana di scienza politica* 38 (3): 417–43.

Müller, Wolfgang C., and Kaare Strøm, eds. 2000. *Coalition Governments in Western Europe.* Oxford: Oxford University Press.

Müller, Wolfgang C., and Kaare Strøm. 2008. Coalition Agreements and Cabinet Governance. In *Coalition Bargaining: The Democratic Life Cycle in Western Europe*, edited by Kaare Strøm, Wolfgang C. Müller, and Torbjorn Bergman, 159–199. Oxford: Oxford University Press.

Müller, Wolfgang C., and Thomas M. Meyer. 2010. Mutual Veto? How Coalitions Work. In *Reform Processes and Policy Change: Veto Players and Decision-Making in Modern Democracies*, edited by Thomas König, George Tsebelis and Marc Debus, 99–124. New York: Springer.

Namenwirth, J. Zvi, and Robert P. Weber. 1987. *Dynamics of Culture.* London: Allen & Unwin.

Nannestad, Peter. 1989. *Reactive Voting in Danish General Elections, 1971–1979.* Aarhus: Aarhus University Press.

Newell, James L. 2000. *Parties and Democracy in Italy.* Aldershot: Ashgate.

Neidhart, Leonard. 1970. *Plebiszit und pluralitäre Demokratie: Eine Analyse der Funktionen des schweizerischen Gesetzesreferendum.* Bern: Francke.

Nicholson-Crotty, Sean. 2009. The Politics of Diffusion: Public Policy in the American States. *Journal of Politics* 71 (1): 192–205.

Nicolet, Sarah, and Pascal Sciarini, eds. 2010. *Le destin électoral de la gauche: Analyse du vote socialiste et vert en Suisse.* Geneva: Georg.

Norporth, Helmut, and Bruce Buchanan. 1992. Wanted: The Education President; Issue Trespassing by Political Candidates. *Public Opinion Quarterly* 56 (1): 87–99.

Norton, Philip. 2005. *Parliament in British Politics.* Basingstoke: Palgrave Macmillan.

Oesch, Daniel. 2008. Explaining Workers' Support for Right-Wing Populist Parties in Western Europe: Evidence from Austria, Belgium, France, Norway and Switzerland. *International Political Science Review* 29 (3): 349–73.

Palau, Anna M., and Laura Chaqués-Bonafant. 2012. The Europeanization of Law-Making Activities in Spain. In *The Europeanization of Domestic Legislatures: The Empirical Implications of the Delors' Myth in Nine Countries*, edited by Sylvain Brouard, Olivier Costa, and Thomas Köning, 173–96. New York: Jon Springer.

Pedersen, Mogens N. 1987. The Danish "Working Multiparty System": Breakdown or

Adaptation. In *Party Systems in Denmark, Austria, Switzerland, the Netherlands, and Belgium*, edited by Hans Daalder, 1–60. London: Frances Pinter.

Pedersen, Mogens N. 1988. The Defeat of All Parties: The Danish Folketing Election, 1973. In *When Parties Fail*, edited by Kay Lawson and Peter H. Merkl, 257–81. Princeton: Princeton University Press.

Peterson, Robert L., and Martine M. De Ridder. 1986. Government Formation as a Policy-Making Arena. *Legislative Studies Quarterly* 11 (4): 565–81.

Petrocik, John R. 1996. Issue Ownership in Presidential Elections with a 1980 Case Study. *American Journal of Political Science* 40 (3): 825–50.

Pétry, François, and Benoît Collette. 2009. Measuring How Political Parties Keep Their Promises: A Positive Perspective from Political Science. In *Do They Walk Like They Talk?*, edited by Louis Imbeau, 65–80. New York: Springer.

Rasch, Bjørn-Erik, and George Tsebelis, eds. 2011. *The Role of Governments in Legislative Agenda Setting*. London: Routledge.

Rice, James J., and Michael J. Prince. 2000. *Changing Politics of Canadian Social Policy*. Toronto: University of Toronto Press.

Riker, William. 1962. *The Theory of Political Coalitions*. New Haven: Yale University Press.

Riker, William. 1996. *The Strategy of Rhetoric: Campaigning for the American Constitution*. New Haven: Yale University Press.

Risse, Thomas, Maria G. Cowles, and James Caporaso. 2001. Europeanization and Domestic Change: Introduction. In *Transforming Europe: Europeanization and Domestic Change*, edited by Maria G. Cowles, James Caporaso, and Thomas Risse, 1–20. Ithaca: Cornell University Press.

Risse, Thomas, and Marianne van de Steeg. 2003. An Emerging European Public Sphere? Empirical Evidence and Theoretical Clarifications. Paper presented at the Europeanisation of the Public Spheres, Political Mobilisation, Public Communication and the European Union, 20–22 June.

Robertson, David. 1976. *A Theory of Party Competition*. London: Wiley.

Rose, Richard. 1980. *Do Parties Make a Difference?* London: Macmillan.

Rose, Richard. 1983. Still the Era of Party Government. *Parliamentary Affairs* 36 (3): 282–99.

Rose, Richard, and Phillip L. Davies. 1994. *Inheritance in Public Policy: Change without Choice in Britain*. New Haven: Yale University Press.

Royed, Terry. 1996. Testing the Mandate Model in Britain and the United States: Evidence from the Reagan and Thatcher Eras. *British Journal of Political Science* 26 (1): 45–80.

Russell, Meg, and Maria Sciara. 2007. Why Does the Government Get Defeated in the House of Lords? The Lords, the Party System and British Politics. *British Politics* 2 (3): 299–322.

Sánchez Cuenca, Ignacio, and Alejandro Mújica. 2006. Consensus and Parliamentary Opposition: The Case of Spain. *Government and Opposition* 41 (1): 86–108.

Sartori, Giovanni. 1976. *Parties and Party Systems: A Theoretical Framework*. Cambridge: Cambridge University Press.

Savoie, Donald. 1999. *Governing from the Centre: The Concentration of Power in Canadian Politics*. Toronto: University of Toronto Press.

Savoie, Donald. 2008. *Court Government and the Collapse of Accountability in Canada and the United Kingdom*. Toronto: University of Toronto Press.

Scharpf, Fritz W. 1988. The Joint Decision Trap: Lessons from German Federalism and European Integration. *Public Administration* 66 (3): 239–78.

Schattschneider, Elmer E. 1960. *The Semisovereign People: A Realist's View of Democracy in America*. New York: Holt, Rinehart & Winston.

Schmidt, Manfred G. 1987. West Germany: The Policy of the Middle Way. *Journal of Public Policy* 7 (2): 135–77.

Schmidt, Manfred G. 1996. When Parties Matter: A Review of the Possibilities and Limits of Partisan Influence on Public Policy. *European Journal of Political Research* 30 (2): 155–83.

Sciarini, Pascal. 2007. The Decision-Making Process. In *Handbook of Swiss Politics/ Handbuch der Schweizer Politik*, edited by Ulrich Klöti, Peter Knoepfel, Hanspeter Kriesi, Yannis Papadopoulos, and Pascal Sciarini, 465–500. Zurich: Verlag Neue Zürcher Zeitung.

Shepsle, Kenneth A. 1979. Institutional Arrangements and Equilibrium in Multi-dimensional Voting Models. *American Journal of Political Science* 23 (1): 23–57.

Shipan, Charles R., and Craig Volden. 2006. Bottom-Up Federalism: The Diffusion of Antismoking Policies from US Cities to States. *American Journal of Political Science* 50 (4): 825–43.

Shipan, Charles R., and Craig Volden. 2008. The Mechanisms of Policy Diffusion. *American Journal of Political Science* 52 (4): 840–57.

Sigelman, Lee, and Emmett H. Buell. 2004. Avoidance or Engagement? Issue Convergence in U.S. Presidential Campaigns, 1960–2000. *American Journal of Political Science* 48 (4): 650–61.

Simeon, Richard, and Ian Robinson. 2009. The Dynamics of Canadian Federalism. In *Canadian Politics*, 5th ed., edited by James Bickerton and Alain-G. Gagnon, 155–78. Toronto: University of Toronto Press.

Skjæveland, Asbjørn. 2005. Dimensionaliteten i Folketinget: Er der en ny politisk dimension? *Politica* 37 (4): 411–22.

Skenderovic, Damir. 2009. *The Radical Right in Switzerland: Continuity and Change, 1945–2000*. Oxford and New York: Berghahn Books.

Smiley, Donald. 1987. *The Federal Condition in Canada*. Toronto: McGraw-Hill Ryerson.

Soroka, Stuart N. 2002. *Agenda-setting Dynamics in Canada*. Vancouver: University of British Columbia Press.

Soroka, Stuart N., and Christopher Wlezien. 2010. *Degrees of Democracy: Politics, Public Opinion and Policy*. Cambridge: Cambridge University Press.

Stimson, James. 2000. *Public Opinion in America*. 2nd ed. New York: Perseus.

Stimson, James A., Michael B. MacKuen, and Robert S. Erikson. 1995. Dynamic Representation. *American Political Science Review* 89 (3): 543–65.

Stokes, Donald E. 1963. Spatial Models of Party Competition. *American Political Science Review* 57: 368–77.

Stokes, Susan. 2001. *Mandates and Democracy*. Cambridge: Cambridge University Press.

Stone, Clarence. 2006. Peter Bachrach and Morton S. Baratz, 1962: "Two Faces of Power." *American Political Science Review* 56 (4): 947–52.

Strøm, Kaare, and Wolfgang C. Muller. 1999. Political Parties and Hard Choices. In *Policy, Office, or Votes? How Political Parties in Western Europe Make Hard Choices*, edited by Kaare Strøm and Wolfgang Muller. Cambridge: Cambridge University Press.

Strøm, Kaare, and Wolfgang C. Müller. 1999. The Keys to Togetherness: Coalition Agreements in Parliamentary Democracies. *Journal of Legislative Studies* 5 (3–4): 255–82.

Strøm, Kaare, Wolfgang C. Müller, and Torbjorn Bergman, eds. 2008. *Coalition Bargaining: The Democratic Life Cycle in Western Europe*. Oxford: Oxford University Press.

Stubager, Rune. 2010. The Development of the Education Cleavage: Denmark as a Critical Case. *West European Politics* 33 (3): 505–33.

Stubager, Rune, Jakob Holm, Maja Smidstrup, and Katrine Kramp. 2013. De danske vælgere 1971–2011. Aarhus: Det danske valgprojekt. www.valgprojektet.dk.

Sulkin, Tracy. 2005. *Issue Politics in Congress*. Cambridge: Cambridge University Press.

Svensson, Palle. 1996. *Demokratiets krise?* Aarhus: Politica.

Swank, Duane. 2002. *Global Capital, Political Institutions, and Policy Change in Developed Welfare States*. New York: Cambridge University Press.

Swenden, Wilfried, and Maarten T. Jans. 2006. Will It Stay or Will It Go? Federalism and the Sustainability of Belgium. *West European Politics* 29 (5): 877–94.

Thesen, Gunnar. 2013. When Good News Is Scarce and Bad News Is Good: Government Responsibilities and Opposition Possibilities in Political Agenda-Setting. *European Journal of Political Research* 52 (3): 364–89.

Thomassen, Jacques, ed. 2005. *The European Voter*. Oxford: Oxford University Press.

Thome, Helmut. 1999. Party Mandate Theory and Time-Series Analysis: A Methodological Comment. *Electoral Studies* 18 (4): 569–85.

Tiberj, Vincent. 2012. La politique des deux axes: votes sociaux et votes de valeurs en France (1988–2007). *Revue française de science politique* 62 (1): 71–106.

Timmermans, Arco. 2003. *High Politics in the Low Countries. An Empirical Study of Coalition Agreements in Belgium and the Netherlands*. Aldershot: Ashgate.

Timmermans, Arco. 2006. Standing Apart and Sitting Together: Enforcing Coalition Agreements in Multiparty Systems. *European Journal of Political Research* 45 (2): 263–83.

Timmermans, Arco. 2011. The Netherlands: Legislative Agenda Setting and the Politics of Strategic Lock-In. In *The Role of Governments in Legislative Agenda Setting*, edited by Bjørn Erik Rasch and George Tsebelis. London: Routledge.

Timmermans, Arco, and Rudy B. Andeweg. 2000. Coalition Cabinets in the Netherlands: Still the Politics of Accommodation? In *Coalition Governments in Western Europe*, edited by Wolfgang C. Mülller and Kaare Strøm. Oxford: Oxford University Press.

Timmermans, Arco, and Catherine Moury. 2006. Coalition Governance in Belgium and the Netherlands: Rising Government Stability against All Electoral Odds. *Acta Politica* 41: 389–407.

Tresch, Anke, Pascal Sciarini, and Frédéric Varone. 2013. The Relationship between Media and Political Agendas: Variations across Decision-Making Phases. *West European Politics* 36 (5): 897–918.

Tsebelis, George. 2002. *Veto Players: How Political Institutions Work*. Princeton: Princeton University Press.

Verzichelli, Luca, and Maurizio Cotta. 2003. Italy: From "Constrained" Coalitions to Alternating Governments. In *Coalition Governments in Western Europe*, edited by Wolfgang Müller and Kaare Strøm, 433–97. Oxford: Oxford University Press.

Vliegenthart, Rens, and Stefaan Walgrave. 2011. Content Matters: The Dynamics of Parliamentary Questioning in Belgium and Denmark. *Comparative Political Studies* 44 (4): 1031–59.

Vliegenthart, Rens, Stefaan Walgrave, and Corinne Meppelink. 2011. Inter-Party Agenda-Setting in Belgian Parliament: The Contingent Role of Party Characteristics and Competition. *Political Studies* 59 (2): 368–88.

Vliegenthart, Rens, Stefaan Walgrave, and Brandon Zicha. 2013. How Preferences, Information and Institutions Interactively Drive Agenda-Setting: Questions in the Belgian Parliament, 1993–2000. *European Journal of Political Research* 52 (3): 390–418.

Volkens, Andrea. 2002. *Manifesto Coding Instructions: Discussion Paper FS III 02-201*. Berlin: WZB.

von Beyme, Klaus. 1985. Policy-Making in the Federal Republic of Germany: A Systematic Introduction. In *Policy and Politics in the Federal Republic of Germany*, edited by Klaus von Beyme and Manfred G. Schmidt, 1–26. New York: St. Martin's Press.

von Beyme, Klaus. 1998. *The Legislator: German Parliament as a Centre of Political Decision-Making*. Aldershot: Ashgate.

von Hagen, Jürgen, and Ian Harden. 1996. Budget Processes and Commitment to Fiscal Discipline. IMF Working Paper.

Walgrave, Stefaan, and Michiel Nuytemans. 2009. Friction and Party Manifesto Change in 25 Countries, 1945–1998. *American Journal of Political Science* 53 (1): 190–206.

Walgrave, Stefaan, Frédéric Varone, and Patrick Dumont. 2006. Policy with or without Parties? A Comparative Analysis of Policy Priorities and Policy Change in Belgium, 1991 to 2000. *Journal of European Public Policy* 13 (7): 1021–38.

Walgrave, Stefaan, Rens Vliegenthart, and Brandon Zicha. 2010. Towards a General Theory of Agenda-Setting: How Preferences, Information, and Institutions Drive Agenda-Setting. ESF workshop on Parties and Agendas, Manchester.

Walker, Jack L. 1969. The Diffusion of Innovations among the American States. *American Political Science Review* 63 (3): 880–99.

Warwick, P. V. 1994. *Government Survival in Parliamentary Democracies*. Cambridge: Cambridge University Press.

Warwick, Paul V. 2006. *Policy Horizons and Parliamentary Government*. Basingstoke and New York: Palgrave Macmillan.

Werder, Hans. 1978. *Die Bedeutung der Volksinitiativen in der Nachkriegszeit*. Berne: Francke.

Weyland, Kurt. 2005. Theories of Policy Diffusion: Lessons from Latin American Pension Reform. *World Politics* 57 (2): 262–95.

Wlezien, Christopher. 1995. The Public as Thermostat: Dynamics of Preferences for Spending. *American Journal of Political Science* 39 (4): 981–1000.

Young, Robert A., Philippe Faucher, and André Blais. 1984. The Concept of Province-Building: A Critique. *Canadian Journal of Political Science* 17 (4): 783–818.

Zicha, Brandon C., and Isabelle Guinaudeau. 2009. Introducing the Comparative Agendas Project Manifesto Coding Method. Paper presented at the PolEtmaal Conference.

Zucchini, Francesco. 2011a. Government Alternation and Legislative Agenda Setting. *European Journal of Political Research* 50 (6): 749–74.

Zucchini, Francesco. 2011b. Italy: Government Alternation and Legislative Agenda Setting. In *The Role of Governments in Legislative Agenda Setting*, edited by Bjørn Erik Rasch and George Tsebelis. London: Routledge.

Notes on Contributors

Shaun Bevan is a research fellow at the Mannheim Centre for European Social Research (MZES), University of Mannheim, Germany. His research interests include agenda setting, public policy, interest groups, public opinion, time-series analysis, event history analysis, and measurement.

Enrico Borghetto is a postdoctoral fellow at CESNOVA, Nova University of Lisbon, Portugal. His research focuses mainly on legislative studies and European Union public policies.

Gerard Breeman is assistant professor at the Public Administration and Policy Group, Wageningen University, Netherlands. His research interests are policy agenda setting, trust and policy-making, environmental policies, and the common agricultural policy.

Christian Breunig is professor of comparative politics at the University of Konstanz, Germany. His research concentrates on public policy in advanced democracies, comparative political economy, political methodology, and budgetary politics.

Sylvain Brouard is senior research fellow FNSP at Centre Émile Durkheim, Sciences Po Bordeaux, France, where he is currently a codirector of the French Agendas Project. He is also a coconvener of the law and courts standing group of the European Consortium for Political Research as well as the French Politics Group of the American Political Science Association. His research and teaching focus on comparative politics and political institutions (mainly Parliaments and constitutional courts).

Marcello Carammia is a lecturer at the Institute for European Studies, University of Malta. His research focuses on comparative and European Union public policy.

Laura Chaqués-Bonafont is professor of political science at the University of Barcelona, Spain. She leads the Spanish Policy Agendas Project. Her present research activities focus on analyses of the interrelation of the political agenda, the media agenda, and public opinion.

Isabelle Engeli is assistant professor at the University of Ottawa, Canada. Her main areas of expertise are comparative public policies, agenda setting, and policy change, as well as political representation and gender.

Martial Foucault is full professor of political science at Sciences Po Paris,

France. His current research concentrates on political economy, fiscal policies, political behavior, and policy agendas. Since 2011 he has been the director of the European Union Center for Excellence (University of Montreal/McGill University)

Roy Gava is a doctoral candidate in political science at the University of Geneva. His research interests include comparative public policy, financial services regulation, and internationalization.

Christoffer Green-Pedersen is professor of political science at Aarhus University, Denmark. His research focuses on agenda setting and party competition in a comparative perspective. He is the initiator of the Danish Policy Agendas Project.

Emiliano Grossman is senior researcher and associate professor at Sciences Po Paris, France. He has written widely on interest groups, political institutions, and agenda setting in France. His current research deals with the role of media in political agenda setting.

Isabelle Guinaudeau is CNRS senior researcher at Pacte, Sciences Po Grenoble. Her research deals with the conditions, modalities and consequences of party competition. Her publications have maily focused on Europeanization of party competition, party strategies and parties' influence on policies.

Anne Hardy is a doctoral candidate and teaching assistant at the University of Antwerp, Belgium. She is responsible for the Belgian media coding in the Comparative Agendas Project. Her research focuses on the determinants, mechanisms, and consequences of media storms.

Will Jennings is a reader in politics at the University of Southampton and a research associate at the Centre for Analysis of Risk and Regulation at the London School of Economics, England. He specializes in the fields of executive politics and the governance of risk in megaprojects, as well as in the quantitative analysis of politics, policy, and society (in particular in the application of time-series methods).

Peter John is professor of political science and public policy at University College London, England. He has completed two books using British policy agendas data and is carrying out a series of randomized controlled trials with policy makers seeking to encourage prosocial behavior.

Jeroen Joly is a doctoral student in political science and researcher at the University of Antwerp, Belgium. His main research interest is the comparative politics of public policy-making. His current research focuses on the impact and role of the domestic determinants of foreign-policy decision making.

Bryan D. Jones is the J. J. "Jake" Pickle Regent's Chair in Congressional Studies at the University of Texas at Austin and director of the U.S. Policy Agendas Project. With Frank R. Baumgartner, he is the coauthor of *Agendas and Instability in American Politics* (1993) and *The Politics of Attention: How Government Prioritizes Problems* (2005).

Éric Montpetit is chair of the political science department at the University of Montreal, Canada, and specializes in comparative and Canadian public policy. His current research centers on domains requiring scientific knowledge (notably biotechnology) in North America and Europe. In particular, he examines the role of scientists, policy learning, and disagreements generated by the making of policy choices in these domains.

Luz M. Muñoz Márquez is a lecturer in political science at the University of Barcelona, Spain. She is finishing her doctoral dissertation on nongovernmental organizations in Spain. Her research is focused mainly on interest-group organizations and policy dynamics.

Anna M. Palau is a postdoctoral researcher in political science at the University of Barcelona, Spain. Her research focuses on public policy, specifically food safety policy, and also on the study of agenda-setting dynamics and the role of the mass media as a political actor.

Pascal Sciarini is professor of Swiss and comparative politics at the University of Geneva, Switzerland. His main research topics are decision-making processes, direct democracy, Europeanization, and political behavior.

Arco Timmermans is professor of public affairs at Campus The Hague, University of Leiden, Netherlands. His research focuses on comparative agendas in European Union member states and in the European Union, on interest group strategies and on coalition building.

Tobias Van Assche was a member of the M²P working group at the University of Antwerp from 2008 to 2010 and remains affiliated with the University of Antwerp, Belgium. He received his doctorate in political science from Syracuse University, New York. His areas of specialization are political psychology, political leadership, and foreign-policy decision making.

Frédéric Varone is a professor of policy analysis and public administration at the University of Geneva, Switzerland. His current research interests include comparative public policy, program evaluation, and public-sector reforms.

Stefaan Walgrave is a professor of political science at the University of Antwerp, Belgium. His research interests are media and politics, public opinion, elections, and protest and social movements. He leads the research group M²P in Antwerp.

Michelle Whyman is a graduate student in the government department at the University of Texas at Austin and a graduate fellow at the Policy Agendas Project. Her research interests center on American political institutions, public policy, lawmaking, and interbranch relations, with an emphasis on the role of the Supreme Court.

Brandon C. Zicha earned his doctorate in political science from Binghamton University, State University of New York, in 2010 with a dissertation on working to fuse information-processing and preference-processing models of policy-making. He has been a researcher with the Comparative Agendas Project since 2008 and served as a methodologist in the Belgian Agenda Setting Project at the University of Antwerp from 2008 until 2011. Currently he is an assistant professor of media politics at Leiden University College in The Hague, Netherlands, where he studies how democracies process information to make policy in different contexts.

Francesco Zucchini is associate professor at the University of Milan and acting director of the Ph.D. Program in political studies of the Graduate School in Social and Political Sciences (http://www.graduateschool.unimi.it/). His research focuses on legislative studies, the Italian Parliament, and the Italian Constitutional Court. He has published in several journals, including the *European Journal of Political Research*, *West European Politics*, and *Public Choice*.

General Index

acts of Parliament (United Kingdom), 25; coding, 26; decline in number of, 26; issue attention in, 26–33; party influence on, 31, 32, 33; regulatory requirements in, 34; Speech from the Throne compared with, 32

agendas, political. *See* political agendas

agenda-setting theory: agenda setting as "second face of power," 1, 220, 228; for analyzing competition between levels of political system, 227; on attention and institutions in agenda dynamics, 131; on attention as scarce and consequential, 8; Comparative Manifesto Group compared with, 14; in comparative research, 230; counterintuitive results in, 228; integrating capacity of, 221; integrating with classic approaches to politics, 229–30; for investigating issue attention, 221; on issue divergence in Belgium, 146, 162–63; and mandate theory, 166–68, 180–81; methodological approach of, 9–11; on party manifestos and policy outputs, 187, 198; and party-system change, 72–73; and policy-diffusion theories, 202–3; turning agenda setting from approach to theory, 220–30

agriculture: in Canada, 204, 211; in Comparative Agendas Project, 231; in Germany, 128, 129, 134, 135, 139, 141, 142; in Netherlands, 95, 97; in Spain, 195, 196, 197, 198; in Switzerland, 109, 110, 115, 116, 118; in United Kingdom, 24, 26; in United States, 46, 47, 48, 50

Amato, Giuliano, 172

attention, political. *See* political attention

autoregressive distributed lag (ADL) model, 26

Aznar, José, 189, 191, 192, 193, 194, 195

banking, finance, and commerce: in Canada, 204, 211, 217; in Comparative Agendas Project, 231; in Germany, 128, 142, 143; in Netherlands, 97, 98; in Spain, 196; in

United Kingdom, 24, 29, 32, 34; in United States, 46, 48

Basque Nationalist Party (Spain), 192

Belgium, 145–63; approaches to political stalemate in, 163; checks and balances in, 150; devolution competes with other issues in, 226–27; issue divergence between party elites in, 149–51; as partitocracy, 150–51; political parties split along linguistic lines, 147, 148; record for longest period of government formation, 145, 163; state reform of 1993, 147, 155; summary of findings about, 223; two political systems in, 147–49

Berlusconi, Silvio, 164, 170, 171, 174, 177

Blair, Tony, 29, 32

Blocher, Christoph, 108, 121n4, 122n5

Bush, George H. W., 50

Bush, George W., 36, 50, 51

Canada, 201–19; "cartel" of government clubs in, 204; "club government" attributed to, 203; Constitution Act of 1867, 204; federalism in, 201–5, 208–18, 227; intergovernmental relations in, 203–5, 208–10; province building in, 205; state building in, 205; summary of findings about, 223; territorial clusters of correlations of issue attention in, 210, 215, 218

capacity limits of legislative agenda, 87, 92, 93, 97, 98, 100–102

Carter, Jimmy, 49

Casa della Libertà (House of Freedoms; CdL) (Italy), 172, 176, 178

center parties: in Denmark, 71, 80; versus niche parties, 61, 64

Centre Démocrate Humaniste (CDH) (Belgium), 152, 156, 157

Christen-Democratisch en Vlaams (CD&V) (Belgium), 152, 156, 157, 160

Christian Democratic Party (Denmark), 79, 83

Christian Democratic Party (Italy), 164, 168, 169, 171, 172, 174, 175, 176, 178

69, 70, 83; impact of party policy priorities on Italian lawmaking from First to Second Republic, 1983–2006, 164–82; issue priorities and party competition in France, 53–68; issue priorities of Belgian parties, 1987–2010, 145–63; and legislative agendas in Germany, 125–44; multiple objectives of, 21; niche parties, 55–56, 61–64, 66, 155, 225; party-system development in Denmark, 69–85; and the policy agenda in the United Kingdom, 19–35; spatial models of party competition, 19, 58, 185; testing issue-ownership hypothesis, 58–60; varying impact across institutional arenas, 34. *See also* center parties; left-wing parties; new parties; party manifestos; party-system agenda; right-wing parties; *and by name*
politics: class politics, 76, 108; new politics, 77–78, 85n5; political attention as crucial for understanding, 3, 8–9, 149; reacts to real world, 7, 223–24; as struggle for control of political agenda, 1. *See also* political agendas; political attention; political parties
popular initiatives (referendums): general absence of, 121; in Swiss consensus democracy, 111, 122n6; of Swiss People's Party, 105, 112, 113–14, 117–19, 120
preferences: in agenda-setting approach, 13–14, 165, 221; incoming information shapes, 167; integrating with issue priorities in agenda-setting theory, 229; in issue prioritization, 6–7, 13, 106, 185, 228–29; of political parties, 20, 23; in veto-player theory, 229
prioritization of issues. *See* issue prioritization
prioritization of policies. *See* policy prioritization
Prodi, Romano, 172
Progress Party (Denmark), 71, 79, 81
proportional representation, 89, 103, 112, 169
public lands and water management: in Canada, 212; in Comparative Agendas Project, 231; in Germany, 128; in Spain, 196, 197; in United Kingdom, 24; in United States, 48
Public Laws Database, 38
public mood, 44
public opinion: British Speech from the

Throne influenced by, 29; and Canadian government, 203, 206; and coalition governments in Netherlands, 104; and direction of legislation, 37; issue attention data from, 207; and party influence on public policy, 21; public policy influenced by, 33; retrospective evaluations of, 40; and size of statutory agenda, 37, 44–45, 48, 51, 52
punctuated equilibria, 3–4

Queen's Speech (United Kingdom). *See* Speech from the Throne (Queen's Speech) (United Kingdom)

Rassemblement pour la République (Rally for the Republic; RPR) (France), 55, 57, 58, 59, 61, 62, 63, 64, 66
Reagan, Ronald, 41, 49–50
referendums. *See* popular initiatives (referendums)
right-wing parties: in Belgium, 152, 162, 163; in Denmark, 70, 71, 72, 81, 82, 84; in France, 65; and globalization, 72; issue ranking in, 59; policies associated with, 19, 21, 146; populist, 105–6, 115, 118, 152, 162; respond to their electorate, 20; in Spain, 189, 192; in Switzerland, 105, 108, 116, 118
Rodríguez Zapatero, José Luis, 189, 190, 191, 192, 194, 195

salience of issues. *See* issue salience
Schmidt, Helmut, 138
Schröder, Gerhard, 138
science. *See* space, science, technology, and communications
Shannon's H, 61–62, 67n12
Social Democratic Party (Denmark), 71, 80, 81, 84
Social Democratic Party (Germany), 137–38, 139
Social Democratic Party (Netherlands), 95
Social Democratic Party (Switzerland), 107, 112, 115, 116, 117, 118, 119, 121
Socialistische Partij Anders (Sp.a) (Belgium), 152, 156, 160
Socialist Party (PS) (Belgium), 152, 156, 160
Socialist Party (PS) (France), 55, 57, 58, 59, 61, 62, 63, 64, 66
Socialist People's Party (Denmark), 71
Social Liberal Party (Denmark), 71, 80, 81, 82

Vlaamse Liberalen en Democraten (VLD)
(Belgium), 152, 156, 160
Volksunie (VU) (Belgium), 152
vote seeking: popular initiatives offer opportunities for, 111, 114; by Swiss People's
Party, 106, 108, 113, 114, 119, 120, 225
voting, issue, 54, 65, 74, 79

water management. *See* public lands and
water management
watertight-compartment federalism, 204,
227

welfare: in Canada, 205, 208, 209, 212, 217;
in Comparative Agendas Project, 231; in
Denmark, 70, 77, 78, 79, 81, 85n5; in Germany, 126, 127, 128, 129, 132, 133, 134, 135,
138, 139, 140, 143, 144; in Netherlands,
94, 95; party differences regarding, 21; in
Spain, 183, 184, 188, 190, 191, 198, 200n4;
in Switzerland, 105, 108, 112, 116, 118,
119; in United Kingdom, 24, 29; in United
States, 46, 47, 48, 50

Index of Cited Authors

Lightning Source UK Ltd.
Milton Keynes UK
UKOW02f0114300716

279519UK00002B/338/P